the Ultimate cake mix COOKIE BOOK

more than 375 DELECTABLE COOKIE RECIPES
That Begin with a Box of Cake Mix

CAMILLA V. SAULSBURY

CUMBERLAND HOUSE™

Published by Cumberland House, an imprint of Sourcebooks, Inc.
P.O. Box 4410, Naperville, Illinois 60567-4410
(630) 961-3900
Fax: (630) 961-2168
www.sourcebooks.com

Library of Congress Cataloging-in-Publication Data

Saulsbury, Camilla V.
  The ultimate cake mix cookie book : more than 375 delectable cookie recipes that begin with a box of cake mix / Camilla V. Saulsbury.—2nd ed.
      p. cm.
  Rev. ed. of: Cake mix cookies / Camilla V. Saulsbury. c2005.
  Includes index.
  1. Cookies. I. Saulsbury, Camilla V. Cake mix cookies. II. Title.
  TX772.S2578 2011
  641.8'654—dc23
                                    2011022483

Printed and bound in the United States of America.
      VP 10 9 8 7 6 5 4 3 2

To Nick, my favorite cookie monster.

contents

foreword

As this new edition of The Ultimate Cake Mix Cookie Book heads to the printer, I've been musing about the exciting developments that have occurred since it was first published in 2005.

Topping the list is the sheer popularity of the book, something I merely hoped and dreamed of back in the early days of testing and writing recipes. I knew then how much I loved making cookies with cake mix, but it has been a thrill to share the joy with others.

I've especially reveled in the notes and letters from fans, letting me know which recipes are loved most, and what kinds of recipes they would still love to see. After chatting with countless home bakers across the country, I know that it's the simplest recipes with an innovative twist that everyone's after. It has to taste terrific, first and foremost, but if it's versatile, can be made in minutes, has an especially short list of ingredients, and looks gorgeous, all the better.

So, in addition to the familiar favorites from the first edition, you'll find here more than two hundred brand-new recipes, all of which reflect feedback from fellow cake-mix-cookie-aficionados. I am confident you'll love each and every offering, from the ease of baking the cookie to the subsequently stellar results. Think Hazelnut and Chocolate Chip Butter Cookies, Deluxe Nut Jumbles, Chocolate-Covered Marshmallow Pillows, and Vanilla Malt Gooey Bars; it just gets better and better.

And if those new options don't have your mouth watering, just wait until you try two of the hottest new trends for using cake mix: cake balls and whoopie pies.

Cake balls are tiny cookie-like confections made from mixing crumbled, baked cake with frosting, molding the mixture into tiny balls, then coating all with chocolate. Yum! I've created eighteen scrumptious varieties for you to try, such as German Chocolate, Cinnamon Roll, Berries-and-Cream,

Key Lime, and Cheesecake. Be forewarned: they are highly addictive to make and eat (and absolutely adorable, to boot).

Second, whoopie pies. The oversized, soft cookie sandwiches, stuffed with a variety of creamy frostings, are nothing short of cookie nirvana. Think Red Velvet Whoopies, Caramel Latte Whoopies, and Lemon Buttermilk Whoopies, to name but a few. Forget the cupcakes: make whoopie pies for your next party to score an excess of points.

Beyond the new recipes, I am compelled to mention that with this new edition, what ultimately excites me above all else is that it further celebrates American home cooks' enduring embrace of home baking in general, and home-baked cookies in particular. No matter how many cookies in our repertoire, we have a boundless zeal for new ideas, from techniques to flavor combinations, and we cannot wait to share them. That's the real story of American home cooking and baking.

That being said, I hope you'll experience as much delight in creating these cookies in your home as I have had crafting them in mine. Few things gratify me as much as sharing a plate of cookies with friends, including the conversation and camaraderie that typically coincide. If this book helps you do the same, I will be truly pleased.

introduction

It's always a good time to rediscover the age-old comfort of cookies. Try conjuring an image more comforting than a warm kitchen, infused with the scents of sweet vanilla, fragrant cinnamon, and fresh butter, and, on the kitchen counter, a cooling rack piled high with fresh-from-the-oven delights studded with chocolate chips and crunchy pecans. It is a cause for celebration in itself—even more so when the cookie recipe is as quick and convenient as opening a package of cake mix.

That's right—cake mix. A standard 18.25-ounce package of cake mix is the secret to a wealth of homemade cookies. Even better, the results are assuredly irresistible. A package of cake mix gives home bakers the same head start for baking cookies as for baking cakes. Cake mix simplifies steps and ingredients and offers insurance (in the form of accurately premeasured and mixed flour, sugar, and leavening) that the time spent baking will lead to sweet success time and again. With a few extra ingredients, turns of the spoon, and whirs of the mixer, cake mix can make any home cook a prize cookie baker.

And oh, what cookies to choose from! You may have come across a handful of cake mix cookie recipes here and there, but never a collection as extensive as this. Turn the pages and you'll find an enticing array of cookie options: think easy-as-can-be drop cookies, made from spoonfuls of dough dropped onto a cookie sheet; formed, fancy, and filled cookies, that are either shaped into balls, rolled and cut into fun shapes, or filled with jams, candies, and other treasures; and blissful bar cookies, baked with ease in square or rectangular baking pans, then cut into handheld pieces. They're all here, and they're all scrumptious, satisfying, simple to make, and pretty to serve.

Quite a few all-American favorites can be found throughout the book: Chocolate Chip Cookies, Oatmeal Raisin Cookies, Nutty Jam Thumbprints, and Dark Chocolate Brownies are but a few. New takes on classic European cookies are also well-represented, including crunchy Italian biscotti, tender French madeleines, and rich Viennese teacakes.

Finally, a hearty helping of serendipity is stirred up to create a host of modern cookie options, guaranteed to tempt one and all, and destined to become classics in their own right. How about a Giant Cookie Pizza for your next birthday party? Or Granola Chocolate Chunkers or Fresh Berry Cheesecake Bars for a picnic at the park? How about a holiday cookie plate filled to overflowing with White Chocolate Cranberry Bars, Caramel-Macchiato Thumbprints, Spumoni Chunk Cookies, and Crushed Peppermint Snowballs? And why not surprise (and thrill) your family on a busy week-day morning with healthy Whole Wheat Pumpkin Breakfast Cookies or Chocolate-Nut Power Bars? This is the stuff of which sweet dreams are made.

Once the cookie baking commences, one thing will immediately become self-evident: each and every cookie in this collection will lead home bakers—and the lucky recipients of their efforts—straight to the comfort zone. So why wait? Don an apron, grab a bowl, and start mixing up some delicious fun. Be it ever so humble, there's no taste like a homemade cookie.

SMART COOKIE TIPS

- Read the recipe thoroughly. Note the required ingredients and the equipment needed, as well as the chilling, baking, and cooling times.

- Gather the necessary ingredients, checking for freshness. (See the Ingredients section that follows for tips on specific ingredients.)

- Gather the necessary equipment, including oven mitts and cooling racks.

- Prep the ingredients—such as chopping nuts, zesting lemons, softening cream cheese, or melting butter, as needed—before you begin to assemble the recipe.

- Prepare any baking pans or cookie sheets as specified in the recipe. If no advance preparation is needed, set the pan or sheet aside so that it is ready to be used when needed.

- Re-read the recipe.

- Preheat the oven. Turn the oven to the specified temperature for 10 to 15 minutes prior to baking to give the oven adequate time to heat up to the correct point.

- Use an oven thermometer. Indispensable, inexpensive, and readily available in the baking sections of most supermarkets, or at any kitchen supply store, these handy devices allow you to check the accuracy and consistency of your oven temperature. Oven temperatures tend to be higher or lower than the dial indicates; armed with the correct information from your thermometer, you can adjust accordingly.

- Precisely measure all of the ingredients. Baking is a science, hence small variations can have a significant effect on the final product. See the Measuring Ingredients section for tips on measuring dry, liquid, and moist ingredients.

- Mix ingredients according to recipe specifications.

- Use a kitchen timer. This allows for precision and helps ensure the end product is not over-baked. One or two minutes can make a world of difference in cookie baking, so ensure your results with a reliable timer.

- Check the baked goods at the earliest time specified. For example, if a recipe reads "Bake for 30 to 35 minutes until toothpick inserted near the center comes clean," then check for doneness at 30 minutes. Continue baking if needed and continue checking every minute.

EQUIPMENT

Cake mix cookies require minimal equipment. Here is a short list of what you'll need:

BAKING PANS AND SHEETS

- ✓ Aluminum cookie sheets (at least two)
- ✓ 8-inch square pan
- ✓ 9-inch square pan
- ✓ Jelly roll pan (10 x 15 inches)
- ✓ Madeleine pan (3 x 1¼-inch shell molds)

MEASURING AND MIXING

- ✓ Dry measuring cups in graduated sizes: ¼, ⅓, ½, and 1 cup
- ✓ Liquid measuring cup (preferably clear glass or plastic)
- ✓ Measuring spoons in graduated sizes: ⅛, ¼, ½, and 1 teaspoon, as well as 1 tablespoon
- ✓ Wooden spoon(s)
- ✓ Mixing bowls (at least one each of small, medium, and large sizes)

✓ Rubber or silicone spatula (for scraping the sides of a mixing bowl)

APPLIANCES

✓ Electric mixer (handheld or stand mixer)

✓ Food processor

✓ Kitchen timer

UTENSILS

✓ Rolling pin or mallet (for crushing cookies, graham crackers, and candies)

✓ Wire whisk

✓ Chef's knife

✓ Wooden spoon

✓ Spring-loaded cookie or ice cream scoop, small (typically 2 teaspoons) and medium (typically 1 tablespoon)

✓ Kitchen spoons (everyday place-setting soupspoons for drop cookies)

✓ Metal pastry scraper (the ideal tool for cutting sheets into perfect squares and bars)

✓ Zester

✓ Metal spatula or pancake turner for removing cookies from sheets

✓ Pastry brush (a clean 1-inch paintbrush from the hardware store works fine)

✓ Rolling pin (only for a few recipes)

✓ Assorted cookie cutters

✓ Metal icing spatula

MISCELLANEOUS

✓ Wire cooling racks

✓ Cutting board(s)

✓ Oven mitts or pot holders

✓ Aluminum foil

✓ Plastic wrap

✓ Wax paper

✓ Parchment paper

✓ Toothpicks

INGREDIENTS

CAKE MIXES

All of the recipes in this book calling for cake mix were tested using 18.25-ounce boxes of cake mix. These included name-brand mixes such as Betty Crocker, Duncan Hines, and Pillsbury, as well as store-brand mixes such as Kroger and Safeway. Flavors vary slightly by manufacturer, so take note if you prefer one brand over another.

Cake mixes contain flour, sugar, leavening (baking powder and baking soda), fat, salt, flavoring, and coloring in precise, premeasured proportions. They have a one-year shelf life, so it is a great idea to stock up, particularly when cake mixes are on sale (which is often). For spur-of-the-moment cookie baking, try keeping one or two each of chocolate, yellow, lemon, white, and spice cake mixes in the pantry.

FLOUR

All-purpose flour: Made from a blend of high-gluten hard wheat and low-gluten soft wheat, all-purpose flour is a fine-textured flour milled from the inner part of the wheat kernel and contains neither the germ nor the bran. All-purpose flour comes either bleached or unbleached; they can be used interchangeably.

Whole wheat flour: Whole wheat flour is milled from hard red wheat; it has a fuller flavor and is far more nutritious than all-purpose flour because it contains the wheat bran and sometimes the germ. Because of its higher fat content, it should be stored in the refrigerator to prevent rancidity.

OATS

Two types of oats are used throughout this collection: old-fashioned and quick-cooking. Old-fashioned oats are rolled and are made from the entire oat kernel. With quick-cooking oats the oat kernel is cut into pieces before being rolled thinly. Use the oats specified in the recipe for best results. Avoid using instant oatmeal, which consists of oats that have been very finely cut and processed. Store oats in a tightly covered container, in a cool, dry place, for up to six months. Oats may also be frozen in a zip-top plastic freezer bag for up to one year. Oats do not spoil but may become stale with age.

GRAHAM CRACKERS

Both whole graham crackers and graham cracker crumbs are used throughout this collection, particularly for the no-bake cookie options. Graham crackers are rectangular whole wheat crackers that have been lightly sweetened. Use only fresh, crisp graham crackers for best results.

Where graham cracker crumbs are specified in a recipe, ready-made graham cracker crumbs may be used. Look for them in the baking section of the grocery store where flour is shelved.

BUTTER

Butter is used in many of the recipes throughout the book to bolster the flavor of the cookies, brownies, and bars. Either unsalted or lightly salted butter may be used where butter is listed as an ingredient in this book.

Fresh butter should have a delicate cream flavor and pale yellow color. Butter quickly picks up off-flavors during storage and when exposed to oxygen; once the carton is opened, place it in a resealable plastic storage bag or airtight container. Store it away from foods with strong odors, especially items such as onions or garlic.

Avoid using butter to coat baking pans and sheets. Because butter melts at a lower temperature than other "greasing" ingredients, such as vegetable shortening, it may leave ungreased gaps on cookie sheets and pans, causing baked goods to stick. Second, butter can burn, particularly when baking above 350°F. At best, what you're baking will be overly brown; at worst, scorched.

Melting butter: Melted butter is used in many recipes throughout this book. For best results, cut the specified amount of butter into small pieces, place in a small saucepan, and allow it to melt over the lowest heat setting of the burner. Once the butter has melted, remove pan from heat and cool. To speed the cooling, pour the melted butter into a small bowl or liquid measuring cup.

Softening butter: Softened butter is also required in several recipes throughout the book. The traditional method for softening butter is to remove the needed amount from the refrigerator and let it stand for 30 to 45 minutes at room temperature. Cutting the butter into small chunks will reduce the softening time to about 15 minutes. If time is really limited, try grating the cold butter on the large holes of a cheese grater. The small bits of butter will be soft in just a few minutes.

Soften butter until it yields to light pressure from your fingertips. Overly softened butter (i.e., it looks greasy and/or begins to collapse) will cause the cookies to spread too much in the oven. Return the butter to the refrigerator for 5 to 10 minutes until it re-firms slightly.

Alternatively, place the cold butter between sheets of wax paper and hit it several times with a rolling pin. Avoid softening butter in the microwave. It will typically melt at least part of the butter, even if watched closely.

CHOCOLATE

Two general types of chocolate are used throughout this book. The first type is chocolate chips, available in semisweet, milk, white, and miniature semisweet. Some premium brands offer bittersweet chocolate chips, which may be used interchangeably with semisweet chocolate chips.

The second general type, used in a short number of recipes, is baking chocolate, which is typically available in 6- or 8-ounce packages, with the chocolate most often individually wrapped in 1-ounce squares or occasionally in 2-ounce bars. It is available in unsweetened, bittersweet, semisweet, milk, and white chocolate varieties.

- Six ounces of chocolate chips or baking chips measure 1 level cup.
- For a cookie more densely populated with chocolate chips, feel free to increase the amount by ¼ cup for every 1 cup of chocolate chips in the recipe.

Store both chocolate chips and baking chocolate in a dry, cool place, between 60°F and 78°F. Wrapping chocolate in moisture-proof wrap or in a zip-top plastic bag is a good idea if the temperature is higher or the humidity is above 50 percent. Chocolate can also be stored in the fridge, but let it stand at room temperature before using.

Blooming chocolate: If the chocolate from your pantry has a white, crusty-looking film on it, don't toss it. This is commonly called "bloom" and develops when the chocolate is exposed to varying temperatures, from hot to cold. The change in heat allows the cocoa butter to melt and rise to the surface of the chocolate. Bloom does not affect the quality or flavor of the chocolate. The chocolate will look normal again once it is melted or used in baking.

CREAM CHEESE

All of the recipes in this book use "brick"-style cream cheese, which is typically packaged in 3-ounce and 8-ounce rectangular packages. For best results avoid using soft-spread, flavored, or whipped cream cheese.

To soften cream cheese, unwrap it and cut it into chunks with a sharp knife. Let it stand at room temperature for 30 to 45 minutes until softened. For speed softening, place the chunks of cream cheese on a microwavable plate or in a microwavable bowl and microwave on high for 15 seconds. If necessary, microwave 5 or 10 seconds longer.

EGGS

Use large eggs in all of the recipes in this book. Select clean, fresh eggs that have been handled properly and refrigerated. Do not use dirty, cracked, or leaking eggs that may have a bad odor or unnatural color when cracked open. They may have become contaminated with harmful bacteria such as salmonella. Cold eggs are easiest to separate; eggs at room temperature beat to high volume.

Eggs may be checked for freshness by filling a deep bowl with enough cold water to cover an egg. Place the egg in the water. If the egg lies on its side on the bottom of the bowl, it is fresh. If the egg stands up and bobs on the bottom, it isn't quite as fresh, but is still acceptable for baking. If the egg floats on the surface, it should be discarded.

MARGARINE

Margarine may be substituted for butter, but it is not recommended because it lacks the rich flavor that butter offers. However, if using margarine in place of butter, it is essential that it is a 100 percent vegetable oil, solid stick.

Margarine spreads—in tub or stick form—will alter the liquid and fat combination of the recipe, leading to either unsatisfactory or downright disastrous results. You can determine the fat percentage in one of two ways. In some cases, the percentage is printed on the box. If it reads anything less than 100 percent oil, it is a spread and should be avoided for baking purposes. If the percentage is not printed on the outside of the box, flip it over and check the calories. If it is 100 calories per tablespoon, it is 100 percent vegetable oil; any less, and it is less than 100 percent and should not be used in these recipes.

GRANULATED WHITE SUGAR

Granulated white sugar is the most common sweetener used throughout this collection. It is refined cane or beet sugar. If a recipe in the book calls for sugar without specifying which one, use granulated white sugar. Once opened, store granulated sugar in an airtight container, in a cool, dry place.

BROWN SUGAR

Brown sugar is granulated sugar that has some molasses added to it. The molasses gives the brown sugar a soft texture. Light brown sugar has less molasses and a more delicate flavor than dark brown sugar. If a recipe in the book calls for brown sugar without specifying which one, use light brown sugar. If you are out of brown sugar, substitute 1 cup granulated white sugar plus 2 tablespoons molasses for each cup of brown sugar. Once opened, store brown sugar in an airtight container or zip-top plastic bag to prevent clumping.

TURBINADO SUGAR

Turbinado sugar is raw sugar that has been steam-cleaned. The coarse crystals are blond in color and have a delicate molasses flavor. They are typically used for decoration and texture atop baked goods.

CONFECTIONERS' SUGAR

Confectioners' sugar (also called powdered sugar) is granulated sugar that has been ground to a fine powder. Cornstarch is added to prevent the sugar from clumping together. It is used in recipes where regular sugar would be too grainy. If you are out of confectioners' sugar, place 1 cup granulated white sugar plus ⅛ teaspoon cornstarch in a food processor or blender, then process on high speed until finely powdered. Once opened, store confectioners' sugar in an airtight container or zip-top plastic bag to prevent clumping.

CORN SYRUP

Corn syrup is a thick, sweet syrup made by processing cornstarch with acids or enzymes. Light corn syrup is further treated to remove any color. Light corn syrup is very sweet but does not have much flavor. Dark corn syrup has coloring and flavoring added to make it caramel-like. Unopened containers of corn syrup may be stored at room temperature. After opening, store corn syrup in the refrigerator to protect against mold. Corn syrup will keep indefinitely when stored properly.

HONEY

Honey is the nectar of plants that has been gathered and concentrated by honeybees. Unopened containers of honey may be stored at room temperature. After opening, store honey in the refrigerator to protect against mold. Honey will keep indefinitely when stored properly.

MAPLE SYRUP

Maple syrup is a thick liquid sweetener made by boiling the sap from maple trees. Maple syrup has a strong, pure maple flavor. Unopened containers of maple syrup may be stored at room temperature. After opening, store maple syrup in the refrigerator to protect against mold. Maple syrup will keep indefinitely when stored properly.

MOLASSES

Molasses is made from the juice of sugar cane or sugar beets, which is boiled until a syrupy mixture remains. Light molasses is lighter in flavor and color and results from the first boiling of the syrup. Dark molasses, dark in both flavor and color, is not as sweet as light molasses. It comes from the second boiling of the syrup. Light and dark molasses may be used interchangeably in the recipes in this collection. Blackstrap molasses is thick, very dark, and has a bitter flavor; it is not recommended for the recipes in this collection. Unopened containers of molasses may be stored at room temperature. After opening, store molasses in the refrigerator to protect against mold. Molasses will keep indefinitely when stored properly.

NONSTICK COOKING SPRAY

Nonstick cooking spray, such as PAM, may also be used for "greasing" pans because of its convenience. However, solid vegetable shortening, such as Crisco, may also be used. Both are flavorless and coat pans and cookie sheets evenly.

When spraying or greasing baking pans for brownies, be sure to coat only the bottom of the pan. If the inside walls of the pan are coated, the brownies will not rise properly. When making bars, the entire inside of the pan may be coated in cooking spray. Cookie sheets should be given only a very light spraying or greasing for best results.

SHELLED NUTS

Use plain, unsalted nuts unless specified otherwise in the recipe. To determine whether shelled nuts are fresh, taste them: they should taste and smell fresh, not rancid with an off-flavor. Frozen nuts are prone to freezer burn if stored improperly and may taste old or stale (old, stale, or rancid nuts will ruin the baked product). Shelled nuts should also have a crisp texture, should be relatively uniform in color, and should not be shriveled or discolored in spots.

Toasting nuts: Toasting nuts before adding them to a recipe can greatly intensify their flavor and hence their contribution to a recipe. To toast without turning on the oven, place them in an ungreased skillet over medium heat (3 to 4 minutes), stirring frequently, until golden brown (note that this method works best with chopped, as opposed to whole, nuts). To oven-toast, spread the nuts in a single layer in a baking pan or on a cookie sheet. Bake at 350°F for 8 to 10 minutes, stirring occasionally, or until golden brown. Cool the nuts before adding them to the recipe. Watch nuts carefully as they toast, checking at the minimum suggested time, as nuts can burn quickly.

SPICES

All of the recipes in this book use ground, as opposed to whole, spices. Freshness is everything with ground spices. The best way to determine if a ground spice is fresh is to open the container and smell it. If it still has a strong fragrance, it is still acceptable for use. If not, toss it and make a new purchase.

VANILLA EXTRACT

Vanilla extract adds a sweet, fragrant flavor to baked goods and is particularly good for enhancing the flavor of chocolate. It is produced by extracting the flavor of dried vanilla beans with an alcohol-and-water mixture. It is then aged for several months. The three most common types of beans used to make vanilla extract are Bourbon-Madagascar, Mexican, and Tahitian.

Store vanilla extract in a cool, dark place, with the bottle tightly closed, to prevent it from evaporating and losing flavor. It will stay fresh for about two years unopened and for one year after being opened. Imitation vanilla flavoring can be substituted for vanilla extract, but it may have a slight or prominent artificial taste depending on the brand. It is about half the cost of real vanilla extract; however, it's worth the extra expense of splurging on the real thing.

OTHER EXTRACTS AND FLAVORINGS

Other extracts and flavorings, such as maple, rum, lemon, and brandy, are used in recipes throughout this book. They can be found in the baking aisle alongside the vanilla extract. Store in a cool, dark place to maintain optimal flavor.

PEANUT BUTTER

Peanut butter is a spreadable blend of ground peanuts, vegetable oil, and salt. Two types of peanut butter are used throughout this collection: creamy and chunky. Avoid using natural or old-fashioned peanut butter in all of the recipes in this book because the consistency is significantly different from the commercial styles of peanut butter.

MARSHMALLOWS AND MARSHMALLOW CREME

Marshmallows are white, spongy, pillow-shaped confections made from sugar, corn syrup, gelatin, and egg whites. They are available ready-made in both large and miniature sizes. Opened packages of marshmallows should be placed in a large, zip-top plastic bag to preserve their freshness. Marshmallow creme (also called marshmallow fluff) is available in jar form and looks like melted marshmallow.

EVAPORATED MILK

Evaporated milk is a canned milk product that is made by evaporating milk to half of its volume, producing a creamy texture and rich taste. All of the recipes in this book that require evaporated milk were tested using regular (as opposed to low-fat) evaporated milk.

SWEETENED CONDENSED MILK

Sweetened condensed milk is canned evaporated milk that has been reduced further and sweetened with sugar. It is available in fat-free varieties, too; either the regular or fat-free varieties may be used.

READY, SET, BAKE!

Before you begin, I'm going to stand on my soapbox and make a plea for attention to the following four baking issues, each of which is elementary to cookie baking, yet frequently taken for granted, if not overlooked entirely. I'm talking about choosing the correct cookie sheets and baking pans, getting to know your oven, and using an oven thermometer. So if you're looking to make every batch of cookies, brownies, bars, and biscotti edible perfection, read on.

1. CHOOSE THE BEST COOKIE SHEETS

People have strong opinions about their preferred cookie sheets, so consider the following recommendations as guidelines rather than inflexible rules. I find that the more information I have about the baking process, the easier it is to "foolproof" recipes. For example, knowing that different sheets and pans can produce different results, and why, can reduce the possibility of your favorite recipe tasting wonderful one time, okay the next, and positively inedible on the occasion you plan to share it at a potluck party.

When baking cookies, choose light-colored, dull-finished, heavy-gauge cookie sheets. Shiny sheets work best for cookies that should not brown too much on the bottom.

Except for bar cookies, avoid using cookie sheets with high sides. Such pans can deflect heat as well as make it difficult to remove the cookies for cooling. As a general rule, cookie sheets should be two inches narrower and shorter than the oven to allow for even baking.

It is best to avoid dark aluminum cookie sheets. These sheets have a brown or almost black finish and may absorb heat, causing bottoms of cookies to brown more quickly. If using these sheets is the only option, decrease the baking time and lower the temperature slightly (by about 25°).

Nonstick cookie sheets are easier to clean and help ensure even baking; however, the dough may not spread as much and you may end up with a thicker cookie. On the other hand, rich cookies can spread if baked on a greased sheet. Follow the manufacturer's instructions if using a cookie sheet with a nonstick coating; the oven temperature may need to be reduced by 25°.

Also follow the manufacturer's instructions if using insulated cookie sheets, which are made from two sheets of metal with a layer of air between for insulation. Cookies will not brown as much on the bottom, so it may hard to tell when the cookies are done. Also, cookies may take slightly longer to bake. If you don't have enough cookie sheets, you can invert a jelly roll pan or use heavy-duty foil.

2. SELECT THE RIGHT BAKING PAN

Just as the right cookie sheet is essential for drop and shaped cookies, so too is using the correct size baking pan for brownies and bars. Brownies and bars made in too-large pans, for example, will be over-baked, and those in too-small pans will be under-baked.

If you only have a few pans, and none are the pan size specified, a solution still exists. Use the pan size that you have. If it's larger than what is called for, use a shorter bake time. If it's smaller than what is called for, use a longer bake time and reduce the oven temperature by 25°.

For best results, use shiny metal pans for all of the bar recipes in this book. Not only do metal pans make the bars easier to remove but they also allow the crusts of layered bars to become crispy. If possible, avoid using dark pans. If a dark pan is all you have, reduce the oven temperature by 25°.

3. GET TO KNOW YOUR OVEN

Whether you use it a little or a lot, it is worth taking a few minutes to familiarize yourself with your oven's myriad functions. Some ovens have specialty features specific to baking, such as precision temperature settings and extra-large interior capacities that allow for multiple items baking at once, so take advantage of these for delicious baked results. Also, give the interior a good cleaning. This is especially important if you have no idea when it last got a thorough wipe-down or if you recently baked or roasted something particularly aromatic. Lingering odors or scents can alter the flavor and smell of your cookies and desserts.

The three most common types of baking ovens for the home kitchen are conventional (gas or electric), convection, and toaster.

Conventional oven: This is the most common type of oven. All of the recipes in this book were tested using a standard, conventional oven. The heat source is located in the bottom of conventional ovens, allowing for the heat to rise up through the oven in a more or less even manner.

Convection oven: By contrast, the heat source in a convection oven is located behind the oven wall. In addition, convection ovens have a fan that continuously circulates air through the oven cavity. When hot air is blowing onto food, as opposed to merely surrounding it (as in a conventional oven), the food tends to cook more quickly and evenly, ideal for baking perfect, evenly browned cookies. The circulating air may alter the amount of time needed for baking, so you may need to do a small experimental batch to get a sense of how to adjust the baking time.

Toaster oven: I do not recommend baking any of the cookies or other desserts in this book in a toaster oven. The exceptions to this rule are the combination toaster/convection ovens that have appeared on the market in the last few years. These ovens offer more even circulation of heat than traditional toaster ovens. Drop cookies are the best option for baking small batches of cookies in these ovens, but follow the manufacturer's guidelines for adapting recipe baking times.

4. PURCHASE AND USE AN OVEN THERMOMETER

If I could make a single plea to home bakers it would be this: buy an oven thermometer to check your oven temperatures. Unless you have a state-of-the-art oven (and even then, temperature discrepancies can still occur), it is very likely that your oven temperature is inaccurate. It may be off as few as 5° or as many as 50°, but whatever the discrepancy, it will affect your results.

The good news is that an easy, inexpensive, readily available remedy exists: an oven thermometer. You can find this simple tool in the baking section of most supermarkets or superstores (e.g., Kmart, Target, and Walmart), kitchen stores, and hardware stores (typically, if they have a pots-and-pans section they will carry oven thermometers).

Simply place or attach the oven thermometer in your oven (see package instructions) and preheat. Once your oven indicates that it has reached the temperature setting, check your oven thermometer. If the oven temperature is higher on the thermometer than the setting you selected, you will need to set your oven that many degrees lower. For example, if the thermometer reads 375°F and you had set your oven for 350°F, you know that you will need to set your oven to 325° in the future for it to reach 350°F. Leave the oven thermometer in the oven and check it every time you preheat the oven to monitor temperature accuracy.

While few ovens are precise, most are consistent. That is, if it is 25° hotter than the selected temperature, it tends to stay 25° too hot all of the time. This may shift slightly at extremely high temperatures (exceeding 400°F). However, temperatures lower than 400°F are used for all of the baking recipes in this book.

MEASURING INGREDIENTS
MEASURING DRY INGREDIENTS

When measuring a dry ingredient such as sugar, spices, or salt, spoon it into the appropriate-size dry measuring cup or measuring spoon, heaping it up over the top. Next, slide a straight-edged utensil, such as a knife, across the top to level off the extra. Be careful not to shake or tap the cup or spoon to settle the ingredient or you will have more than you need.

MEASURING LIQUID INGREDIENTS

Use a clear plastic or glass measuring cup or container with lines up the sides to measure liquid ingredients. Set the container on the counter and pour the liquid to the appropriate mark. Lower your head to read the measurement at eye level.

MEASURING SYRUPS, HONEY, AND MOLASSES

Measure syrups, honey, and molasses as you would other liquid ingredients, but lightly spray the measuring cup or container with nonstick cooking spray before filling. The syrup, honey, or molasses will slide out of the cup without sticking, allowing for both accurate measuring and easy cleanup.

MEASURING MOIST INGREDIENTS

Some moist ingredients, such as brown sugar, coconut, and dried fruits, must be firmly packed into the measuring cup to be measured accurately. Use a dry measuring cup for these ingredients. Fill the measuring cup to slightly overflowing, then pack down the ingredient firmly with the back of a spoon. Add more of the ingredient and pack down again until the cup is full and even with the top of the measure.

MEASURING BUTTER

Butter is typically packaged in stick form with markings on the wrapper indicating tablespoon and cup measurements. Use a sharp knife to cut off the amount needed for a recipe.

¼ cup = ½ stick = 4 tablespoons = 2 ounces
½ cup = 1 stick = ¼ pound = 4 ounces
1 cup = 2 sticks = ½ pound = 8 ounces
2 cups = 4 sticks = 1 pound = 16 ounces

MEASURING CREAM CHEESE

Like sticks of butter, bricks of cream cheese are typically packaged with markings on the wrapper indicating tablespoon and cup measurements. Use a sharp knife to cut off the amount needed for a recipe.

MEASURING SPICES, SALT, BAKING POWDER, AND BAKING SODA

Use the standard measuring spoon size specified in the recipe and be sure the spoon is dry when measuring. Fill a standard measuring spoon to the top and level with a spatula or knife. When a recipe calls for a dash of a spice or salt, use about one-sixteenth of a teaspoon. A pinch is considered to be the amount of salt that can be held between the tips of the thumb and forefinger, and is also approximately one-sixteenth of a teaspoon.

MEASURING NUTS

Spoon nuts into a dry measuring cup to the top. Four ounces of whole nuts is the equivalent of 1 cup chopped nuts.

MEASURING EXTRACTS AND FLAVORINGS

Fill the standard measuring spoon size specified in the recipe to the top, being careful not to let any spill over. It's a good idea to avoid measuring extracts or flavorings over the mixing bowl because the spillover will go into the bowl and you will not know the amount of extract or flavoring you have added.

MAKING, BAKING, AND STORING COOKIES

PREHEATING THE OVEN

For perfectly baked cookies, preheat the oven, which takes about 10 to 15 minutes, depending on your oven.

CENTER OF THE OVEN

If baking just one sheet or pan of cookies at a time, place it on a rack set in the center of the oven and change from back to front halfway through the baking cycle. Leave at least 2 inches of space on all sides between the edge of the sheet and the oven walls for proper air circulation.

FOIL-LINE YOUR BAKING PANS

Lining baking pans with aluminum foil is a great way to avoid messy cleanup whenever you bake bar cookies and brownies. Doing so also makes it easy to remove the entire batch of brownies or bars from the pan, making the cutting of perfectly uniform squares and bars a snap.

When bars are cool or nearly cool, simply lift them out of the pan, peel back the foil, and cut. Foil-lining is also a boon during holiday baking seasons, allowing for the production of multiple batches of bars and brownies in no time, with virtually no clean-up.

Foil-lining is simple. Begin by turning the pan upside down. Tear off a piece of aluminum foil longer than the pan, and shape the foil over the pan. Carefully remove the foil and set aside. Flip the pan over and gently fit the shaped foil into the pan, allowing the foil to hang over the sides (the overhanging ends will work as "handles" when the brownies or bars are removed).

TWO COOKIE SHEETS AT A TIME: SWITCH THE RACKS

It's okay to bake more than one sheet of cookies at a time. Use the upper and lower thirds of the oven, reversing sheets from upper to lower and front to back about halfway through the baking period to ensure even baking. Even the best ovens can build up hot spots in certain areas.

Keep in mind, too, that two sheets of cookies in the oven may require a slightly longer baking time than one sheet.

CHECKING FOR DONENESS

Bake cookies the minimum amount of time, even though the center may look slightly under-baked. To check cookies for doneness, press down lightly in the middle to see if it bounces back.

Bake sliced cookies until the edges are firm and the bottoms are lightly browned. Generally, cookies are done when the edges begin to brown, or when they are golden. Every pan bakes differently, depending on the material, thickness, weight, and surface reflection.

Remember to open and close the oven door quickly to maintain the proper baking temperature. Most importantly, watch carefully, especially batches of individual cookies that bake for very short amounts of time. While a watched pot may never boil, unwatched cookies will likely burn.

COOLING COOKIE SHEETS IN BETWEEN BATCHES

Always cool the cookie sheet before baking another batch. A warm pan causes the dough to melt, which can cause overspreading, deformed cookies, or altered baking times. To cool cookie sheets quickly between baking, rinse under cold water until the sheet is completely cooled. Dry and proceed with the next batch of cookies.

COOLING COOKIES

Most of the drop and formed cookies in this collection require that the baked cookies cool on the sheets one or more minutes before removing to a wire cooling rack. This allows the cookies to continue baking (carryover baking) and also allows delicate or crumbly cookies to set up more firmly before being moved.

When ready to remove the baked cookies from the cookie sheet, use a wide spatula, unless the recipe states other cooling directions. Place cookies in a single layer on wire racks to cool evenly, so the bottoms don't get soggy. If the cookie bends or breaks when transferring, wait another minute before trying. Thoroughly cool cookies before storing them to prevent them from becoming soggy.

QUICK COOKIE SHEET Q&A: WHY DO COOKIES STICK?

If cookies stick, it is most likely due to one of the following easily remedied causes:

- The cookie sheets were not sufficiently cleaned between uses.
  SOLUTION: Wash and dry sheets between uses if pieces of cookie remain on sheet, or line the sheets with parchment paper to avoid clean-up altogether).

- The cookie sheets were not greased and the recipe called for greasing.
  SOLUTION: Double-check recipe directions before placing cookies on cookie sheet.

- The cookies were underbaked.
  SOLUTION: Return cookies to oven for one or more minutes.

- The cookies were left on cookie sheets too long before removal.
  SOLUTION: Remove cookies according to the time directed in recipe.

- The cookie batter was too warm.
  SOLUTION: Place batter in refrigerator in between batches. If batter gets too warm, chill 15 to 30 minutes.

- The cookie sheets were warm or hot before baking.
  SOLUTION: Rinse cookie sheets in cold water between batches.

STORING COOKIES

Once cookies are baked, keep them delicious by taking care with their storage. Most importantly, store them in an airtight container for optimal freshness. Sturdier cookies, such as drop cookies, can be placed in a zip-top plastic bag, but more delicate filled and formed cookies are better off stacked between layers of wax paper in a plastic container.

Bar cookies can be stacked in a container between layers of wax paper or stored in their baking pan. I prefer to cut them first and then place them back in the pan for easy removal. Cover the top tightly with aluminum foil, wrap, or a lid. For delicate, crisp cookies, store in a sturdy container such as a cookie jar or tin.

Lay extra-fragile cookies flat in a wide container with parchment or wax paper between the layers. If you have iced or decorated cookies, let them dry before storing. (If freezing, freeze on a pan in a single layer, and then carefully stack layers with wax paper between layers).

FREEZING ALREADY-BAKED COOKIES

To enjoy your cookies for several weeks, or even months, freeze them. For best results, freeze the cookies as soon as possible after they are completely cooled.

Both individual and bar cookies can be frozen with equal success. With either type, it is best to frost at a future date when the cookies have been thawed. Place the cookies in freezer bags or airtight freezer containers for up to 12 months. Double-wrap cookies to prevent them from getting freezer burn or absorbing odors from the freezer. Label the cookies clearly with the name of the cookie and the date. Cookies can be frosted after thawing at room temperature for 15 minutes.

SHIPPING COOKIES

A care package full of home-baked cookies may be the best gift ever. To ensure perfect delivery, follow my tips below:

- Biscotti, bar, and drop cookies can best withstand mailing; tender, fragile cookies are apt to crumble when shipped.

- Line a heavy cardboard box, cookie tin, or empty coffee can with aluminum foil or plastic wrap. Wrap four to six cookies of the same size together in aluminum foil, plastic wrap, or plastic food bags and seal securely with tape; repeat until the container is full.

- Place the heaviest cookies at the bottom of the container and layer the wrapped cookies with bubble wrap or crumpled paper towels. Use either of these to line the container. Seal the container with tape.

drop cookies

Drop cookies are just that, cookies made from spoonfuls of dough dropped onto a cookie sheet, then baked to perfection. Think of chocolate chip, oatmeal raisin, and applesauce cookies, and you know drop cookies. Most of my favorite cookies from childhood—and most likely yours, too—fit into this yummy category. Perhaps it's because these were the first cookies that I was able to help make alongside my mother, from stirring in chocolate chips, raisins, or oats, to spooning up blobs of the delicious dough and plopping them onto cookie sheets. Or maybe it is simply because they are the homiest cookies: uncomplicated, typically lumpy-bumpy, and blissful with a cold glass of milk or a warm mug of cocoa.

Whichever the case, drop cookies are typically the simplest cookies to make and bake. And when you begin with a box of cake mix, they are that much easier. With a short list of ingredients and minimal steps, a range of fresh-from-the-oven cookies—both classics and exciting new twists—are mere minutes away.

Cake Mix WHITE	# CHOCOLATE CHIP COOKIES

Hats off to Ruth Wakefield. Back in the 1930s the clever home baker and proprietor of the Toll House Inn "invented" (whether by mistake or design—the jury is still out on this one) what we now know as the chocolate chip cookie. American cookie baking has never been the same since, and thank goodness. This quick and easy cake-mix version of Mrs. Wakefield's classic creation earns its blue-ribbon tag.

PREHEAT OVEN TO 350°F

MAKES 4½ DOZEN COOKIES

COOKIE SHEETS, GREASED OR LINED WITH PARCHMENT PAPER

1 (18.25-ounce) package white cake mix

½ cup (1 stick) butter, softened

2 large eggs

3 tablespoons packed light brown sugar

1 teaspoon vanilla extract

1½ cups semisweet chocolate chips

Optional: 1 cup chopped pecans or walnuts, toasted

1. Place the cake mix, butter, eggs, brown sugar, and vanilla in a large bowl. Mix with an electric mixer on low speed 1 minute or until blended. Mix in the chocolate chips and (optional) nuts with a wooden spoon.
2. Drop by tablespoonfuls, 2 inches apart, onto prepared cookie sheets.
3. Bake 10 to 13 minutes or until golden at the edges and just barely set at center when lightly touched. Cool 1 minute on sheets, then remove cookies with spatula to wire racks to cool completely.

VARIATIONS *for Chocolate Chip Cookies*

CHERRY (OR CRANBERRY) MILK CHOCOLATE CHIPPERS: Prepare as directed but replace semisweet chocolate chips with milk chocolate chips and add ⅔ cup dried tart cherries or dried cranberries instead of nuts.

MINT CHOCOLATE CHIP COOKIES: Prepare as directed but replace the vanilla extract with ¾ teaspoon peppermint extract. Sprinkle cookie tops with crushed red-and-white-striped peppermint candies or candy canes just before baking (about 1 cup total).

MOCHA CHOCOLATE CHIP COOKIES: Prepare as directed but dissolve 1 tablespoon instant coffee powder in the vanilla extract before adding.

TOFFEE CHOCOLATE CHIP COOKIES: Prepare as directed but add ¾ cup toffee baking bits to the dough instead of nuts.

FAMOUS NAMELESS CHOCOLATE CHIP COOKIES

I love these cookies. A friend shared a version of the recipe with me back in graduate school and they fast became favorites, mostly because they are so incredibly good, but also because they are made entirely with pantry ingredients (great for spur-of-the-moment cookie baking). The mayonnaise takes the place of both eggs and oil, producing a delicate crunch. And if you're wondering about the name: it rhymes with the name of a brand of famous chocolate chip cookies popular in the 1980s.

PREHEAT OVEN TO 350°F

MAKES 4 DOZEN COOKIES

COOKIE SHEETS, GREASED OR LINED WITH PARCHMENT PAPER

1 (18.25-ounce) package white cake mix

2 (4-serving size) packages cook-and-stir (not instant) butterscotch pudding mix

1¼ cups mayonnaise (not reduced fat)

1 (12-ounce) package (2 cups) semisweet chocolate chips

1 cup chopped pecans (preferably toasted)

1. Mix the cake mix, dry pudding mixes, and mayonnaise in a large bowl with an electric mixer set on medium speed 1 to 2 minutes until blended. Mix in the chocolate chips and pecans with a wooden spoon.
2. Drop the dough by tablespoonfuls, 2 inches apart, onto prepared cookie sheets.
3. Bake 9 to 10 minutes or until just barely set at edges (cookies will continue to bake on the hot sheets). Cool 5 minutes on sheets, then remove cookies with spatula to wire racks to cool completely.

Tip: Be sure to let the cookies sit the full 5 minutes on the sheets; they are very delicate right out of the oven but will firm up as they cool on the sheets.

VARIATION *for Famous Nameless Chocolate Chip Cookies*

FAMOUS NAMELESS WHITE CHOCOLATE CHIP COOKIES: Prepare as directed but use vanilla cake mix and white chocolate chips.

WHITE CHOCOLATE AND MACADAMIA COOKIES

Cake Mix
WHITE

These are premium-tasting cookies. Make them for the next bake sale and you can expect them to fly off the plate.

PREHEAT OVEN TO 350°F

MAKES 4 DOZEN COOKIES

COOKIE SHEETS, GREASED OR LINED WITH PARCHMENT PAPER

Buy butter when it goes on sale (often near the spring and winter holidays) and freeze until needed. Defrost overnight in the refrigerator before using.

1 (18.25-ounce) package white cake mix

1 cup all-purpose flour

¾ cup (1½ sticks) butter, melted

½ cup packed light brown sugar

2 large eggs

1 teaspoon vanilla extract

1½ cups white chocolate chips

1 cup chopped macadamia nuts

¾ cup quick-cooking oats

1. Mix the cake mix, flour, melted butter, brown sugar, eggs, and vanilla in a large bowl with an electric mixer set on medium speed 1 to 2 minutes until blended. Mix in the white chocolate chips, nuts, and oats with a wooden spoon.
2. Drop the dough by tablespoonfuls, 2 inches apart, onto prepared cookie sheets.
3. Bake 10 to 13 minutes or until just set and bottoms of cookies are lightly browned. Cool 5 minutes on sheets, then remove cookies with spatula to wire racks to cool completely.

BANANA, PECAN, AND CHOCOLATE CHUNK COOKIES

Cake Mix
YELLOW

Bananas, pecans, and chunks of chocolate? This cookie is Americana personified.

PREHEAT OVEN TO 350°F

MAKES 4½ DOZEN COOKIES

COOKIE SHEETS, GREASED OR LINED WITH PARCHMENT PAPER

1 large, very ripe banana, peeled

1 (18.25-ounce) package yellow cake mix

½ cup (1 stick) butter, melted

⅓ cup packed light brown sugar

1 large egg

1 cup old-fashioned rolled oats

1 cup semisweet chocolate chunks or chips

1 cup chopped pecans

1. Mash the banana in a large bowl with a potato masher or fork. Mix in the cake mix, melted butter, brown sugar, and egg with a wooden spoon until blended. Stir in the oats and chocolate chunks.
2. Drop by tablespoonfuls, 2 inches apart, onto prepared cookie sheets. If desired, sprinkle tops of cookies with chopped nuts; gently press nuts into dough.
3. Bake 10 to 13 minutes or until set at edges and just barely set at center when lightly touched (do not overbake). Cool 1 minute on sheets, then remove cookies with spatula to wire racks to cool completely.

Tip! **TIPS FOR BAKING DROP COOKIES**

1. Cookies bake best one sheet at a time in the oven. If you need to reuse a cookie sheet, give it a quick rinse in cold water, then wipe clean in between batches.
2. Bake drop cookies until the edges are golden brown (or just set if the dough is dark, such as a chocolate dough); the centers may look slightly underbaked. The cookies will continue to bake on the cookie sheet once they are removed from the oven. Follow the recipe instructions for letting the cookies remain on the cookie sheet; the cookies will deflate and firm up as they cool and will be easier to transfer to a cooling rack.
3. Be sure to leave the specified amount of room between the drops of cookie dough. If placed too close together, the sides of the cookies will fuse as the cookies bake.
4. If cookies bake unevenly (i.e., some are overdone, some underdone, others just right), it is most likely due to one of the following reasons: (1) there are hot spots in the oven (correct this in the next batch by rotating the cookie sheet halfway through baking); (2) the dough was not mixed thoroughly; or (3) the drops of dough were of different sizes (a cookie scoop can easily solve this problem).

TRAIL MIX COOKIES

Good-for-you ingredients abound in these sweet and salty energy cookies. They're great travelers, so make plenty for lunch bags, backpacks, and afternoon snacks.

PREHEAT OVEN TO 350°F

MAKES 2½ DOZEN LARGE COOKIES

COOKIE SHEETS, GREASED OR LINED WITH PARCHMENT PAPER

1 (18.25-ounce) package white cake mix

1 cup vegetable oil

3 large eggs

1 teaspoon ground cinnamon

1½ cups quick-cooking oats

¾ cup carob chips or milk chocolate chips

¾ cup roasted, lightly salted cashew pieces or peanuts

½ cup toasted wheat germ

½ cup dried cranberries

1. Place the cake mix, oil, and eggs in a large bowl. Blend with electric mixer set on low speed for 1 minute until blended. Mix in the oats, carob chips, cashews, wheat germ, and dried cranberries with a wooden spoon.
2. Drop the dough by level ¼-cupfuls, 3 inches apart, onto prepared cookie sheets. Flatten slightly with your palm or a spatula.
3. Bake 13 to 17 minutes or until edges are firm and center is just barely set when lightly touched. Cool 1 minute on sheets, then remove cookies with spatula to wire racks to cool completely.

ICED ALMOND COOKIES

For anyone who loves the flavor of almonds, these cookies are the perfect choice. A sour cream-enriched cookie is finished with an elegant almond icing and sprinkle of toasted almonds.

PREHEAT OVEN TO 350°F

MAKES 4 DOZEN COOKIES

COOKIE SHEETS, GREASED OR LINED WITH PARCHMENT PAPER

1 (18.25-ounce) package white cake mix

1 (8-ounce) container sour cream (not reduced fat)

⅓ cup (1 stick) butter, softened

2 large eggs

¾ teaspoon almond extract, divided

2 cups confectioners' sugar

2 tablespoons half and half (light cream)

½ cup sliced almonds, toasted

1. Place the cake mix, sour cream, butter, eggs, and ¼ teaspoon almond extract in a large bowl. Blend with electric mixer set on low speed for 1 minute until blended.

2. Drop by tablespoonfuls, 2 inches apart, onto prepared cookie sheets.

3. Bake 9 to 12 minutes or until edges are firm and center is just barely set when lightly touched. Cool 1 minute on sheets, then remove cookies with spatula to wire racks to cool completely.

4. Mix the confectioners' sugar, half and half, and remaining ¼ teaspoon almond extract in a small bowl until blended. Spread cooled cookies with icing and sprinkle with almonds.

GINGERBREAD-OATMEAL COOKIES

These oatmeal cookies are a rich, dark brown from the addition of molasses to the dough, and then loaded with all of the familiar spices of classic gingerbread. They are pure comfort in every bite.

PREHEAT OVEN TO 375°F

MAKES 4 DOZEN COOKIES

COOKIE SHEETS, GREASED OR LINED WITH
    PARCHMENT PAPER

1 (18.25-ounce) package spice cake mix

⅓ cup vegetable oil

¼ cup dark molasses

2 large eggs

1 tablespoon ground ginger

1 teaspoon ground cinnamon

¼ teaspoon ground cloves

1⅔ cups quick-cooking oats

KNOW YOUR OATS

Old-fashioned and quick-cooking (not instant) oats may be used interchangeably in any recipe in this collection. Old-fashioned oats will produce a moister, coarser cookie, while quick-cooking oats will result in a finer-textured cookie.

1. Mix the cake mix, oil, molasses, eggs, ginger, cinnamon, and cloves in a large bowl with an electric mixer set on medium speed 1 to 2 minutes until blended. Mix in the oats with a wooden spoon.

2. Drop the dough by tablespoonfuls, 2 inches apart, onto prepared cookie sheets.

3. Bake 8 to 11 minutes or until just set and bottoms of cookies are lightly browned. Cool 5 minutes on sheets, then remove cookies with spatula to wire racks to cool completely.

HONEY-LEMON DROPS

Cake Mix
WHITE

These honey-sweetened lemon cookies are a sophisticated offering any time of the year. They're particularly good for tea time, so brew a pot of your favorite fragrant tea such as jasmine or Earl Gray.

PREHEAT OVEN TO 350°F

MAKES 4½ DOZEN COOKIES

COOKIE SHEETS, GREASED OR LINED WITH
    PARCHMENT PAPER

1 (18.25-ounce) package white cake mix

½ cup vegetable shortening

¼ cup honey

1 large egg

1 tablespoon grated lemon peel

2 cups confectioners' sugar

1½ tablespoons fresh lemon juice

1. Place the cake mix, shortening, honey, egg, and lemon peel in large bowl. Mix with an electric mixer on low speed 1 minute or until blended.
2. Drop by tablespoonfuls, 2 inches apart, onto prepared cookie sheets.
3. Bake 9 to 12 minutes or until just barely set at center when lightly touched. Cool 1 minute on sheets, then remove cookies with spatula to wire racks to cool completely.
4. Mix the confectioners' sugar and lemon juice in a small bowl until smooth. Drizzle icing over cooled cookies.

COCONUT CHEWIES WITH CHOCOLATE DRIZZLE

Cake Mix
WHITE

Chewy and rich with coconut and chocolate, these quick and easy cookies are winners at any occasion.

MAKES 3½ DOZEN COOKIES

COOKIE SHEETS, UNGREASED OR LINED WITH
    PARCHMENT PAPER

1 (18.25-ounce) package white cake mix

1 (14-ounce) bag sweetened flake coconut

1 (14-ounce) can sweetened condensed
    milk (not evaporated)

⅓ cup whole or lowfat milk

1 cup semisweet chocolate chips

2 teaspoons vegetable shortening

1. Mix the cake mix, coconut, condensed milk, and whole or lowfat milk in a large bowl with a wooden spoon until blended. Cover and chill 2 hours.

2. Preheat oven to 375°F. Drop the dough by tablespoonfuls, 2 inches apart, onto prepared cookie sheets.

3. Bake 10 to 14 minutes or until just set and bottoms of cookies are lightly browned. Cool 5 minutes on sheets, then remove cookies with spatula to wire racks to cool completely.

4. Microwave the chocolate chips and shortening in a medium microwaveable bowl on High, 1 minute, stirring after 30 seconds, until melted and smooth. Using a fork, drizzle tops of cooled cookies with the melted chocolate. Chill cookies 10 minutes to set the chocolate.

VARIATION *for Coconut Chewies with Chocolate Drizzle*

GERMAN CHOCOLATE CHEWIES: Prepare as directed but use a German Chocolate cake mix and milk chocolate chips.

Cake Mix
DEVIL'S FOOD

CHOCOLATE FUDGE BANANA CHIPPERS

These tender, chocolate-banana cookies are packed with chocolate chips times two (melted into the batter, and stirred in whole) then given some salty-sweet crunch with some roasted cashews.

PREHEAT OVEN TO 375°F

MAKES 4 DOZEN COOKIES

COOKIE SHEETS, UNGREASED OR LINED WITH PARCHMENT PAPER

1 (12-ounce) bag (2 cups) semisweet chocolate chips, divided

6 tablespoons (¾ stick) butter

1 (18.25-ounce) package devil's food cake mix

¾ cup mashed ripe banana (about 2 small)

1 large egg

1 cup roasted, lightly salted cashew pieces, coarsely chopped

1. Microwave 1 cup of the chocolate chips with the butter in a large microwaveable bowl on High, 1 minute and 30 seconds, stirring after 30 seconds, until melted and smooth. Mix in the cake mix, mashed banana, and egg with a wooden spoon until blended. Mix in the cashews and remaining 1 cup chocolate chips.

2. Drop the dough by tablespoonfuls, 2 inches apart, onto ungreased cookie sheets.

3. Bake 9 to 12 minutes or until just set. Cool 2 minutes on sheets, then remove cookies with spatula to wire racks to cool completely.

Tip!

JUMBO DROP COOKIES: HERE'S THE SCOOP

Longing to make giant cookies like the ones in the pastry case at the coffee shop? You can with any drop cookie.

First, prepare the dough as directed. Use a larger cookie scoop (3 to 4 tablespoons) to scoop the dough onto the cookie sheet, leaving about 3 inches between the mounds of dough (you might want to try a few to start with to see what size you like and to see how much they spread). Bake at a lower temperature (25°F lower than the recipe calls for) to prevent drying out the cookie, and bake for a few minutes more per batch (usually about 13 to 15 minutes). Try a test batch of 2 or 3 cookies before baking an entire sheet.

Cake Mix
WHITE

TRIPLE-CHIP COOKIES

Simple is so often best: three types of chips, one easy dough, and you're done. Bring on the applause.

PREHEAT OVEN TO 350°F

MAKES 4 DOZEN COOKIES

COOKIE SHEETS, GREASED OR LINED WITH PARCHMENT PAPER

1 (18.25-ounce) package white cake mix
½ cup quick-cooking oats
½ cup vegetable oil
2 large eggs
½ cup butterscotch chocolate chips
½ cup semisweet chocolate chips
½ cup white chocolate chips

1. Mix the cake mix, oats, oil, and eggs in a large bowl with an electric mixer set on medium speed 1 to 2 minutes until blended. Mix in all of the chips with a wooden spoon.
2. Drop the dough by tablespoonfuls, 2 inches apart, onto prepared cookie sheets.
3. Bake 9 to 12 minutes or until just set at edges. Cool 5 minutes on sheets, then remove cookies with spatula to wire racks to cool completely.

SPUMONI CHUNK COOKIES

Cake Mix
WHITE

Spumoni, a colorful Italian dessert made of multiple layers of ice cream, candied fruits, chocolate, and nuts, was the inspiration for this over-the-top cookie.

PREHEAT OVEN TO 350°F

MAKES 4½ DOZEN COOKIES

COOKIE SHEETS, GREASED OR LINED WITH
PARCHMENT PAPER

1 (18.25-ounce) package white cake mix

½ cup (1 stick) butter, softened

2 large eggs

½ teaspoon almond extract

1 cup dried cherries, coarsely chopped

1 cup semisweet chocolate chunks

1 cup roasted, salted, shelled pistachio nuts, coarsely chopped

1. Place the cake mix, butter, eggs, and almond extract in large bowl. Mix with an electric mixer on low speed 1 minute or until blended. Mix in the cherries, chocolate chips, and pistachios with a wooden spoon.
2. Drop by tablespoonfuls, 2 inches apart, onto prepared cookie sheets.
3. Bake 10 to 13 minutes or until just barely set at center when lightly touched. Cool 1 minute on sheets, then remove cookies with spatula to wire racks to cool completely.

DARK CHOCOLATE-DIPPED APRICOT COOKIES

Cake Mix
WHITE

Inspired by premium glacé apricots that have been dunked in dark chocolate, these cookies are studded with sweet chunks of tart-sweet apricots, scented with orange peel, then dipped in dark chocolate—pure decadence!

PREHEAT OVEN TO 350°F

MAKES 4 DOZEN COOKIES

COOKIE SHEETS, GREASED OR LINED WITH
PARCHMENT PAPER

1 (18.25-ounce) package white cake mix

½ cup (1 stick) butter, softened

1 large egg

1 teaspoon grated orange peel

1¼ cups chopped dried apricots

2 cups bittersweet or semisweet chocolate chips, divided

2 teaspoons vegetable shortening

1. Place the cake mix, butter, egg, and orange peel in large bowl. Mix with an electric mixer on low speed 1 minute or until blended. Mix in the dried apricots with a wooden spoon.
2. Drop by tablespoonfuls, 2 inches apart, onto prepared cookie sheets.
3. Bake 10 to 13 minutes or until just barely set at center when lightly touched. Cool 1 minute on sheets, then remove cookies with spatula to wire racks to cool completely.
4. In small microwavable bowl, microwave the chocolate chips and vegetable shortening on High 1 to 1½ minutes or until melted and smooth. Dip half of each cookie into melted chocolate. Place on waxed paper and chill 10 minutes until set.

Cake Mix
WHITE

SALTY-SWEET NUTTY CHIPPERS

The taste of chocolate, peanut butter, the surprise of salty potato chips, and crunchy nuts in these cookies is a taste of pure indulgence. If you've got a really sweet tooth, consider dipping the cooled cookies in melted chocolate.

PREHEAT OVEN TO 375°F
MAKES 4 DOZEN COOKIES
COOKIE SHEETS, GREASED OR LINED WITH PARCHMENT PAPER

1 (18.25-ounce) package white cake mix
1 cup creamy peanut butter (not old-fashioned or natural style)
2 large eggs
⅓ cup whole or lowfat milk
1 cup crushed plain potato chips
1 cup semisweet chocolate chips
1 cup chopped lightly salted mixed nuts

1. Mix the cake mix, peanut butter, eggs, and milk in a large bowl with a wooden spoon until blended. Stir in the crushed potato chips, chocolate chips, and nuts.
2. Drop by tablespoonfuls, 2 inches apart, onto prepared cookie sheets. Gently flatten cookies with palm or spatula.
3. Bake 9 to 12 minutes or until edges are firm and center is just barely set when lightly touched. Cool 3 minutes on sheets, then remove cookies with spatula to wire racks to cool completely.

Cake Mix
CHOCOLATE FUDGE
or CHOCOLATE

CHOCOLATE, PEANUT BUTTER, AND BANANA COOKIES

Chocolate, peanut butter, and banana cookie dough and peanut butter baking chips…it's a great new way to savor the classic chocolate-peanut butter combination.

PREHEAT OVEN TO 350°F

MAKES 4½ DOZEN COOKIES

COOKIE SHEETS, GREASED OR LINED WITH
PARCHMENT PAPER

1 large, very ripe banana, peeled

1 (18.25-ounce) package chocolate fudge or
chocolate cake mix

½ cup creamy or chunky-style peanut butter

1 large egg

2 tablespoons vegetable oil

1½ cups peanut butter baking chips

¾ cup quick-cooking oats

1. Mash the banana in a large bowl with a potato masher or fork. Mix in the cake mix, peanut butter, egg, and oil with a wooden spoon until blended. Mix in the peanut butter chips and oats.
2. Drop by tablespoonfuls, 2 inches apart, onto prepared cookie sheets.
3. Bake 10 to 13 minutes or until set at edges and just barely set at center when lightly touched (do not overbake). Cool 1 minute on sheets, then remove cookies with spatula to wire racks to cool completely.

Cake Mix
DEVIL'S FOOD

BLACK BEAUTIES

These rich, triple-chocolate cookies—chocolate dough, chocolate chips, and chocolate dip—are the wickedly decadent antithesis of vanilla wafers—the only cookie choice for passionate chocoholics.

PREHEAT OVEN TO 350°F

MAKES 4 DOZEN COOKIES

COOKIE SHEETS, GREASED OR LINED WITH
PARCHMENT PAPER

1 (18.25-ounce) package devil's food cake mix

½ cup (1 stick) butter, softened

2 large eggs

3 cups bittersweet or semisweet chocolate
chips, divided

1 cup chopped macadamia nuts or pecans
(preferably toasted)

2 teaspoons vegetable shortening

1. Place the cake mix, butter, and eggs in a large bowl. Mix with an electric mixer on low speed 1 minute or until blended. Mix in 1 cup chocolate chips and the nuts with a wooden spoon.
2. Drop by tablespoonfuls, 2 inches apart, onto prepared cookie sheets.
3. Bake 10 to 13 minutes or until just barely set at center when lightly touched. Cool 1 minute on sheets, then remove cookies with spatula to wire racks to cool completely.
4. In small microwavable bowl, microwave the remaining chocolate chips and vegetable shortening on High 1 to 1½ minutes or until melted and smooth. Dip half of each cookie into melted chocolate. Place on waxed paper and chill 10 minutes until set.

Cake Mix WHITE COCONUT MACAROONS

I'm a bit of a snob about macaroons—I like the kind that strike a good balance between chewy and crisp with just a slight nuance of almond flavor. This recipe fits the bill. Better still, you can bang out a batch in well under an hour.

PREHEAT OVEN TO 350°F

MAKES 6 DOZEN COOKIES

COOKIE SHEETS, GREASED OR LINED WITH PARCHMENT PAPER

1 (18.25-ounce) package white cake mix

1 cup water

⅓ cup vegetable oil

3 large egg whites

¾ teaspoon almond extract

2 (14-ounce) packages sweetened flaked coconut

1. Place the cake mix, water, oil, egg whites, and almond extract in a large bowl. Blend with an electric mixer set on medium speed for 2 minutes until blended. Stir in the coconut with a wooden spoon.
2. Drop the dough by tablespoonfuls onto prepared sheets.
3. Bake 12 to 14 minutes or until golden brown. Cool 1 minute on sheets, then remove cookies with spatula to wire racks to cool completely.

VARIATION *for Coconut Macaroons*

CHOCOLATE CHIP MACAROONS: Prepare as directed but add 2 cups miniature semisweet chocolate chips to the batter along with the coconut.

BLACK-AND-WHITE COOKIES

These cake-like cookies, with their dramatic chocolate and vanilla icings, are New York classics.

PREHEAT OVEN TO 350°F

MAKES 3 DOZEN COOKIES

COOKIE SHEETS, UNGREASED OR LINED WITH
    PARCHMENT PAPER

1 (18.25-ounce) package white cake mix

⅓ cup buttermilk

¼ cup (½ stick) butter, softened

2 large eggs

1 teaspoon grated lemon peel

Icings:

3 cups confectioners' sugar

2 tablespoons light corn syrup

1 tablespoon fresh lemon juice

½ teaspoon vanilla extract

3 tablespoons water

½ cup unsweetened Dutch-process cocoa
    powder

1. Mix the cake mix, buttermilk, butter, eggs, and lemon peel in a large bowl with a wooden spoon until blended.
2. With medium cookie scoop or by the heaping tablespoon, drop the dough 3 inches apart onto ungreased cookie sheets.
3. Bake 12 to 15 minutes or until edges are light golden brown. Cool 5 minutes on sheets, then remove cookies with spatula to wire racks to cool completely.
4. Mix the confectioners' sugar, corn syrup, lemon juice, vanilla, and 2 tablespoons water in a small bowl until smooth. Transfer half of icing to another bowl and stir in cocoa, adding more water, ½ teaspoon at a time, to thin to same consistency as white icing.
5. Spread white icing over half of the bottom (flat side) of each cookie and chocolate over other half.

GIANT DOUBLE-PEANUT-BUTTER OAT COOKIES

My father is a certified peanut butter fanatic, so I created these cookies just for him. But I'm confident that they will be loved by peanut butter lovers everywhere.

PREHEAT OVEN TO 350°F

MAKES 3 DOZEN GIANT COOKIES

COOKIE SHEETS, GREASED OR LINED WITH
    PARCHMENT PAPER

1 (18.25-ounce) package white cake mix

1 cup creamy peanut butter

½ cup (1 stick) butter, melted

2 large eggs

⅓ cup whole or lowfat milk

1 cup quick-cooking oats

1 (10-ounce) package peanut butter baking chips

1. Place the cake mix, peanut butter, melted butter, eggs, and milk in a large bowl. Mix with an electric mixer on medium speed 1 to 2 minutes until blended. Mix in the oats and baking chips until blended.

2. Drop by ¼-cupfuls, 3 inches apart, onto prepared cookie sheets.

3. Bake 11 to 15 minutes or until edges are firm and center is just barely set when lightly touched. Cool 1 minute on sheets, then remove cookies with spatula to wire racks to cool completely.

MELTING BUTTER

Butter has a lower smoking point than most other fats, so be sure to watch it carefully when melting.

VARIATION *for Giant Double-Peanut-Butter Oat Cookies*

GIANT PEANUT BUTTER, OAT, AND CHOCOLATE JUMBLES: Prepare as directed, but use 1 cup candy-coated milk chocolate candies (e.g., M&Ms) and 1 cup semisweet or milk chocolate chips in place of peanut butter baking chips.

POTATO CHIP COOKIES

The combination of salty and sweet has been getting more and more popular in dessert offerings, and do I have a winner for you here: a brown sugar-y cookie, plump with butterscotch chips and crunchy-salty with crushed potato chips. Trust me on this one—you will love them, and so will everyone else who gets a taste.

PREHEAT OVEN TO 350°F

MAKES 4 DOZEN COOKIES

COOKIE SHEETS, GREASED OR LINED WITH
    PARCHMENT PAPER

1 (18.25-ounce) package white cake mix

½ cup (1 stick) butter, softened

¼ cup packed light brown sugar

2 large eggs

2 cups crushed plain potato chips

1 cup butterscotch chocolate chips

1. Mix the cake mix, butter, brown sugar, and eggs in a large bowl with an electric mixer set on medium speed 1 to 2 minutes until blended. Mix in the potato chips and butterscotch chips with a wooden spoon.
2. Drop the dough by tablespoonfuls, 2 inches apart, onto prepared cookie sheets.
3. Bake 9 to 12 minutes or until just set at edges. Cool 5 minutes on sheets, then remove cookies with spatula to wire racks to cool completely.

HUMMINGBIRD COOKIES

Hummingbird cake is a rich, *moist, old-fashioned Southern cake loaded with banana, pineapple, nuts, and spice, then gilded with cream cheese frosting. I've captured all of the flavors of the beloved cake in this moist and delicious cookie.*

PREHEAT OVEN TO 350°F

MAKES 4 DOZEN COOKIES

COOKIE SHEETS, GREASED OR LINED WITH PARCHMENT PAPER

1 (18.25-ounce) package spice cake mix

1 (8-ounce) can crushed pineapple, drained, 2 tablespoons juice reserved

⅓ cup mashed very ripe banana (about 1 small)

¼ cup all-purpose flour

¼ cup (½ stick) butter, melted

1 large egg

1 teaspoon ground cinnamon

1 cup chopped pecans

1 cup (½ a 16-ounce tub) ready-to-spread cream cheese frosting

1. Mix the cake mix, drained pineapple, banana, flour, melted butter, egg, and cinnamon with a wooden spoon until blended.
2. Drop the dough by tablespoonfuls, 2 inches apart, onto prepared cookie sheets. Sprinkle tops of cookies with pecans.
3. Bake 10 to 13 minutes or until set at edges and just barely set at center when lightly touched. Cool 1 minute on sheets, then remove cookies with spatula to wire racks to cool completely.
4. Whisk the frosting with reserved 2 tablespoons pineapple juice in a small bowl until smooth. Drizzle or spread frosting over cooled cookies.

ICED APPLESAUCE-OATMEAL COOKIES

Applesauce cookies and oatmeal cookies are equally nostalgic cookie favorites, so I thought it was fitting to combine the two in one easy, old-fashioned cookie. According to all of the tasters, they're winners (especially with a drizzle of maple icing on top).

PREHEAT OVEN TO 375°F

MAKES 4 DOZEN COOKIES

COOKIE SHEETS, GREASED OR LINED WITH
    PARCHMENT PAPER

1 (18.25-ounce) package spice cake mix

½ cup chunky applesauce

¼ cup vegetable oil

¼ cup packed light brown sugar

1 large egg

1½ cups quick-cooking oats

1 cup raisins

Icing:

2 cups confectioners' sugar

3 tablespoons pure maple syrup or maple-
    flavored pancake syrup

3 tablespoons water

1. Mix the cake mix, applesauce, oil, brown sugar, and egg in a large bowl with an electric mixer set on medium speed 1 to 2 minutes until blended. Mix in the oats and raisins with a wooden spoon.

2. Drop the dough by tablespoonfuls, 2 inches apart, onto prepared cookie sheets.

3. Bake 10 to 13 minutes or until just set and bottoms of cookies are lightly browned. Cool 1 minute on sheets, then remove cookies with spatula to wire racks to cool completely.

4. Whisk the confectioners' sugar, syrup, and water in a small bowl until blended and smooth. Drizzle icing over top of cooled cookies using a fork.

DOUBLE-CHOCOLATE COCONUT COOKIES

Cake Mix
CHOCOLATE

While I was developing the new recipes for this book, these cookies became an obsession. With their perfect ratio of chocolate to coconut to butter to almond flavor, they are almost irresistible. At a recent party, I put them out at 6 p.m. and by 6:20 p.m., they were gone!

PREHEAT OVEN TO 375°F

MAKES 4 DOZEN COOKIES

COOKIE SHEETS, GREASED OR LINED WITH
PARCHMENT PAPER

1 (18.25-ounce) package chocolate cake mix

½ cup quick-cooking oats

2 large eggs

½ cup (1 stick) butter, melted

½ teaspoon almond extract

2 cups sweetened flaked coconut

1 cup semisweet or white chocolate chips

1. Mix the cake mix, oats, eggs, melted butter, and almond extract in a large bowl with an electric mixer set on medium speed 1 to 2 minutes until blended. Mix in the coconut and chocolate chips with a wooden spoon.
2. Drop the dough by tablespoonfuls, 2 inches apart, onto prepared cookie sheets.
3. Bake 9 to 12 minutes or until just set and bottoms of cookies are lightly browned. Cool 2 minutes on sheets, then remove cookies with spatula to wire racks to cool completely.

NO-BAKE PEANUT BUTTER CHEWIES

Cake Mix
WHITE

No need to turn on the oven—these rich and chewy cookies are prepared on the stovetop, then dropped onto wax paper to cool. That's it!

MAKES 3½ DOZEN COOKIES

COOKIE SHEETS, LINED WITH FOIL OR WAX
PAPER

1½ cups honey or light corn syrup

1 cup creamy peanut butter

1 (18.25-ounce) package white cake mix

7 cups crisp rice cereal (e.g., Kellogg's Rice Krispies)

1½ cups roasted, salted peanuts

1. Place the honey in a Dutch oven or extra-large, heavy-bottom pot. Bring to a boil over

medium heat. Stir in the peanut butter until blended, then stir in cake mix. Cook, stirring constantly, 2 minutes longer.

2. Remove mixture from heat and immediately stir in the cereal and nuts with a wooden spoon.

3. Working quickly, drop by tablespoonfuls onto prepared cookie sheets. Flatten slightly with spoon or spatula. Cool completely on sheets. Store at room temperature 1 week.

Cake Mix DEVIL'S FOOD — CHOCOLATE-ALMOND COOKIES

Almond filling—available in the baking section where pie fillings are shelved—*makes these European-inspired cookies short work.*

PREHEAT OVEN TO 350°F

MAKES 3½ DOZEN COOKIES

COOKIE SHEETS, GREASED OR LINED WITH PARCHMENT PAPER

1 (18.25-ounce) package devil's food cake mix

1 (12.5-ounce) can almond filling

¼ cup butter, melted

2 large eggs

1½ cups miniature semisweet chocolate chips

1. Mix the cake mix, almond filling, melted butter, and eggs in a large bowl with a wooden spoon until blended. Mix in the chocolate chips.

2. Drop by tablespoonfuls, 2 inches apart, onto prepared cookie sheets.

3. Bake 9 to 12 minutes or until edges are firm and center is just barely set when lightly touched. Cool 1 minute on sheets, then remove cookies with spatula to wire racks to cool completely.

VARIATIONS *for Chocolate-Almond Cookies*

WHITE CHOCOLATE-ALMOND COOKIES: Prepare as directed but use a white cake mix and add 1½ cups white chocolate chips.

ALMOND SPICE COOKIES: Prepare as directed but use a spice cake mix and add 1½ teaspoons pumpkin pie spice. Omit chocolate chips. Sprinkle cooled cookies with confectioners' sugar.

HEALTHY CHOCOLATE-PUMPKIN COOKIES

These two-ingredient cookies—or three ingredients if you decide to add some chocolate chips— *are a healthy way to satisfy a sweet tooth.*

PREHEAT OVEN TO 350°F

MAKES 3 DOZEN COOKIES

COOKIE SHEETS, GREASED OR LINED WITH
PARCHMENT PAPER

1 (18.25-ounce) package devil's food or
chocolate cake mix

1 (15-ounce) can unsweetened pumpkin puree

Optional: ⅔ cup miniature semisweet
chocolate chips

1. Mix the cake mix and pumpkin puree in a large bowl with a wooden spoon until blended (dough will be stiff). If desired, mix in the chocolate chips.
2. Drop by tablespoonfuls, 2 inches apart, onto prepared cookie sheets.
3. Bake 8 to 11 minutes or until edges are firm and center is just barely set when lightly touched. Cool 1 minute on sheets, then remove cookies with spatula to wire racks to cool completely.

VARIATION *for Healthy Chocolate-Pumpkin Cookies*

HEALTHY PUMPKIN-SPICE COOKIES: Prepare as directed, but use a spice or yellow cake mix and add 1½ teaspoons pumpkin pie spice or cinnamon. If desired, add ⅔ cup chopped dried cranberries or raisins.

CHOCOLATE CAKE COOKIES

These have the taste and texture of perfect, bite-size chocolate cakes.

PREHEAT OVEN TO 350°F

MAKES 4 DOZEN COOKIES

COOKIE SHEETS, GREASED OR LINED WITH
PARCHMENT PAPER

1 (18.25-ounce) package devil's food cake mix

1 box (4-serving size) chocolate instant
pudding and pie filling mix

1 cup sour cream

¼ cup water

2 large eggs

Optional: 1½ cups semisweet, milk, or
white chocolate chips

1. Mix the cake mix, pudding mix, sour cream, water, and eggs in a large bowl with a wooden spoon until blended (dough will be stiff). If desired, mix in the chocolate chips.
2. Drop by tablespoonfuls, 2 inches apart, onto prepared cookie sheets.
3. Bake 9 to 12 minutes or until edges are firm and center is just barely set when lightly touched. Cool 1 minute on sheets, then remove cookies with spatula to wire racks to cool completely.

VARIATIONS *for Chocolate Cake Cookies*

VANILLA CAKE COOKIES: Prepare as directed, but use a white cake mix, vanilla pudding mix, and white chocolate chips.

BIRTHDAY CAKE COOKIES: Prepare as directed, but use a confetti cake mix, vanilla pudding mix, and omit chocolate chips. Frost cooled cookies with prepared vanilla or cream cheese frosting.

Cake Mix
SPICE

SPICED YOGURT COOKIES

These spiced, cake-like cookies are the perfect accompaniment to a cup of tea on a chilly day.

PREHEAT OVEN TO 350°F

MAKES 4 DOZEN COOKIES

COOKIE SHEETS, GREASED OR LINED WITH
    PARCHMENT PAPER

1 (18.25-ounce) package spice cake mix

1 box (4-serving size) vanilla instant
    pudding and pie filling mix

1 cup plain yogurt (not fat-free)

¼ cup oil

2 large eggs

1 teaspoon pumpkin pie spice or ground
    cinnamon

Optional: 1 cup chopped pecans or walnuts

1. Mix the cake mix, pudding mix, yogurt, oil, eggs, and pumpkin pie spice in a large bowl with a wooden spoon until blended (dough will be stiff).
2. Drop by tablespoonfuls, 2 inches apart, onto prepared cookie sheets. If desired, sprinkle tops of cookies with the chopped nuts.
3. Bake 9 to 12 minutes or until edges are firm and center is just barely set when lightly touched. Cool 1 minute on sheets, then remove cookies with spatula to wire racks to cool completely.

APPLE HARVEST COOKIES

Cranberries, apples, and nuts, covered in a quick and spicy dough, make for a festive, fuss-free cookie. If other nuts, such as almonds or pecans, are what you have on hand, use them interchangeably with the walnuts, or leave them out altogether if you prefer.

PREHEAT OVEN TO 350°F

MAKES 4½ DOZEN COOKIES

COOKIE SHEETS, GREASED OR LINED WITH
    PARCHMENT PAPER

1 (18.25-ounce) package spice cake mix

⅓ cup vegetable oil

2 large eggs

1 teaspoon ground cinnamon

1 cup peeled, cored, and finely chopped
    tart apple (e.g., Granny Smith)

⅔ cup dried cranberries

1 cup chopped walnuts

1. Mix the cake mix, oil, eggs, and cinnamon with a wooden spoon until blended. Mix in the apple and cranberries.
2. Drop the dough by tablespoonfuls, 2 inches apart, on prepared cookie sheets. Sprinkle tops with the chopped walnuts, gently pressing into dough.
3. Bake 9 to 12 minutes or until set at edges and just barely set at center when lightly touched. Cool 1 minute on sheets, then remove cookies with spatula to wire racks to cool completely.

APPLESAUCE COOKIES

This slightly spicy, nostalgic cookie is simple and good, with lots of familiar flavors and a soft, old-fashioned texture—just what you want to bake on a cool autumn day.

PREHEAT OVEN TO 350°F

MAKES 4 DOZEN COOKIES

COOKIE SHEETS, GREASED OR LINED WITH
    PARCHMENT PAPER

1 (18.25-ounce) package spice cake mix

½ cup vegetable oil

½ cup applesauce

1 large egg

1 cup raisins or dried cranberries

1. Place the cake mix, oil, applesauce, and egg in a large bowl. Blend with electric mixer set on low speed for 1 minute until blended. Mix in the raisins with a wooden spoon.

2. Drop by tablespoonfuls, 2 inches apart, onto prepared cookie sheets.
3. Bake 9 to 12 minutes or until edges are firm and center is just barely set when lightly touched. Cool 1 minute on sheets, then remove cookies with spatula to wire racks to cool completely.

APRICOT-COCONUT COOKIES

Apricot fans rejoice—this is an exceptional cookie, crisp-chewy and rich with fruit.

PREHEAT OVEN TO 375°F

MAKES 4 DOZEN COOKIES

COOKIE SHEETS, GREASED OR LINED WITH
    PARCHMENT PAPER

1 (18.25-ounce) package white cake mix

½ cup quick-cooking oats

2 large eggs

½ cup vegetable oil

2 teaspoons grated orange peel

1 cup chopped dried apricots

½ cup sweetened flaked coconut

1. Mix the cake mix, oats, eggs, oil, and orange peel in a large bowl with an electric mixer set on medium speed 1 to 2 minutes until blended. Mix in the apricots and coconut with a wooden spoon.
2. Drop the dough by tablespoonfuls, 2 inches apart, onto prepared cookie sheets.
3. Bake 8 to 11 minutes or until just set and bottoms of cookies are lightly browned. Cool 5 minutes on sheets, then remove cookies with spatula to wire racks to cool completely.

BANANA COOKIES

How is it that such simple foods, like these soft, nutmeg-scented banana cookies, have such wide appeal? My guess is that it's because, like many favorite things, the familiar comforts are what we like best.

PREHEAT OVEN TO 350°F

MAKES 4 DOZEN COOKIES

COOKIE SHEETS, GREASED OR LINED WITH
    PARCHMENT PAPER

1 large, very ripe banana, peeled

1 (18.25-ounce) package yellow cake mix

1 large egg

2 tablespoons vegetable oil

½ teaspoon ground nutmeg

Optional: 1 cup chopped walnuts (or pecans)

1. Mash the banana in a large bowl with a potato masher or fork. Mix in the cake mix, egg, oil, and nutmeg with a wooden spoon until blended.
2. Drop by tablespoonfuls, 2 inches apart, onto prepared cookie sheets. If desired, sprinkle tops of cookies with chopped nuts; gently press nuts into dough.
3. Bake 10 to 13 minutes or until set at edges and just barely set at center when lightly touched (do not overbake). Cool 1 minute on sheets, then remove cookies with spatula to wire racks to cool completely.

OATMEAL RAISIN COOKIES

Cake Mix
YELLOW

Oatmeal cookies are a nostalgic choice anytime.

PREHEAT OVEN TO 375°F

MAKES 4 DOZEN COOKIES

COOKIE SHEETS, GREASED OR LINED WITH
    PARCHMENT PAPER

1 (18.25-ounce) package yellow cake mix

1¼ cups quick-cooking oats

2 large eggs

½ cup vegetable oil

1½ teaspoons ground cinnamon

1¼ cups raisins

1. Mix the cake mix, oats, eggs, oil, and cinnamon in a large bowl with an electric mixer set on medium speed 1 to 2 minutes until blended. Mix in the raisins with a wooden spoon.
2. Drop the dough by tablespoonfuls, 2 inches apart, onto prepared cookie sheets.
3. Bake 8 to 11 minutes or until just set and bottoms of cookies are lightly browned. Cool 5 minutes on sheets, then remove cookies with spatula to wire racks to cool completely.

OATMEAL SCOTCHIES

I can still remember the first time I had an oatmeal-butterscotch cookie. It was a friend's birthday party and I didn't know what it was, but I knew that it was my new favorite cookie. They still rank near the top of my list.

PREHEAT OVEN TO 375°F

MAKES 4 DOZEN COOKIES

COOKIE SHEETS, GREASED OR LINED WITH PARCHMENT PAPER

1 (18.25-ounce) package yellow cake mix

½ cup butter, softened

2 large eggs

3 tablespoons packed light brown sugar

1¼ cups quick-cooking oats

1 cup butterscotch baking chips

1. Mix the cake mix, butter, eggs, and brown sugar in a large bowl with an electric mixer set on medium speed 1 to 2 minutes until blended. Mix in the oats and butterscotch chips with a wooden spoon.
2. Drop the dough by tablespoonfuls, 2 inches apart, onto prepared cookie sheets.
3. Bake 8 to 11 minutes or until just set and bottoms of cookies are lightly browned. Cool 5 minutes on sheets, then remove cookies with spatula to wire racks to cool completely.

GIANT CRANBERRY, ORANGE, AND OATMEAL COOKIES

I love a giant oatmeal cookie, even more so when it is loaded with dried cranberries and fresh orange flavor. The brown sugar, vanilla extract, and butter heighten the rich, old-fashioned flavor of these easily assembled goodies.

PREHEAT OVEN TO 350°F

MAKES 2 DOZEN LARGE COOKIES

COOKIE SHEETS, GREASED OR LINED WITH PARCHMENT PAPER

1 (18.25-ounce) package spice cake mix

1 cup (2 sticks) butter, softened

2 large eggs

⅓ cup packed dark brown sugar

1 tablespoon finely grated orange peel

2 cups quick-cooking oats

1¼ cups dried cranberries

1. Mix the cake mix, butter, eggs, brown sugar, and orange peel in a large bowl with an electric

mixer set on medium speed 1 to 2 minutes until blended. Mix in the oats and dried cranberries with a wooden spoon (dough will be very stiff).

2. Drop the dough by level ¼-cupfuls, 2 inches apart, onto prepared cookie sheets, then flatten slightly with palm or a spatula.

3. Bake 13 to 17 minutes or until set at edges and just barely set at center when lightly touched. Cool 1 minute on sheets, then remove cookies with spatula to wire racks to cool completely.

Cake Mix
DEVIL'S FOOD

BITTERSWEET CHOCOLATE BLACKOUT COOKIES

The list of what's great about these very chocolate, crisp-chewy cookies is long. In addition to an over-the-top chocolate intensity, they're quite practical: you can make several dozen premium cookies with a few flicks of a spoon and have a delicious chocolate bounty ready and waiting.

PREHEAT OVEN TO 350°F

MAKES 4 DOZEN COOKIES

COOKIE SHEETS, GREASED OR LINED WITH
    PARCHMENT PAPER

2 tablespoons instant coffee powder

⅓ cup water

1 (18.25-ounce) package devil's food cake mix

¼ cup (½ stick) butter, melted

1 large egg

1⅓ cups bittersweet or semisweet chocolate chips or chunks

1. Combine the coffee powder and water in a large bowl, stirring to dissolve. Mix in the cake mix, melted butter, and egg with an electric mixer set on medium speed 1 to 2 minutes until blended. Mix in the chocolate chips or chunks with a wooden spoon.

2. Drop the dough by tablespoonfuls, 2 inches apart, on prepared cookie sheets.

3. Bake 9 to 12 minutes or until set at edges and just barely set at center when lightly touched. Cool 1 minute on sheets, then remove cookies with spatula to wire racks to cool completely.

VARIATION *for Bittersweet Chocolate Blackout Cookies*

BLACK-AND-WHITE BLACKOUT COOKIES: Prepare as directed but substitute 1⅓ cups white chocolate chips for the bittersweet chocolate chips.

BLUEBERRY POWER COOKIES

Whether you're hitting the trails, headed to the gym, or just running late to work or school, grab one of these healthy and delicious cookies—they'll power you along for hours, deliciously.

PREHEAT OVEN TO 350°F

MAKES 3 DOZEN COOKIES

COOKIE SHEETS, GREASED OR LINED WITH PARCHMENT PAPER

1 (18.25-ounce) package white cake mix

⅓ cup whole or lowfat milk

¼ cup toasted wheat germ

¼ cup canola oil

2 large egg whites

½ cup dried blueberries

½ cup sliced almonds

¼ cup miniature semisweet chocolate chips

1. Place the cake mix, milk, wheat germ, oil, and egg whites in a large bowl. Mix with an electric mixer set on medium speed 1 to 2 minutes until blended. Mix in the blueberries, almonds, and chocolate chips with a wooden spoon.
2. Drop the dough by tablespoonfuls, 2 inches apart, on prepared cookie sheets.
3. Bake 9 to 12 minutes or until set at edges and just barely set at center when lightly touched. Cool 1 minute on sheets, then remove cookies with spatula to wire racks to cool completely.

LIME IN THE COCONUT COOKIES

Lime and coconut are a natural pairing, made even better in these buttery cookies.

PREHEAT OVEN TO 350°F

MAKES 3 DOZEN COOKIES

COOKIE SHEETS, GREASED OR LINED WITH PARCHMENT PAPER

1 (18.25-ounce) package white cake mix

6 tablespoons (¾ stick) butter, melted

¼ cup lime juice

1 large egg

1 tablespoon grated lime peel

1 cup sweetened flake coconut

1. Place the cake mix, melted butter, lime juice, egg, and lime peel in a large bowl. Mix with an electric mixer set on medium speed 1 to 2 minutes until blended. Mix in the coconut with a wooden spoon.

2. Drop the dough by tablespoonfuls, 2 inches apart, on prepared cookie sheets.
3. Bake 9 to 12 minutes or until set at edges and just barely set at center when lightly touched. Cool 1 minute on sheets, then remove cookies with spatula to wire racks to cool completely.

THE BIG SQUEEZE

To extract the most juice from a lemon or lime, roll it with your hand on the kitchen counter, or microwave for 20 to 30 seconds before cutting and squeezing.

Cake Mix
DEVIL'S FOOD

BLACK FOREST OATMEAL COOKIES

The combination of chocolate and cherry is always a crowd pleaser, which is why these easily assembled cookies are a guaranteed hit. Be sure to make an extra batch during the holiday season—a plateful will only last so long.

PREHEAT OVEN TO 375°F

MAKES 4 DOZEN COOKIES

COOKIE SHEETS, GREASED OR LINED WITH
   PARCHMENT PAPER

1 (18.25-ounce) package devil's food cake mix

½ cup vegetable oil

2 large eggs

½ teaspoon almond extract

1 cup quick-cooking oats

1 cup miniature semisweet chocolate chips

¾ cup tart dried cherries or dried
   cranberries, roughly chopped

1. Place the cake mix, oil, eggs, and almond extract in a large bowl. Blend with electric mixer set on low speed for 1 minute until blended. Mix in the oats, chocolate chips, and dried cherries or cranberries with a wooden spoon.
2. Drop by tablespoonfuls, 2 inches apart, onto prepared cookie sheets.
3. Bake 9 to 12 minutes or until edges are firm and center is just barely set when lightly touched. Cool 1 minute on sheets, then remove cookies with spatula to wire racks to cool completely.

LEMON-BLUEBERRY COOKIES

A touch of lemon, plus the intense flavor of dried blueberries, make this cookie a double winner.

PREHEAT OVEN TO 350°F

MAKES 3 DOZEN COOKIES

COOKIE SHEETS, GREASED OR LINED WITH
    PARCHMENT PAPER

1 (18.25-ounce) package white cake mix

6 tablespoons (¾ stick) butter, melted

¼ cup lemon juice

1 large egg

1 tablespoon grated lemon peel

1 cup dried blueberries

1. Place the cake mix, melted butter, lemon juice, egg, and lemon peel in a large bowl. Mix with an electric mixer set on medium speed 1 to 2 minutes until blended. Mix in the blueberries with a wooden spoon.
2. Drop the dough by tablespoonfuls, 2 inches apart, on prepared cookie sheets.
3. Bake 9 to 12 minutes or until set at edges and just barely set at center when lightly touched. Cool 1 minute on sheets, then remove cookies with spatula to wire racks to cool completely.

CHINESE FIVE-SPICE COOKIES

The fragrant blend called five-spice powder—now available in the spice section of most well-stocked grocery stores—turns humble butter cookies into something sophisticated.

PREHEAT OVEN TO 350°F

MAKES 4½ DOZEN COOKIES

COOKIE SHEETS, GREASED OR LINED WITH
    PARCHMENT PAPER

1 (18.25-ounce) package white cake mix

½ cup (1 stick) butter, softened

2 large eggs

3 tablespoons packed light brown sugar

2 teaspoons Chinese five-spice powder

1 teaspoon vanilla extract

½ cup sliced almonds

Optional: 3 tablespoons turbinado (raw)
    sugar

1. Place the cake mix, butter, eggs, brown sugar, five-spice powder, and vanilla in a large bowl.

Mix with an electric mixer on low speed 1 minute or until blended. Mix in the almonds with a wooden spoon.

2. Drop by tablespoonfuls, 2 inches apart, onto prepared cookie sheets. If desired, sprinkle tops of cookies with sugar.

3. Bake 10 to 13 minutes or until golden at the edges and just barely set at center when lightly touched. Cool 1 minute on sheets, then remove cookies with spatula to wire racks to cool completely.

Cake Mix WHITE

BANANA SPLIT CRUNCH COOKIES

All the flavors of a decadent banana split sundae in petite, handheld form.

PREHEAT OVEN TO 350°F

MAKES 4½ DOZEN COOKIES

COOKIE SHEETS, GREASED OR LINED WITH PARCHMENT PAPER

1 (18.25-ounce) package white cake mix

½ cup (1 stick) butter, softened

2 large eggs

1 cup banana chips, coarsely crushed

1 cup semisweet chocolate chips

½ cup maraschino cherries, drained, coarsely chopped

1 cup chopped walnuts and pecans

1. Place the cake mix, butter, and eggs in a large bowl. Mix with an electric mixer on low speed 1 minute or until blended. Mix in the crushed banana chips, chocolate chips, and cherries with a wooden spoon.

2. Drop by tablespoonfuls, 2 inches apart, onto prepared cookie sheets. Sprinkle tops of cookies with nuts.

3. Bake 10 to 13 minutes or until golden at the edges and just barely set at center when lightly touched. Cool 1 minute on sheets, then remove cookies with spatula to wire racks to cool completely.

Cake Mix CHOCOLATE	# CHOCOLATE-CHERRY CORDIAL COOKIES

I created these cookies in celebration of my maternal grandmother, Gran, who loved chocolate-covered cherries.

PREHEAT OVEN TO 350°F

MAKES 4½ DOZEN COOKIES

COOKIE SHEETS, GREASED OR LINED WITH
    PARCHMENT PAPER

1 (18.25-ounce) package chocolate cake mix

½ cup (1 stick) butter, softened

2 large eggs

½ teaspoon almond extract

1½ cups maraschino cherries, drained,
    coarsely chopped (about 1 10-ounce jar)

1 cup semisweet chocolate chips

1. Place the cake mix, butter, eggs, and almond extract in a large bowl. Mix with an electric mixer on low speed 1 minute or until blended. Mix in the cherries and chocolate chips with a wooden spoon.
2. Drop by tablespoonfuls, 2 inches apart, onto prepared cookie sheets.
3. Bake 10 to 13 minutes or until golden at the edges and just barely set at center when lightly touched. Cool 1 minute on sheets, then remove cookies with spatula to wire racks to cool completely.

Cake Mix YELLOW	# FRUITCAKE JUMBLES

There's no middle ground when it comes to fruitcake—one person's beloved portent of the Christmas season is another's bitter pill. But there's no better cookie than this brandy-accented one to convince even the most stalwart of skeptics.

PREHEAT OVEN TO 350°F

MAKES 4½ DOZEN COOKIES

COOKIE SHEETS, GREASED OR LINED WITH
    PARCHMENT PAPER

1 (18.25-ounce) package yellow cake mix

¼ cup brandy, dark rum, or apple juice

¼ cup (½ stick) butter, melted

1 large egg

1 cup candied mixed fruit

⅔ cup raisins or dried cranberries

½ cup quick-cooking oats

1 cup chopped walnuts (or pecans)

1. Mix the cake mix, brandy (or rum or juice), melted butter, and egg in a large bowl with a wooden spoon until blended. Mix in the candied fruit, raisins or cranberries, and oats.
2. Drop by tablespoonfuls, 2 inches apart, onto prepared cookie sheets. Sprinkle tops of cookies with nuts, gently pressing into dough.
3. Bake 10 to 13 minutes or until edges are firm and center is just barely set when lightly touched. Cool 1 minute on sheets, then remove cookies with spatula to wire racks to cool completely.

VARIATION *for Fruitcake Jumbles*

CHOCOLATE FRUITCAKE JUMBLES: Prepare as directed but use a devil's food cake mix and replace the raisins or cranberries with 1 cup semisweet chocolate chips.

Cake Mix
WHITE

BUTTERSCOTCH COOKIES

These cookies have magical properties—they disappear almost as quickly as they are made.

PREHEAT OVEN TO 350°F

MAKES 4½ DOZEN COOKIES

COOKIE SHEETS, UNGREASED OR LINED WITH PARCHMENT PAPER

1 (18.25-ounce) package white cake mix

⅓ cup butter, melted

¼ cup packed dark brown sugar

2 large eggs

1½ cups butterscotch baking chips

1. Place the cake mix, melted butter, brown sugar, and eggs in a large bowl. Mix with an electric mixer on low speed 1 minute or until blended. Mix in the butterscotch chips with a wooden spoon.
2. Drop by tablespoonfuls, 2 inches apart, onto ungreased cookie sheets.
3. Bake 10 to 13 minutes or until edges are firm and center is just barely set when lightly touched. Cool 1 minute on sheets, then remove cookies with spatula to wire racks to cool completely.

CHOCOLATE CHIP GRAHAM COOKIES

Whip up a batch of these home-style cookies anytime—together with a cold glass of milk, they are the perfect after school treat.

PREHEAT OVEN TO 350°F

MAKES 4½ DOZEN COOKIES

COOKIE SHEETS, UNGREASED OR LINED WITH
   PARCHMENT PAPER

1 (18.25-ounce) package yellow cake mix

½ cup (1 stick) butter, melted

2 large eggs

3 tablespoons packed dark brown sugar

1¼ cups graham-cracker crumbs

1 cup milk chocolate chips

1. Mix the cake mix, melted butter, eggs, and brown sugar in a large bowl with a wooden spoon until blended. Mix in the graham-cracker crumbs and chocolate chips with a wooden spoon.
2. Drop by tablespoonfuls, 2 inches apart, onto ungreased cookie sheets.
3. Bake 10 to 13 minutes or until edges are firm and center is just barely set when lightly touched. Cool 1 minute on sheets, then remove cookies with spatula to wire racks to cool completely.

WHITE CHOCOLATE AND COCONUT COOKIES

With a subtle zing of ginger, the tropical flavor of coconut, and the creamy richness of white chocolate, these cookies are a mini-vacation in a mouthful.

PREHEAT OVEN TO 350°F

MAKES 4½ DOZEN COOKIES

COOKIE SHEETS, UNGREASED OR LINED WITH
   PARCHMENT PAPER

1 (18.25-ounce) package white cake mix

½ cup (1 stick) butter, melted

2 large eggs

1 teaspoon vanilla extract

1 teaspoon ground ginger

1 cup sweetened flake coconut

1 cup white chocolate chips

1. Mix the cake mix, melted butter, eggs, vanilla, and ginger in a large bowl with a wooden spoon until blended. Mix in the coconut and white chocolate chips with a wooden spoon.
2. Drop by tablespoonfuls, 2 inches apart, onto ungreased cookie sheets.

3. Bake 10 to 13 minutes or until edges are firm and center is just barely set when lightly touched. Cool 1 minute on sheets, then remove cookies with spatula to wire racks to cool completely.

Cake Mix
YELLOW

CARAMEL APPLE COOKIES

In general, and as a guiding rule, tamper with tradition and that wonderful thing called nostalgia only up to a certain point. Case in point: these cookies, which showcase all the best flavors of classic caramel apples but in convenient cookie form.

PREHEAT OVEN TO 350°F

MAKES 4½ DOZEN COOKIES

COOKIE SHEETS, UNGREASED OR LINED WITH
    PARCHMENT PAPER

1 (18.25-ounce) package yellow cake mix

½ cup vegetable oil

2 large eggs

1 cup quartered chocolate-covered caramel candies (e.g., Rolos)

1 (5- or 6-ounce) package dried apples, chopped

1. Mix the cake mix, oil, and eggs in a large bowl with a wooden spoon until blended. Mix in the candies and dried apples.

2. Drop by tablespoonfuls, 2 inches apart, onto prepared cookie sheets.

3. Bake 10 to 13 minutes or until edges are firm and center is just barely set when lightly touched. Cool 2 minutes on sheets, then remove cookies with spatula to wire racks to cool completely.

VARIATION *for Caramel Apple Cookies*

CHOCOLATE CARAMEL APPLE COOKIES: Prepare as directed but use a devil's food cake mix.

CARAMEL CHOCOLATE CHIP COOKIES

Chocolate-coated caramel candies sweeten the deal in these incredible double-chocolate chippers. They are over-the-top good when eaten slightly warm, while the caramel and chocolate are still a bit gooey.

PREHEAT OVEN TO 350°F

MAKES 4½ DOZEN COOKIES

COOKIE SHEETS, GREASED OR LINED WITH
    PARCHMENT PAPER

1 (18.25-ounce) package yellow cake mix

⅓ cup butter, softened

2 large eggs

1 teaspoon vanilla extract

1 cup quartered chocolate-covered caramel candies (e.g., Rolos or Milk Duds)

1 cup semisweet or milk chocolate chips

1. Place the cake mix, butter, eggs, and vanilla in a large bowl. Blend with electric mixer set on low speed for 1 minute until blended. Mix in the candies and chocolate chips with a wooden spoon.
2. Drop by tablespoonfuls, 2 inches apart, onto prepared cookie sheets.
3. Bake 9 to 12 minutes or until edges are firm and center is just barely set when lightly touched. Cool 2 minutes on sheets, then remove cookies with spatula to wire racks to cool completely.

CARROT-CRANBERRY COOKIES WITH LEMON CREAM CHEESE ICING

Looking for a friendly good time? Perhaps few things could be more conducive to such than the pure congeniality that comes from baking a batch of these carrot cookies, plump with cranberries and spices and finished with a drizzle of cream cheese icing.

PREHEAT OVEN TO 350°F

MAKES 4½ DOZEN COOKIES

COOKIE SHEETS, GREASED OR LINED WITH
    PARCHMENT PAPER

1 (18.25-ounce) package carrot cake mix

½ cup (1 stick) butter, melted

¼ cup all-purpose flour

2 large eggs

1 teaspoon pumpkin pie spice or ground
    cinnamon

1 cup dried cranberries

¾ cup ready-to-spread cream cheese
    frosting

1½ tablespoons lemon juice

1. Place the cake mix, melted butter, flour, eggs, and pumpkin pie spice in a large bowl. Blend with electric mixer set on low speed for 1 minute until blended. Mix in the dried cranberries with a wooden spoon.
2. Drop by tablespoonfuls, 2 inches apart, onto prepared cookie sheets.
3. Bake 10 to 13 minutes or until edges are firm and center is just barely set when lightly touched. Cool 1 minute on sheets, then remove cookies with spatula to wire racks to cool completely.
4. Mix the cream cheese frosting and lemon juice in a small bowl. Drizzle over tops of cooled cookies.

ZUCCHINI-CHOCOLATE COOKIES

An excess of late summer zucchini is the perfect reason to bake a batch of these exceptionally delicious, moist, double-chocolate cookies. Just like your favorite version of carrot cake or zucchini bread, the zucchini in these cookies is transformed by the oven's heat, rendering these cookies soft and cakey—a faultless foil for a double dose of chocolate!

PREHEAT OVEN TO 350°F

MAKES 4½ DOZEN COOKIES

COOKIE SHEETS, GREASED OR LINED WITH
    PARCHMENT PAPER

1 (18.25-ounce) package devil's food cake mix

⅓ cup vegetable oil

2 large eggs

¾ teaspoon ground cinnamon

1½ cups grated peeled zucchini

1 cup miniature semisweet chocolate chips

Optional: 1 cup finely chopped walnuts or pecans

1. Place the cake mix, oil, eggs, and cinnamon in a large bowl. Blend with electric mixer set on low speed for 1 minute until blended. Mix in the zucchini and chocolate chips with a wooden spoon.

2. Drop by tablespoonfuls, 2 inches apart, onto prepared cookie sheets. If desired, sprinkle tops of cookies with chopped nuts.

3. Bake 11 to 14 minutes or until edges are firm and center is just barely set when lightly touched. Cool 2 minutes on sheets, then remove cookies with spatula to wire racks to cool completely.

VARIATION *for Zucchini-Chocolate Cookies*

SPICED ZUCCHINI AND GOLDEN RAISIN COOKIES: Prepare as directed but use a spice cake mix and replace the chocolate chips with 1 cup golden raisins.

CASHEW BRICKLE COOKIES

Toffee fans beware: these cookies are highly addictive. Other roasted nuts may be substituted, but buttery cashews make for a very special confection.

PREHEAT OVEN TO 350°F

MAKES 4½ DOZEN COOKIES

COOKIE SHEETS, UNGREASED OR LINED WITH
PARCHMENT PAPER

1 (18.25-ounce) package yellow cake mix

1 cup coarsely chopped, lightly salted
roasted cashews

¾ cup toffee baking bits

⅔ cup quick-cooking oats

½ cup (1 stick) butter, melted

2 large eggs

3 tablespoons dark brown sugar

1. Mix the cake mix, cashews, toffee bits, oats, melted butter, eggs, and brown sugar in a large bowl with a wooden spoon until all dry ingredients are moistened.
2. Drop by tablespoonfuls, 2 inches apart, onto ungreased cookie sheets.
3. Bake 10 to 13 minutes or until cracked in appearance and just barely set at center when lightly touched. Cool 1 minute on sheets, then remove cookies with spatula to wire racks to cool completely.

CHAI SPICE COOKIES

These quick cookies capture the unique flavor of chai, an aromatic spiced tea drink long favored in the East Indies. Warm and wonderful, they will fill the house with their distinctive fragrance as they bake.

PREHEAT OVEN TO 350°F

MAKES 3½ DOZEN COOKIES

COOKIE SHEETS, GREASED OR LINED WITH
PARCHMENT PAPER

1 (18.25-ounce) package spice cake mix

⅓ cup butter, melted

2 large eggs

2 teaspoons pumpkin pie spice

½ teaspoon ground cardamom

1 cup slivered almonds

Optional: 1 cup (½ a 16-ounce tub) ready-
to-spread vanilla frosting

1. Place the cake mix, melted butter, eggs, pumpkin pie spice, and cardamom in a large bowl. Blend with electric mixer set on low speed for 1 minute until blended.

2. Drop by tablespoonfuls, 2 inches apart, onto prepared cookie sheets. Sprinkle tops of cookies with almonds, gently pressing into dough.

3. Bake 9 to 12 minutes or until edges are firm and center is just barely set when lightly touched. Cool 1 minute on sheets, then remove cookies with spatula to wire racks to cool completely.

4. If desired, microwave the frosting in a small microwaveable bowl 30 to 45 seconds until melted enough to drizzle. Drizzle over cooled cookies.

CARDAMOM

Cardamom is a fragrant, exotic spice popular in Scandinavian baking as well as in both sweet and savory dishes throughout Africa, India, and the Middle East. Look for it where other spices are sold. For a bargain, purchase a small amount in bulk from health food stores or Middle Eastern stores that sell spices in bulk.

Cake Mix
YELLOW

CINNAMON CHIP CHEWS

When a magic wand—or, perhaps, a magic cinnamon stick—is waved over classic chocolate chip cookies, this is the sweet and spicy result. Cinnamon chips can be found in the baking aisle of the supermarket alongside the chocolate chips. Tan in color, they look and melt like chocolate chips and are a cinnamon lover's delight.

PREHEAT OVEN TO 350°F

MAKES 4 DOZEN COOKIES

COOKIE SHEETS, GREASED OR LINED WITH PARCHMENT PAPER

1 (18.25-ounce) package yellow cake mix

½ cup water

¼ cup (½ stick) butter, melted

1 large egg

1 teaspoon ground cinnamon

1½ cups cinnamon baking chips (e.g., Hershey's brand)

1. Place the cake mix, water, melted butter, egg, and cinnamon in a large bowl. Blend with electric mixer set on low speed for 1 minute until blended. Mix in the cinnamon chips with a wooden spoon.

2. Drop by tablespoonfuls, 2 inches apart, onto prepared cookie sheets.

3. Bake 9 to 12 minutes or until edges are firm and center is just barely set when lightly touched. Cool 2 minutes on sheets, then remove cookies with spatula to wire racks to cool completely.

MEXICAN-CHOCOLATE CINNAMON DROPS: Prepare as directed but use a devil's food cake mix and add ⅛ teaspoon cayenne pepper.

Cake Mix
WHITE

COCONUT, CASHEW, AND WHITE CHOCOLATE CHEWIES

Newfangled has never been better than with this delectable cookie. Crunchy cashews, chewy coconut, butter, and white chocolate? Hooray for innovation!

PREHEAT OVEN TO 375°F

MAKES 4 DOZEN COOKIES

COOKIE SHEETS, GREASED OR LINED WITH
    PARCHMENT PAPER

1 (18.25-ounce) package white cake mix

⅓ cup water

¼ cup (½ stick) butter, melted

1 large egg

1 cup lightly salted roasted cashews,
    chopped

1 cup white chocolate chips

⅔ cup sweetened flake coconut

1. Mix the cake mix, water, melted butter, and egg with an electric mixer on low speed for 1 minute or until blended. Mix in the cashews, white chocolate chips, and coconut with a wooden spoon.
2. Drop the dough by tablespoonfuls, 2 inches apart, onto prepared cookie sheets.
3. Bake 9 to 12 minutes or until set at edges and just barely set at center when lightly touched. Cool 1 minute on sheets, then remove cookies with spatula to wire racks to cool completely.

CRANBERRY CORNMEAL COOKIES

If ever there was a Thanksgiving cookie, this is it. Cornmeal adds both crunch and color, a fine counterpoint to tart, red, chewy bits of cranberry.

PREHEAT OVEN TO 350°F

MAKES 4 DOZEN COOKIES

COOKIE SHEETS, GREASED OR LINED WITH
    PARCHMENT PAPER

1 (18.25-ounce) package yellow cake mix

⅔ cup plain yellow cornmeal

⅓ cup vegetable oil

2 large eggs

1 tablespoon grated lemon or orange peel

1¼ cups dried cranberries

1. Mix the cake mix, cornmeal, oil, eggs, and lemon or orange peel with an electric mixer on low speed for 1 minute or until blended. Mix in the dried cranberries with a wooden spoon.
2. Drop the dough by tablespoonfuls, 2 inches apart, onto prepared cookie sheets.
3. Bake 9 to 12 minutes or until set at edges and just barely set at center when lightly touched. Cool 1 minute on sheets, then remove cookies with spatula to wire racks to cool completely.

TUSCAN CORNMEAL COOKIES

Cornmeal, citrus zest, olive oil, and fresh rosemary transform a yellow cake mix into a sophisticated cookie with the flavors of Northern Italy.

PREHEAT OVEN TO 350°F

MAKES 4 DOZEN COOKIES

COOKIE SHEETS, GREASED OR LINED WITH
    PARCHMENT PAPER

1 (18.25-ounce) package yellow cake mix

⅔ cup plain yellow cornmeal

½ cup sour cream

¼ cup light olive oil or vegetable oil

2 large eggs

1 tablespoon grated lemon or orange peel

1½ teaspoons finely chopped fresh
    rosemary leaves

1. Mix the cake mix, cornmeal, sour cream, oil, eggs, lemon peel, and rosemary with an electric mixer on low speed for 1 minute or until blended.

2. Drop the dough by tablespoonfuls, 2 inches apart, onto prepared cookie sheets.
3. Bake 9 to 12 minutes or until set at edges and just barely set at center when lightly touched. Cool 1 minute on sheets, then remove cookies with spatula to wire racks to cool completely.

DRIED APPLE CIDER COOKIES

Cake Mix
YELLOW

While fresh apples lead to soft, sometimes cake-like cookies, dried apples create a slightly chewy, toothsome treat. The apple flavor is intensified here with apple cider. All in all, it's a cookie that epitomizes autumn.

PREHEAT OVEN TO 350°F

MAKES 4 DOZEN COOKIES

COOKIE SHEETS, GREASED OR LINED WITH
    PARCHMENT PAPER

1 (18.25-ounce) package yellow cake mix

¼ cup apple cider or apple juice

¼ cup vegetable oil

1 large egg

¾ teaspoon ground cinnamon

1 (5- to 6-ounce) bag dried apples, chopped

Optional: 1¼ cups chopped walnuts or pecans

1. Mix the cake mix, apple cider, oil, egg, and cinnamon with an electric mixer on low speed for 1 minute or until blended. Mix in the dried apples with a wooden spoon.
2. Drop the dough by tablespoonfuls, 2 inches apart, onto prepared cookie sheets. If desired, sprinkle with chopped nuts, gently pressing nuts into dough.
3. Bake 10 to 13 minutes or until set at edges and just barely set at center when lightly touched. Cool 1 minute on sheets, then remove cookies with spatula to wire racks to cool completely.

FRESH PEAR COOKIES

This is a great autumn cookie, loaded with fresh pears and a touch of nutmeg. It's not necessary to peel the pears before chopping and adding them to the dough.

PREHEAT OVEN TO 350°F

MAKES 4 DOZEN COOKIES

COOKIE SHEETS, GREASED OR LINED WITH
   PARCHMENT PAPER

1 (18.25-ounce) package yellow cake mix

½ cup (1 stick) butter, softened

¼ cup packed light brown sugar

2 large eggs

¾ teaspoon ground nutmeg

1½ cups coarsely grated fresh pears (about
   2 medium pears)

½ cup quick-cooking oats

1 cup finely chopped pecans

1. Mix the cake mix, butter, brown sugar, eggs, and nutmeg with an electric mixer on low speed for 1 minute or until blended. Mix in the pears and oats with a wooden spoon.
2. Drop the dough by tablespoonfuls, 2 inches apart, onto prepared cookie sheets. Sprinkle tops of cookies with pecans.
3. Bake 10 to 13 minutes or until set at edges and just barely set at center when lightly touched. Cool 1 minute on sheets, then remove cookies with spatula to wire racks to cool completely.

VARIATIONS *for Fresh Pear Cookies*

FRESH CRANBERRY COOKIES: Prepare as directed but replace the fresh pears with an equal amount of coarsely chopped fresh cranberries and replace the nutmeg with 1 teaspoon ground ginger.

FRESH APPLE COOKIES: Prepare as directed but replace the fresh pears with an equal amount of coarsely grated tart apples and replace the nutmeg with an equal amount of ground cinnamon.

PUMPKIN SOFTIES

Rediscover a family favorite—in minutes—with this quickly assembled cookie. They keep well— that is, if you can keep them from being gobbled up.

PREHEAT OVEN TO 350°F

MAKES 4 DOZEN COOKIES

COOKIE SHEETS, GREASED OR LINED WITH PARCHMENT PAPER

1 (18.25-ounce) package spice cake mix

⅔ cup canned unsweetened pumpkin purée

1 large egg

2 tablespoons vegetable oil

2 teaspoons pumpkin pie spice

1 cup raisins or dried cranberries

½ cup chopped pecans (optional)

1 cup (½ a 16-ounce tub) ready-to-spread vanilla frosting

1. Place the cake mix, pumpkin, egg, oil, and pumpkin pie spice in a large bowl. Blend with electric mixer on low speed for 1 minute or until blended. Mix in raisins or cranberries with a wooden spoon.
2. Drop the dough by tablespoonfuls, 2 inches apart, onto prepared cookie sheets. If desired, sprinkle cookies with pecans, gently pressing into dough.
3. Bake 10 to 13 minutes or until set at edges and just barely set at center when lightly touched. Cool 1 minute on sheets, then remove cookies with spatula to wire racks to cool completely.
4. Microwave the frosting in a small microwaveable bowl 30 to 45 seconds until melted enough to drizzle. Drizzle over cooled cookies.

EGGNOG COOKIES

Here that homogenous blend of eggs, cream, spices, spirits, and plenty of holiday cheer finds form in a delectable, streamlined cookie.

PREHEAT OVEN TO 350°F

MAKES 4 DOZEN COOKIES

COOKIE SHEETS, GREASED OR LINED WITH
  PARCHMENT PAPER

1 (18.25-ounce) package yellow cake mix

⅓ cup butter, melted

2 large eggs

2 teaspoons brandy or rum-flavored extract

1 teaspoon ground nutmeg

¾ teaspoon ground cinnamon

⅓ cup sugar

1. Mix the cake mix, melted butter, eggs, brandy or rum-flavored extract, and nutmeg with an electric mixer on low speed for 1 minute or until blended.
2. Drop the dough by tablespoonfuls, 2 inches apart, onto prepared cookie sheets. Mix the cinnamon and sugar in a small cup, then sprinkle on tops of cookies.
3. Bake 9 to 12 minutes or until set at edges and just barely set at center when lightly touched. Cool 1 minute on sheets, then remove cookies with spatula to wire racks to cool completely.

VARIATIONS *for Eggnog Cookies*

CRANBERRY EGGNOG COOKIES: Prepare as directed, but add 1 cup dried cranberries.

WHITE CHOCOLATE EGGNOG COOKIES: Prepare as directed, but add 1½ cups white chocolate chips.

MAPLE-PECAN COOKIES

Looking for a new Christmas cookie? Give these double-maple treats a try—they're sure to become a fast family favorite, especially if you pair them with mugs of hot cocoa.

PREHEAT OVEN TO 350°F

MAKES 4 DOZEN COOKIES

COOKIE SHEETS, GREASED OR LINED WITH PARCHMENT PAPER

1 (18.25-ounce) package white cake mix

⅓ cup butter, softened

¼ cup packed dark brown sugar

2 large eggs

4 teaspoons maple-flavored extract, divided

1 cup chopped pecans

1 cup (½ a 16-ounce tub) ready-to-spread frosting

1. Place the cake mix, butter, brown sugar, eggs, and 3 teaspoons of the maple extract in a large bowl. Blend with electric mixer set on low speed for 1 minute until blended. Mix in the pecans with a wooden spoon.
2. Drop by tablespoonfuls, 2 inches apart, onto prepared cookie sheets.
3. Bake 9 to 12 minutes or until edges are firm and center is just barely set when lightly touched. Cool 1 minute on sheets, then remove cookies with spatula to wire racks to cool completely.
4. Microwave the frosting in a small microwaveable bowl 30 to 45 seconds until melted enough to drizzle. Mix in the remaining 1 teaspoon maple extract, then drizzle over cooled cookies.

GINGERBREAD SOFTIES

Cake Mix
SPICE

As the weather grows colder and the holidays head in, there's no better time to bake a batch of the kind of cookies that fill every room in the house with the familiar scents of good things to come. These cookies, redolent with sweet vanilla, spicy ginger, and cinnamon, fit the bill.

PREHEAT OVEN TO 350°F

MAKES 4 DOZEN COOKIES

COOKIE SHEETS, GREASED OR LINED WITH
   PARCHMENT PAPER

1 (18.25-ounce) package spice cake mix

½ cup (1 stick) butter, melted

⅓ cup applesauce

¼ cup packed dark brown sugar

1 large egg

2 teaspoons ground ginger

1 teaspoon ground cinnamon

¼ teaspoon ground cloves

1. Place the cake mix, melted butter, applesauce, brown sugar, egg, ginger, cinnamon, and cloves in a large bowl. Blend with electric mixer set on low speed for 1 minute until blended.
2. Drop by tablespoonfuls, 2 inches apart, onto prepared cookie sheets.
3. Bake 9 to 12 minutes or until edges are firm and center is just barely set when lightly touched. Cool 1 minute on sheets, then remove cookies with spatula to wire racks to cool completely.

HOLIDAY FRUIT AND SPICE COOKIES

Cake Mix
SPICE

Meet your new winter holiday tradition. Prepared mincemeat (which can be found in jars at the supermarket in the baking aisle) contains no meat. Rather, it is a spiced compote of apples and raisin, often spiked with rum or brandy. It makes amazing cookies in a flash that are ideal for eating and giving all winter long.

PREHEAT OVEN TO 350°F

MAKES 4 DOZEN COOKIES

COOKIE SHEETS, GREASED OR LINED WITH
   PARCHMENT PAPER

1 (18.25-ounce) package spice cake mix

1 cup prepared mincemeat

½ cup vegetable oil

2 large eggs

1½ teaspoons ground cinnamon

1. Place the cake mix, mincemeat, oil, eggs, and cinnamon in a large bowl. Blend with electric mixer on low speed for 1 minute or until blended.

2. Drop the dough by tablespoonfuls, 2 inches apart, onto prepared cookie sheets.
3. Bake 9 to 12 minutes or until set at edges and just barely set at center when lightly touched. Cool 2 minutes on sheets, then remove cookies with spatula to wire racks to cool completely.

GINGER BUTTER COOKIES

Cake Mix
WHITE

These cookies warrant singular attention. When you taste them—rich with butter, bejeweled with bits of peppery, candied ginger—you will understand why. Don't forget the pot of strong Indian black tea.

PREHEAT OVEN TO 350°F

MAKES 4 DOZEN COOKIES

COOKIE SHEETS, UNGREASED

1 (18.25-ounce) package white cake mix

⅓ cup butter, softened

1 large egg

1 teaspoon ground ginger

½ cup finely chopped crystallized ginger

1. Mix the cake mix, butter, egg, and ginger in a large bowl with an electric mixer set on low speed for 1 minute until blended. Mix in the crystallized ginger with a wooden spoon.
2. Drop by tablespoonfuls, 2 inches apart, onto ungreased cookie sheets.
3. Bake 9 to 12 minutes or until edges are firm and center is just barely set when lightly touched. Cool 1 minute on sheets, then remove cookies with spatula to wire racks to cool completely.

GRANOLA CHOCOLATE CHUNKERS

Cake Mix
WHITE

Excellent travelers, these sturdy cookies are a good choice for care packages, lunch boxes, and also backpacks, when you are heading out on a hike or picnic.

PREHEAT OVEN TO 350°F

MAKES 5 DOZEN COOKIES

COOKIE SHEETS, UNGREASED OR LINED WITH
    PARCHMENT PAPER

1 (18.25-ounce) package white cake mix

½ cup vegetable oil

¼ cup packed light brown sugar

2 large eggs

1½ cups granola

1 cup semisweet chocolate chunks or chips

¾ cup dried fruit (e.g., raisins, dried
    cranberries, chopped dried apricots)

1. Place the cake mix, oil, brown sugar, and eggs in a large bowl. Blend with electric mixer set on low speed for 1 minute until blended. Mix in the granola, chocolate chunks, and dried fruit with a wooden spoon.

2. Drop by tablespoonfuls, 2 inches apart, onto ungreased cookie sheets.

3. Bake 9 to 12 minutes or until edges are firm and center is just barely set when lightly touched. Cool 1 minute on sheets, then remove cookies with spatula to wire racks to cool completely.

> Taste the nuts and dried fruits you intend to use in your cookies before adding them to the dough. If they have no flavor, or if they taste stale or old, do not use them.

Cake Mix WHITE
LIME AND WHITE CHOCOLATE COOKIES

If ever a match was made in culinary heaven, it is lime and white chocolate. These cookies are loaded with lime, then balanced by the smooth sweetness of the white chocolate chips that stud each treat.

PREHEAT OVEN TO 350°F
MAKES 4 DOZEN COOKIES
COOKIE SHEETS, GREASED OR LINED WITH
   PARCHMENT PAPER

1 (18.25-ounce) package white cake mix
⅓ cup butter, softened
1 large egg
3 tablespoons fresh lime juice
1 tablespoon grated lime peel
1½ cups white chocolate chips

1. Place the cake mix, butter, egg, lime juice, and lime peel in a large bowl. Blend with electric mixer set on low speed for 1 minute until blended. Mix in the white chocolate chips with a wooden spoon.

2. Drop by tablespoonfuls, 2 inches apart, onto prepared cookie sheets.

3. Bake 9 to 12 minutes or until edges are firm and center is just barely set when lightly touched. Cool 1 minute on sheets, then remove cookies with spatula to wire racks to cool completely.

VARIATION *for Lime and White Chocolate Cookies*

LEMON AND WHITE CHOCOLATE COOKIES: Prepare as directed but substitute lemon juice for the lime juice and lemon peel for the lime peel.

DOUBLE-CHOCOLATE OATMEAL JUMBLES

When the kitchen is warm from baking and the cookie jar is full with these everything-but-the-kitchen-sink chocolate cookies, who cares if it's cold outside?

PREHEAT OVEN TO 350°F

MAKES 2½ DOZEN LARGE COOKIES

COOKIE SHEETS, GREASED OR LINED WITH
    PARCHMENT PAPER

1 (18.25-ounce) package chocolate or
    devil's food cake mix

1 cup vegetable oil

3 large eggs

2 cups quick-cooking oats

1 cup semisweet or milk chocolate chips

1 cup miniature candy-coated chocolate
    baking pieces (e.g., baking M&Ms)

½ cup raisins or dried cranberries

1. Place the cake mix, oil, and eggs in a large bowl. Blend with electric mixer set on low speed for 1 minute until blended. Mix in the oats, chocolate chips, baking pieces, and raisins or cranberries with a wooden spoon.

2. Drop the dough by level ¼-cupfuls, 3 inches apart, onto prepared cookie sheets. Flatten slightly with your palm or a spatula.

3. Bake 13 to 17 minutes or until edges are firm and center is just barely set when lightly touched. Cool 1 minute on sheets, then remove cookies with spatula to wire racks to cool completely.

KAHLUA COOKIES

Impressive to serve yet simple to prepare, these caffeinated cookies are definitely for adults. The type of chocolate chip chosen really makes a difference in the result. Semisweet chocolate chips make for a European-tasting cookie (consider adding ½ teaspoon ground cinnamon), milk chocolate chips an American-style mocha flavor, and white chocolate chips create a coffee-and-cream cookie.

PREHEAT OVEN TO 350°F

MAKES 4 DOZEN COOKIES

COOKIE SHEETS, GREASED OR LINED WITH PARCHMENT PAPER

⅓ cup Kahlua or other coffee liqueur

1 tablespoon instant coffee powder

1 (18.25-ounce) package white cake mix

¼ cup (½ stick) butter, melted

1 large egg

1½ cups semisweet, milk, or white chocolate chips

1. Mix the Kahlua and coffee powder in a large bowl, stirring until dissolved. Add the cake mix, butter, and egg to bowl. Blend with electric mixer set on low speed for 1 minute until blended. Mix in the chocolate chips with a wooden spoon.

2. Drop by tablespoonfuls, 2 inches apart, onto prepared cookie sheets.

3. Bake 9 to 12 minutes or until edges are firm and center is just barely set when lightly touched. Cool 1 minute on sheets, then remove cookies with spatula to wire racks to cool completely.

OH BABY! COOKIES

At the time, it seemed like my son switched from baby food to solid food overnight: one day, he was happily slurping carrot puree and strained prunes, and the next he was throwing it across the room in protest. So what's a mommy to do? Make cookies, that's what. And, oh baby, what yummy cookies! But you don't need a toddler to make these cookies; just head over to the baby-food section of the grocery store, select your favorite flavor (I suggest avoiding the strained peas), and get baking.

PREHEAT OVEN TO 350°F

MAKES 4 DOZEN COOKIES

COOKIE SHEETS, GREASED OR LINED WITH
  PARCHMENT PAPER

1 (18.25-ounce) package white cake mix

½ cup (1 stick) butter, melted

1 (4-ounce) jar strained plums, apricots,
  pears, or carrots baby food

1 large egg

1 cup chopped dried fruit (e.g., raisins, dried
  cranberries, dried apricots, prunes)

1. Place the cake mix, melted butter, baby food, and egg in a large bowl. Mix with electric mixer set on low speed 1 minute until blended. Mix in the dried fruit with a wooden spoon.
2. Drop by tablespoonfuls, 2 inches apart, onto prepared cookie sheets.
3. Bake 9 to 12 minutes or until edges are firm and center is just barely set when lightly touched. Cool 1 minute on sheets, then remove cookies with spatula to wire racks to cool completely.

LEMON, GINGER, AND CREAM CHEESE SOFTIES

The pleasant bite of ginger coupled with the zing of lemon gives these cookies grown-up appeal.

PREHEAT OVEN TO 350°F

MAKES 3½ DOZEN COOKIES

COOKIE SHEETS, UNGREASED

1 (18.25-ounce) package lemon cake mix

1 (3-ounce) package cream cheese, softened

¼ cup (½ stick) butter, softened

1 large egg

3 tablespoons all-purpose flour

1½ teaspoons ground ginger

2 cups confectioners' sugar

1½ tablespoons lemon juice

1. Place the cake mix, cream cheese, butter, egg, flour, and ginger in a large bowl. Blend with electric mixer set on low speed for 1 to 2 minutes until blended.
2. Drop by tablespoonfuls, 2 inches apart, onto prepared cookie sheets.
3. Bake 9 to 12 minutes or until edges are firm and center is just barely set when lightly touched. Cool 1 minute on sheets, then remove cookies with spatula to wire racks to cool completely.
4. Mix the confectioners' sugar and lemon juice in a small bowl until blended. Drizzle icing over cooled cookies.

Cake Mix
LEMON

LEMON AND POPPY SEED COOKIES

Here's proof positive that joy can be shared in small, sweet ways. Impressive to serve, these lemon-y treats are equally easy to prepare.

PREHEAT OVEN TO 350°F

MAKES 4 DOZEN COOKIES

COOKIE SHEETS, GREASED OR LINED WITH PARCHMENT PAPER

1 (18.25-ounce) package lemon cake mix

⅓ cup vegetable oil

2 large eggs

3 tablespoons poppy seeds

Icing

2 cups confectioners' sugar

1½ tablespoons lemon juice

1. Place the cake mix, oil, eggs, and poppy seeds in a large bowl. Blend with electric mixer set on low speed for 1 minute until blended.
2. Drop by tablespoonfuls, 2 inches apart, onto prepared cookie sheets.
3. Bake 9 to 12 minutes or until edges are firm and center is just barely set when lightly touched. Cool 1 minute on sheets, then remove cookies with spatula to wire racks to cool completely.
4. Mix the confectioners' sugar and lemon juice in a small bowl until blended. Drizzle icing over cooled cookies.

Cake Mix
WHITE

MANDARIN ORANGE COOKIES

Looking for a very special cookie? Sweet-tart mandarin oranges and a bit of orange peel dress up a basic cake mix dough, transforming it from ordinary to extraordinary with minimal effort and expense.

PREHEAT OVEN TO 350°F

MAKES 3½ DOZEN COOKIES

COOKIE SHEETS, GREASED OR LINED WITH
    PARCHMENT PAPER

1 (18.25-ounce) package white cake mix

1 (10-ounce) can mandarin oranges,
    drained and patted dry

¼ cup vegetable oil

1 large egg

1 tablespoon grated orange peel

1. Place the cake mix, drained mandarin oranges, oil, egg, and orange peel in a large bowl. Blend with electric mixer set on low speed for 1 minute until just blended (do not overmix— there should be visible pieces of mandarin orange in dough).
2. Drop by tablespoonfuls, 2 inches apart, onto prepared cookie sheets.
3. Bake 9 to 12 minutes or until edges are firm and center is just barely set when lightly touched. Cool 1 minute on sheets, then remove cookies with spatula to wire racks to cool completely.

Cake Mix
WHITE

MINT JULEP COOKIES

The arrival of spring brings both the Kentucky Derby and the mint julep, a very elegant, very potent potion made of bourbon and fresh mint. Here the libation takes cookie form in a quick, but equally elegant cookie. Be warned—they're potent!

PREHEAT OVEN TO 350°F

MAKES 4 DOZEN COOKIES

COOKIE SHEETS, GREASED OR LINED WITH
    PARCHMENT PAPER

1 (18.25-ounce) package white cake mix

⅓ cup bourbon or whiskey

¼ cup (½ stick) butter, melted

1 large egg

3 tablespoons chopped fresh mint

1. Place the cake mix, bourbon, butter, egg, and chopped mint in a large bowl. Blend with electric mixer set on low speed for 1 minute until blended.
2. Drop by tablespoonfuls, 2 inches apart, onto prepared cookie sheets.

3. Bake 9 to 12 minutes or until edges are firm and center is just barely set when lightly touched. Cool 1 minute on sheets, then remove cookies with spatula to wire racks to cool completely.

VARIATION *for Mint Julep Cookies*

CHOCOLATE MINT JULEP COOKIES: Prepare as directed but substitute chocolate cake mix for the white cake mix. If desired, mix in 1 cup miniature semisweet chocolate chips.

Cake Mix
WHITE
NEAPOLITAN COOKIES

These tricolor cookies are as delightful and delicious as the brick ice cream by the same name.

PREHEAT OVEN TO 350°F

MAKES 4½ DOZEN COOKIES

COOKIE SHEETS, GREASED OR LINED WITH PARCHMENT PAPER

1 (18.25-ounce) package white cake mix

¼ cup vegetable oil

2 large eggs

2 tablespoons water

½ teaspoon almond extract

¾ cup finely chopped maraschino cherries (patted dry between paper towels)

1 cup miniature semisweet chocolate chips

1. Place the cake mix, oil, eggs, water, and almond extract in a large bowl. Blend with electric mixer set on low speed for 1 minute until blended. Mix in the chocolate chips and cherries with a wooden spoon.

2. Drop by tablespoonfuls, 2 inches apart, onto prepared cookie sheets.

3. Bake 9 to 12 minutes or until edges are firm and center is just barely set when lightly touched. Cool 1 minute on sheets, then remove cookies with spatula to wire racks to cool completely.

HERMITS

Hermits—spicy drop cookies filled with fruits and nuts—have been filling American cookie jars since colonial times. Here they are better than ever—and simplified with the help of cake mix.

PREHEAT OVEN TO 350°F

MAKES 4½ DOZEN COOKIES

COOKIE SHEETS, GREASED OR LINED WITH
   PARCHMENT PAPER

1 (18.25-ounce) package spice cake mix

½ cup (1 stick) butter, softened

¼ cup packed dark brown sugar

2 large eggs

1 tablespoon pumpkin pie spice

1 teaspoon ground ginger

1 cup raisins or chopped dates (or a mix of
   the two)

½ cup chopped walnuts or pecans

1 cup (½ a 16-ounce tub) ready-to-spread
   vanilla frosting

1. Mix the cake mix, butter, brown sugar, eggs, pumpkin pie spice, and ginger in a large bowl with an electric mixer on low speed 1 minute or until blended. Mix in the raisins or dates and nuts with a wooden spoon.
2. Drop by tablespoonfuls, 2 inches apart, onto prepared cookie sheets.
3. Bake 10 to 13 minutes or until golden at the edges and just barely set at center when lightly touched. Cool 1 minute on sheets, then remove cookies with spatula to wire racks to cool completely.
4. Microwave the frosting in a small microwaveable bowl 30 to 45 seconds until melted enough to drizzle. Drizzle over cooled cookies.

Cake Mix
WHITE
ORANGE, CHOCOLATE CHIP, AND CREAM CHEESE COOKIES

Here's a cookie with a delicate, tender texture and a subtle tang. Both qualities are owed to the addition of cream cheese to the dough—it's a fine foil for the dark, miniature chocolate chips scattered throughout. Lemon peel may be interchanged for the orange peel with equal success.

PREHEAT OVEN TO 350°F

MAKES 4 DOZEN COOKIES

COOKIE SHEETS, GREASED OR LINED WITH PARCHMENT PAPER

1 (18.25-ounce) package white cake mix

1 (8-ounce) package cream cheese, softened

¼ cup (½ stick) butter, melted

1 large egg

1 tablespoon grated orange peel

1 cup miniature semisweet chocolate chips

1. Place the cake mix, cream cheese, melted butter, egg, and orange peel in a large bowl. Blend with electric mixer set on low speed for 1 minute until blended. Mix in chocolate chips with a wooden spoon.
2. Drop by tablespoonfuls, 2 inches apart, onto prepared cookie sheets.
3. Bake 9 to 12 minutes or until edges are firm and center is just barely set when lightly touched. Cool 1 minute on sheets, then remove cookies with spatula to wire racks to cool completely.

Cake Mix
VANILLA
ORANGE DREAMSICLE COOKIES

Remember those orange and vanilla cream pops from summer vacations past? Vanilla ice cream inside, orange sherbet outside, they always topped my list of ice-pop favorites. Recapture that summertime flavor with these orange and vanilla cookies. But don't limit them to the summer months—they are delicious year-round.

PREHEAT OVEN TO 350°F

MAKES 4½ DOZEN COOKIES

COOKIE SHEETS, UNGREASED

1 (18.25-ounce) package vanilla cake mix

⅓ cup butter, softened

1 large egg

3 tablespoons orange juice

1 tablespoon grated orange peel

1½ cups white chocolate chips

1. Place the cake mix, butter, egg, orange juice, and orange peel in a large bowl. Blend with

electric mixer set on low speed for 1 minute until blended. Mix in the white chocolate chips with wooden spoon.

2. Drop by tablespoonfuls, 2 inches apart, onto prepared cookie sheets.

3. Bake 10 to 13 minutes or until edges are firm and center is just barely set when lightly touched. Cool 1 minute on sheets, then remove cookies with spatula to wire racks to cool completely.

Cake Mix
LEMON

MARMALADE-LEMON COOKIES

Ready for a burst of citrus flavor? All you need is four ingredients to create an unforgettable citrus cookie unlike any other.

PREHEAT OVEN TO 350°F

MAKES 4 DOZEN COOKIES

COOKIE SHEETS, GREASED OR LINED WITH
    PARCHMENT PAPER

1 (18.25-ounce) package lemon cake mix

½ cup vegetable oil

½ cup orange marmalade

1 large egg

1. Place the cake mix, oil, marmalade, and egg in a large bowl. Blend with electric mixer set on low speed for 1 minute until blended.

2. Drop by tablespoonfuls, 2 inches apart, onto prepared cookie sheets.

3. Bake 9 to 12 minutes or until edges are firm and center is just barely set when lightly touched. Cool 1 minute on sheets, then remove cookies with spatula to wire racks to cool completely.

VARIATIONS *for Marmalade-Lemon Cookies*

MARMALADE-SPICE COOKIES: Prepare as directed but use a spice cake mix in place of the lemon cake mix and add 1 teaspoon pumpkin pie spice or ground cinnamon.

DOUBLE-CHOCOLATE MARMALADE COOKIES: Prepare as directed but use a devil's food cake mix. If desired, mix in 1 cup miniature semisweet chocolate chips with a wooden spoon.

APRICOT-LEMON COOKIES: Prepare as directed but use apricot jam in place of the marmalade.

| Cake Mix DEVIL'S FOOD | # RASPBERRY-CHOCOLATE COOKIES |

It's easy to understand why certain flavor combinations become classics—no matter the season or the reason, they please one and all. Case in point: raspberry and chocolate. I've made it easy to enjoy anytime with this quick and easy cookie that has raspberry jam stirred right into the batter.

PREHEAT OVEN TO 350°F

MAKES 4 DOZEN COOKIES

COOKIE SHEETS, GREASED OR LINED WITH PARCHMENT PAPER

1 (18.25-ounce) package devil's food cake mix

½ cup vegetable oil

½ cup seedless raspberry jam

1 large egg

¼ teaspoon almond extract

1 cup miniature semisweet chocolate chips

1. Place the cake mix, oil, raspberry jam, egg, and almond extract in a large bowl. Blend with electric mixer set on low speed for 1 minute until blended. Mix in the chocolate chips with a wooden spoon.

2. Drop by tablespoonfuls, 2 inches apart, onto prepared cookie sheets.

3. Bake 9 to 12 minutes or until edges are firm and center is just barely set when lightly touched. Cool 1 minute on sheets, then remove cookies with spatula to wire racks to cool completely.

| Cake Mix STRAWBERRY | # CHOCOLATE-COVERED STRAWBERRY COOKIES |

If ever there was a Valentine's Day cookie, this is it. Tasting like soft, miniature strawberry cakes, these pretty-in-pink cookies get gorgeous with a drizzle of melted chocolate.

PREHEAT OVEN TO 350°F

MAKES 4 DOZEN COOKIES

COOKIE SHEETS, GREASED OR LINED WITH PARCHMENT PAPER

1 (18.25-ounce) package strawberry cake mix

1½ cups sour cream (not reduced fat)

⅓ cup butter, softened

2 large eggs

Icing

1¼ cups semisweet or white chocolate chips

2 teaspoons vegetable shortening

1. Place the cake mix, sour cream, butter, and eggs in a large bowl. Blend with electric mixer set on low speed for 1 minute until blended.
2. Drop by tablespoonfuls, 2 inches apart, onto prepared cookie sheets.
3. Bake 9 to 12 minutes or until edges are firm and center is just barely set when lightly touched. Cool 1 minute on sheets, then remove cookies with spatula to wire racks to cool completely.
4. Microwave the chocolate chips and shortening in a medium microwaveable bowl on High 1 minute, stirring after 30 seconds, until melted and smooth. Using a fork, drizzle tops of cooled cookies with the melted chocolate. Chill cookies 10 minutes to set the chocolate.

Cake Mix DEVIL'S FOOD

PEANUT BUTTER CHOCOLATE CHUNKERS

A scrumptious pairing of dark chocolate and peanut butter, these chunky cookies call for tall glasses of cold milk and lots of good cheer.

PREHEAT OVEN TO 350°F

MAKES 4 DOZEN COOKIES

COOKIE SHEETS, GREASED OR LINED WITH PARCHMENT PAPER

1 (18.25-ounce) package devil's food cake mix

½ cup chunky-style peanut butter (not old-fashioned or natural style)

½ cup (1 stick) butter, softened

3 large eggs

1 cup semisweet chocolate chunks or chips

1. Place the cake mix, peanut butter, butter, and eggs in a large bowl. Blend with electric mixer set on low speed for 1 minute until blended. Mix in chocolate chunks with a wooden spoon.
2. Drop by tablespoonfuls, 2 inches apart, onto prepared cookie sheets.
3. Bake 10 to 13 minutes or until edges are firm and center is just barely set when lightly touched. Cool 1 minute on sheets, then remove cookies with spatula to wire racks to cool completely.

VARIATION *for Peanut Butter Chocolate Chunkers*

PEANUT BUTTERSCOTCH COOKIES: Prepare as directed but use a yellow cake mix in place of the devil's food cake mix and use 1 cup butterscotch chips in place of the chocolate chunks.

PEANUT BUTTER COOKIES

There's a time for discovering new flavors and a time for savoring old favorites. When you're in the mood for the latter, whip up a batch of these peanut butter cookies.

PREHEAT OVEN TO 375°F

MAKES 4 DOZEN COOKIES

COOKIE SHEETS, GREASED OR LINED WITH
    PARCHMENT PAPER

1 (18.25-ounce) package yellow cake mix

1 cup creamy peanut butter (not old-
    fashioned or natural style)

⅓ cup whole or lowfat milk

2 large eggs

1 teaspoon vanilla extract

⅓ cup granulated sugar

1. Mix the cake mix, peanut butter, milk, eggs, and vanilla in a large bowl with a wooden spoon until blended.
2. Drop by tablespoonfuls, 2 inches apart, onto prepared cookie sheets. Place the sugar in a shallow dish. Gently press a crisscross pattern on top of cookies with fork dipped in the sugar.
3. Bake 9 to 12 minutes or until edges are firm and center is just barely set when lightly touched. Cool 3 minutes on sheets, then remove cookies with spatula to wire racks to cool completely.

PIÑA COLADA COOKIES

All of the flavors of the cool, creamy tropical drink come together in this easy, breezy cookie.

PREHEAT OVEN TO 375°F

MAKES 4 DOZEN COOKIES

COOKIE SHEETS, GREASED OR LINED WITH
    PARCHMENT PAPER

1 (18.25-ounce) package white cake mix

⅓ cup pineapple juice

¼ cup (½ stick) butter, melted

1 large egg

2 teaspoons rum-flavored extract

1½ cups sweetened flake coconut

½ cup chopped dried pineapple

1. Mix the cake mix, pineapple juice, melted butter, egg, and rum extract with an electric mixer on low speed for 1 minute or until blended. Mix in the coconut and dried pineapple with a wooden spoon.

2. Drop the dough by tablespoonfuls, 2 inches apart, onto prepared cookie sheets.
3. Bake 9 to 12 minutes or until set at edges and just barely set at center when lightly touched. Cool 1 minute on sheets, then remove cookies with spatula to wire racks to cool completely.

PINE NUT COOKIES

Cake Mix
WHITE

Pine nuts, also known as pignoli, Indian nuts, and piñons, come from the cones of several varieties of pine trees. Sweet and delicate in flavor, these ivory-colored, torpedo-shaped nuts are used in a wide array of savory and sweet dishes in many cuisines. They are particularly delicious in baked goods, like these subtly spiced, Italian-inspired cookies. Anise is a traditional flavoring in Italian baked goods, but a ½ teaspoon ground nutmeg, mace, or coriander may be substituted.

PREHEAT OVEN TO 350°F

MAKES 4 DOZEN COOKIES

COOKIE SHEETS, GREASED OR LINED WITH
    PARCHMENT PAPER

1 (18.25-ounce) package white cake mix

½ cup (1 stick) butter, softened

2 large eggs

1 teaspoon vanilla extract

1 teaspoon aniseed, crushed in a mortar
    and pestle

1 cup pine nuts

1. Mix the cake mix, butter, eggs, vanilla, and aniseed with an electric mixer on low speed for 1 minute or until blended.
2. Drop the dough by tablespoonfuls, 2 inches apart, onto prepared cookie sheets. Sprinkle tops of cookies with pine nuts, gently pressing into dough.
3. Bake 9 to 12 minutes or until set at edges and just barely set at center when lightly touched. Cool 1 minute on sheets, then remove cookies with spatula to wire racks to cool completely.

Tip: Crush the aniseeds in a mortar and pestle, or place in a heavy-duty plastic zip-top bag and crush with a mallet.

Cake Mix SPICE

PINEAPPLE SOFTIES

This friendly cookie is an ideal choice for giving to new friends and neighbors because it is lush with pineapple, the historic symbol of welcome.

PREHEAT OVEN TO 350°F

MAKES 4 DOZEN COOKIES

COOKIE SHEETS, GREASED OR LINED WITH PARCHMENT PAPER

1 (18.25-ounce) package spice cake mix

1 (8-ounce) can crushed pineapple, drained, 2 tablespoons juice reserved

¼ cup (½ stick) butter, melted

1 large egg

1 teaspoon ground allspice

1. Mix the cake mix, drained pineapple and reserved 2 tablespoons juice, melted butter, egg, and allspice with an electric mixer on low speed for 1 minute or until blended.
2. Drop the dough by tablespoonfuls, 2 inches apart, onto prepared cookie sheets.
3. Bake 10 to 13 minutes or until set at edges and just barely set at center when lightly touched. Cool 1 minute on sheets, then remove cookies with spatula to wire racks to cool completely.

Cake Mix WHITE

AMBROSIA DROPS

I love the tart-sweet splurge of dried cherries, but an equal amount of drained, chopped maraschino cherries, or dried cranberries, may also be used.

PREHEAT OVEN TO 350°F

MAKES 4 DOZEN COOKIES

COOKIE SHEETS, GREASED OR LINED WITH PARCHMENT PAPER

1 (18.25-ounce) package white cake mix

1 (10-ounce) can mandarin oranges, drained, 1 tablespoon juice reserved

1 cup sweetened flake coconut

¾ cup dried cherries, roughly chopped

¼ cup vegetable oil

1 large egg

1. Mix the cake mix, drained oranges, reserved 1 tablespoon juice, coconut, dried cherries, oil, and egg with an electric mixer on low speed for 1 minute or until blended.
2. Drop the dough by tablespoonfuls, 2 inches apart, onto prepared cookie sheets.

3. Bake 10 to 13 minutes or until set at edges and just barely set at center when lightly touched. Cool 1 minute on sheets, then remove cookies with spatula to wire racks to cool completely.

PRALINE COOKIES

This is one great cookie. *The dough will spread out relatively thin as it bakes because the butter recipe cake mix has a higher fat content than other cake mixes. It is very important to let the cookies rest on the sheets before transferring them to cooling racks (they will be too soft when they first come out of the oven). The result is a thin, crispy cookie that really does taste like a praline. For a perfectly round cookie, try using a cookie scoop—it looks like a mini ice cream scooper. Once you taste these you'll agree that a praline in cookie form tastes just as sweet.*

PREHEAT OVEN TO 350°F

MAKES 4½ DOZEN COOKIES

COOKIE SHEETS, UNGREASED OR LINED WITH
    PARCHMENT PAPER

1 (18.25-ounce) package butter recipe
    yellow cake mix

½ cup (1 stick) butter, softened

¼ cup packed dark brown sugar

2 large eggs

1 teaspoon vanilla extract

1¼ cups toffee baking bits

2 cups chopped pecans

1. Place the cake mix, butter, brown sugar, eggs, and vanilla in a large bowl. Blend with electric mixer on low speed for 1 minute or until blended. Mix in toffee bits with a wooden spoon.

2. Drop the dough by tablespoonfuls, 2 inches apart, onto prepared cookie sheets. Generously sprinkle cookie tops with pecans.

3. Bake 10 to 13 minutes or until set at edges and just barely set at center when lightly touched. Cool 3 minutes on sheets, then remove cookies with spatula to wire racks to cool completely.

TEXAS RANGER COOKIES

Chock-full of everything, these Texas Ranger-size cookies are old-time favorites, and with good reason: they taste like home, keep well, and are great travelers for lunch boxes and picnics. Make a batch and there's just one thing left to do—sit, eat, and enjoy.

PREHEAT OVEN TO 350°F

MAKES 2½ DOZEN BIG COOKIES

COOKIE SHEETS, UNGREASED OR LINED WITH
   PARCHMENT PAPER

1 (18.25-ounce) package yellow cake mix

¾ cup vegetable oil

⅓ cup chunky peanut butter (not old-fashioned or natural style)

3 large eggs

1½ cups quick-cooking oats

½ cup semisweet chocolate chips

½ cup raisins or dried cranberries

½ cup sweetened flaked coconut

1. Place the cake mix, oil, peanut butter, and eggs in a large bowl. Blend with electric mixer on low speed for 1 minute or until blended. Mix in the oats, chocolate chips, raisins or cranberries, and coconut with a wooden spoon (dough will be stiff).
2. Drop the dough by ¼-cupfuls, 3 inches apart, onto ungreased cookie sheets. Flatten slightly with palm or spatula.
3. Bake 13 to 17 minutes or until set at edges and just barely set at center when lightly touched. Cool 1 minute on sheets, then remove cookies with spatula to wire racks to cool completely.

RICOTTA COOKIES

Similar to cottage cheese, ricotta is a slightly grainy, very soft, and smooth Italian cheese used in a variety of sweet and savory dishes like cheesecake and lasagna. Here it creates a rich, cake-like cookie with a crisp shell and soft, snowy interior. For a citrus variation, substitute 2 teaspoons of freshly grated lemon, lime, or orange peel for the vanilla.

PREHEAT OVEN TO 350°F

MAKES 4 DOZEN COOKIES

COOKIE SHEETS, UNGREASED OR LINED WITH
PARCHMENT PAPER

1 (18.25-ounce) package white cake mix

¾ cup ricotta cheese (not reduced fat)

¼ cup (½ stick) butter, melted

1 large egg

1 teaspoon vanilla extract

1 cup (½ a 16-ounce tub) ready-to-spread
vanilla frosting

1. Place the cake mix, ricotta cheese, melted butter, egg, and vanilla in a large bowl. Blend with electric mixer on low speed for 1 minute or until blended.
2. Drop the dough by tablespoonfuls, 2 inches apart, onto prepared cookie sheets.
3. Bake 9 to 12 minutes or until set at edges and just barely set at center when lightly touched. Cool 1 minute on sheets, then remove cookies with spatula to wire racks to cool completely.
4. Microwave the frosting in a small microwaveable bowl 30 to 45 seconds until melted enough to drizzle. Drizzle over cooled cookies.

DOUBLE-CHOCOLATE RICOTTA COOKIES

Chocolate trumps all others as the favorite cookie flavor, which makes it fun to play around with the form. Here I've showcased it in a tender ricotta-based cookie, enhanced it with the sweet-nutty flavor of almond extract, and upped the chocolate ante with a generous handful of chocolate chips.

PREHEAT OVEN TO 350°F

MAKES 4 DOZEN COOKIES

COOKIE SHEETS, UNGREASED OR LINED WITH
PARCHMENT PAPER

1 (18.25-ounce) package devil's food cake mix

1 (8-ounce) container ricotta cheese

¼ cup (½ stick) butter, softened

1 large egg

1 teaspoon almond extract

1½ cups semisweet chocolate chips

1. Place the cake mix, ricotta cheese, butter, egg, and almond extract in a large bowl. Blend with electric mixer on low speed for 1 minute or until blended. Mix in the chocolate chips with a wooden spoon.
2. Drop the dough by tablespoonfuls, 2 inches apart, onto prepared cookie sheets.
3. Bake 9 to 12 minutes or until set at edges and just barely set at center when lightly touched. Cool 1 minute on sheets, then remove cookies with spatula to wire racks to cool completely.

Cake Mix
YELLOW

RUM-RAISIN COOKIES

Enhanced with the flavors of rum and nutmeg, these easy raisin cookies are fit for both company and comfort on a chilly night.

PREHEAT OVEN TO 350°F
MAKES 4½ DOZEN COOKIES
COOKIE SHEETS, GREASED OR LINED WITH PARCHMENT PAPER

1 (18.25-ounce) package yellow cake mix
⅓ cup vegetable oil
2 large eggs
3 teaspoons rum-flavored extract, divided
½ teaspoon ground nutmeg
1¼ cups raisins
1 cup (½ a 16-ounce tub) ready-to-spread vanilla frosting

1. Place the cake mix, oil, eggs, 2 teaspoons rum extract, and nutmeg in a large bowl. Blend with electric mixer on low speed for 1 minute or until blended. Mix in the raisins with a wooden spoon.
2. Drop the dough by tablespoonfuls, 2 inches apart, onto prepared cookie sheets.
3. Bake 10 to 13 minutes or until set at edges and just barely set at center when lightly touched. Cool 1 minute on sheets, then remove cookies with spatula to wire racks to cool completely.
4. Microwave the frosting in a small microwaveable bowl 30 to 45 seconds until melted enough to drizzle. Mix in the remaining 1 teaspoon rum extract, then drizzle over cooled cookies.

VARIATION *for Rum-Raisin Cookies*

BRANDIED APRICOT COOKIES: Prepare as directed but substitute chopped dried apricots for the raisins and brandy extract for the rum extract in both the cookies and the icing.

Cake Mix
WHITE

TOASTED ALMOND COOKIES

Five ingredients—that's all it takes to produce these elegant almond cookies. They are a fine choice for teatime.

PREHEAT OVEN TO 350°F

MAKES 4 DOZEN COOKIES

COOKIE SHEETS, GREASED OR LINED WITH
    PARCHMENT PAPER

1 (18.25-ounce) package white cake mix

⅓ cup vegetable oil

2 large eggs

1 teaspoon almond extract

1⅓ cups sliced almonds

1. Place the cake mix, oil, eggs, and almond extract in a large bowl. Blend with electric mixer on low speed for 1 minute or until blended.
2. Drop the dough by tablespoonfuls, 2 inches apart, onto prepared cookie sheets. Sprinkle tops of cookies with the sliced almonds, gently pressing into dough.
3. Bake 10 to 13 minutes or until set at edges and just barely set at center when lightly touched. Cool 1 minute on sheets, then remove cookies with spatula to wire racks to cool completely.

Cake Mix
YELLOW

WALNUT-DATE COOKIES

Dates are one of the first confections, going back more than 5,000 years in culinary history. Although native to the Middle East, they are also plentiful in my home state of California. Here they add brown-sugary sweetness and a toothsome chewiness, a delicious foil to the nutty crunch of walnuts.

PREHEAT OVEN TO 375°F

MAKES 5 DOZEN COOKIES

COOKIE SHEETS, UNGREASED OR LINED WITH
    PARCHMENT PAPER

1 (18.25-ounce) package yellow cake mix

¾ cup (1½ sticks) butter, melted

⅓ cup all-purpose flour

2 large eggs

1 teaspoon ground cinnamon

1 cup quick-cooking oats

1 cup chopped dates

1 cup chopped walnuts

1. Place the cake mix, melted butter, flour, eggs, and cinnamon in a large bowl. Blend with electric mixer on low speed for 1 minute or until blended. Mix in the oats and dates with a wooden spoon.

2. Drop the dough by tablespoonfuls, 2 inches apart, onto ungreased cookie sheets. Sprinkle tops of cookies with walnuts.
3. Bake 9 to 12 minutes or until set at edges and just barely set at center when lightly touched. Cool 1 minute on sheets, then remove cookies with spatula to wire racks to cool completely.

Cake Mix WHITE
VANILLA MALT COOKIES

I've had a strong affection for malt balls since roughly age five, but I've never loved them as much as I do here in these incredibly easy and oh-so-yummy cookies. Kids will clamor for them, but they provide sweet and nostalgic memories for grandmother and grandfather, too.

PREHEAT OVEN TO 350°F

MAKES 4½ DOZEN COOKIES

COOKIE SHEETS, GREASED OR LINED WITH
    PARCHMENT PAPER

1 (18.25-ounce) package white cake mix

½ cup (1 stick) butter, softened

2 large eggs

1 teaspoon vanilla extract

2 cups chocolate-covered malt balls (e.g., Whoppers or Maltesers), coarsely crushed

1. Place the cake mix, butter, eggs, and vanilla in a large bowl. Blend with electric mixer on low speed for 1 minute or until blended. Mix in the crushed malt balls with a wooden spoon.
2. Drop the dough by tablespoonfuls, 2 inches apart, onto prepared cookie sheets.
3. Bake 10 to 13 minutes or until set at edges and just barely set at center when lightly touched. Cool 1 minute on sheets, then remove cookies with spatula to wire racks to cool completely.

Tip: To crush malt balls, place in a large zip-top plastic bag. Seal bag and bang the candies with a mallet or rolling pin until coarsely crushed.

VARIATION *for Vanilla Malt Cookies*

CHOCOLATE MALT COOKIES: Prepare as directed but use a chocolate or devil's food cake mix.

HAZELNUT AND CHOCOLATE CHIP BUTTER COOKIES

Cake Mix
WHITE

It's difficult not to demolish these classic cookies, so why not make two batches at once? You can now find chopped hazelnuts alongside chopped walnuts, pecans, and almonds in the baking aisle of the supermarket.

PREHEAT OVEN TO 375°F

MAKES 4 DOZEN COOKIES

COOKIE SHEETS, UNGREASED OR LINED WITH
    PARCHMENT PAPER

1 (18.25-ounce) package white cake mix

2 large eggs

½ cup (1 stick) butter, melted

¼ teaspoon ground nutmeg

1 cup chopped hazelnuts

1 cup miniature semisweet chocolate chips

1. Place the cake mix, eggs, melted butter, and nutmeg with an electric mixer on low speed for 1 minute or until blended. Mix in the hazelnuts and chocolate chips with a wooden spoon.
2. Drop the dough by tablespoonfuls, 2 inches apart, onto ungreased cookie sheets.
3. Bake 9 to 12 minutes or until set at edges and just barely set at center when lightly touched. Cool 1 minute on sheets, then remove cookies with spatula to wire racks to cool completely.

VARIATIONS *for Hazelnut and Chocolate Chip Butter Cookies*

DOUBLE-CHOCOLATE HAZELNUT BUTTER COOKIES: Prepare as directed, but use a chocolate cake mix in place of the white cake mix.

PISTACHIO AND CHOCOLATE CHIP BUTTER COOKIES: Prepare as directed, but use 1 cup chopped shelled, lightly salted pistachios in place of the hazelnuts.

MANGO COOKIES WITH LIME AND WHITE CHOCOLATE

Cake Mix
WHITE

I could eat dried mangoes by the poundful if left to my own devices—sweet and chewy, they are packed with intense tart-sweet tropical flavor. Better still, they have become readily available at grocery stores and supercenters (look in the dried fruit section), making them an easy add-in to these exotic cookies.

PREHEAT OVEN TO 350°F

MAKES 4 DOZEN COOKIES

COOKIE SHEETS, UNGREASED OR LINED WITH
    PARCHMENT PAPER

1 (18.25-ounce) package white cake mix

½ cup (1 stick) butter, melted

2 large eggs

1 tablespoon grated lime peel

1½ cups white chocolate chips

1 cup chopped dried mango

½ cup quick-cooking oats

1. Mix the cake mix, melted butter, eggs, and lime peel in a large bowl with a wooden spoon until blended. Mix in the white chocolate chips, dried mango, and oats.
2. Drop the dough by tablespoonfuls, 2 inches apart, onto ungreased cookie sheets.
3. Bake 9 to 12 minutes or until set at edges and just barely set at center when lightly touched. Cool 2 minutes on sheets, then remove cookies with spatula to wire racks to cool completely.

TIPSY CHOCOLATE CHEWS

Cake Mix
DEVIL'S FOOD

These cookies belie their easy-as-can-be assembly with a rich, complex chocolate taste and crisp-chewy texture. Use just about any spirit or liqueur you have on hand—experimenting is the most delicious fun.

PREHEAT OVEN TO 375°F

MAKES 4½ DOZEN COOKIES

COOKIE SHEETS, GREASED OR LINED WITH
    PARCHMENT PAPER

1 (18.25-ounce) package devil's food cake
    mix

⅓ cup whiskey, dark rum, or brandy

¼ cup (½ stick) butter, melted

1 large egg

1⅓ cups semisweet chocolate chips

1. Mix the cake mix, whiskey, melted butter, and egg in a large bowl with a wooden spoon until blended. Mix in the chocolate chips.

2. Drop the dough by tablespoonfuls, 2 inches apart, onto prepared cookie sheets.
3. Bake 9 to 12 minutes or until set at edges and just barely set at center when lightly touched. Cool 2 minutes on sheets, then remove cookies with spatula to wire racks to cool completely.

VARIATION *for Tipsy Chocolate Chews*

ORANGE LIQUEUR AND CHOCOLATE CHIP CHEWS: Prepare as directed, but add 1 tablespoon grated orange peel, use a yellow cake mix in place of devil's food cake mix, and use orange liqueur in place of whiskey.

Cake Mix
VANILLA

VANILLA LATTE COOKIES

The inspiration for these cookies sprang from my own coffee obsession: I love vanilla lattes, so why not recreate them in cookie form? I don't think I need to suggest the perfect accompanying beverage.

PREHEAT OVEN TO 375°F

MAKES 4 DOZEN COOKIES

COOKIE SHEETS, GREASED OR LINED WITH PARCHMENT PAPER

⅓ cup whole or lowfat milk

2 tablespoons instant coffee powder

1 (18.25-ounce) package vanilla cake mix

¼ cup (½ stick) butter, melted

1 large egg

1⅓ cups white chocolate chips

1. Mix the milk and coffee powder in a large bowl until dissolved. Add the cake mix, melted butter, and egg and stir with a wooden spoon until blended. Mix in the white chocolate chips.
2. Drop the dough by tablespoonfuls, 2 inches apart, onto prepared cookie sheets.
3. Bake 9 to 12 minutes or until set at edges and just barely set at center when lightly touched. Cool 2 minutes on sheets, then remove cookies with spatula to wire racks to cool completely.

CRISPY RICE AND MARSHMALLOW COOKIES

If you already like rice-crispy treats, you'll love my new interpretation. They are every bit as easy as the original treats, but require one advance step: freezing the marshmallows. Don't skip the step; freezing the marshmallows allows them to keep their shape as the cookies bake. Otherwise, they will ooze out of the cookies.

PREHEAT OVEN TO 375°F

MAKES 4 DOZEN COOKIES

COOKIE SHEETS, GREASED OR LINED WITH PARCHMENT PAPER

1 (18.25-ounce) package white cake mix

½ cup (1 stick) butter, melted

½ cup water

1 large egg

1 teaspoon vanilla extract

2 cups crisp rice cereal (e.g., Kellogg's Rice Krispies)

1½ cups miniature marshmallows, frozen on cookie sheet at least 1 hour

1. Mix the cake mix, melted butter, water, egg, and vanilla in a large bowl with a wooden spoon until blended. Mix in the rice cereal and frozen marshmallows with a wooden spoon.
2. Drop the dough by tablespoonfuls, 2 inches apart, onto prepared cookie sheets.
3. Bake 9 to 12 minutes or until set at edges and just barely set at center when lightly touched. Cool 5 minutes on sheets, then remove cookies with spatula to wire racks to cool completely.

VARIATIONS *for Crispy Rice and Marshmallow Cookies*

CRISPY RICE AND CHOCOLATE CHIP COOKIES: Prepare as directed but use 1 cup semi-sweet chocolate chips in place of the marshmallows.

CHOCOLATE-CRISPY MARSHMALLOW COOKIES: Prepare as directed but use a devil's food cake mix in place of white cake mix.

DATE AND OAT COOKIES

Cake Mix
WHITE

The perfect mid-afternoon cookie—comforting, rich, and easy. Serve with a hot cup of tea, coffee, or cocoa.

PREHEAT OVEN TO 375°F

MAKES 5 DOZEN COOKIES

COOKIE SHEETS, UNGREASED OR LINED WITH
   PARCHMENT PAPER

1 (18.25-ounce) package white cake mix

1 cup (2 sticks) butter, softened

½ cup packed light brown sugar

¼ cup whole or lowfat milk

1 large egg

1½ teaspoons ground cinnamon

2 cups old-fashioned rolled oats

1 cup chopped dates

1. Place the cake mix, butter, brown sugar, milk, egg, and cinnamon in a large bowl. Blend with an electric mixer on medium speed 1 to 2 minutes until blended. Mix in the oats and dates with a wooden spoon (dough will be stiff).
2. Drop the dough by tablespoonfuls, 2 inches apart, onto ungreased cookie sheets.
3. Bake 10 to 13 minutes or until set at edges and just barely set at center when lightly touched. Cool 1 minute on sheets, then remove cookies with spatula to wire racks to cool completely.

DELUXE NUT JUMBLES

Cake Mix
YELLOW

These salty-sweet cookies are packed with flavor—they rank as one of my top-rated cookies!

PREHEAT OVEN TO 350°F

MAKES 4 DOZEN COOKIES

COOKIE SHEETS, UNGREASED OR LINED WITH
   PARCHMENT PAPER

1 (18.25-ounce) package yellow cake mix

½ cup (1 stick) butter, softened

2 large eggs

1 cup lightly salted deluxe mixed nuts,
   roughly chopped

¾ cup milk chocolate chips

¾ cup dried cherries or dried cranberries

1. Place the cake mix, butter, and eggs in a large bowl. Blend with an electric mixer on medium

speed 1 to 2 minutes until blended. Mix in the nuts, chocolate chips, and dried cherries with a wooden spoon.

2. Drop the dough by tablespoonfuls, 2 inches apart, onto ungreased cookie sheets.

3. Bake 10 to 13 minutes or until set at edges and just barely set at center when lightly touched. Cool 1 minute on sheets, then remove cookies with spatula to wire racks to cool completely.

Cake Mix
WHITE

CRISP ALMOND-OAT COOKIES

So often, simple is best. Such is the case with these delicate cookies. They are a great treat with coffee, or serve with ice cream for dessert.

PREHEAT OVEN TO 350°F

MAKES 5 DOZEN COOKIES

COOKIE SHEETS, UNGREASED OR LINED WITH
    PARCHMENT PAPER

1 (18.25-ounce) package white cake mix

1 cup vegetable oil

½ cup sugar

3 large eggs

1 teaspoon almond extract

2 cups quick-cooking oats

1 cup sliced almonds, finely chopped

1. Mix the cake mix, oil, sugar, eggs, and almond extract in a large bowl with a wooden spoon until blended. Mix in the oats.

2. Drop the dough by tablespoonfuls, 2 inches apart, onto ungreased cookie sheets. Sprinkle tops of cookies with chopped almonds.

3. Bake 10 to 13 minutes or until set at edges and just barely set at center when lightly touched. Cool 1 minute on sheets, then remove cookies with spatula to wire racks to cool completely.

COFFEE-TOFFEE COOKIES

Cake Mix
WHITE

Coffee and toffee were meant for one another. My drop-cookie coupling of the two is truly delicious—crunchy round the edges, chewy in the center.

PREHEAT OVEN TO 375°F

MAKES 4 DOZEN COOKIES

COOKIE SHEETS, UNGREASED OR LINED WITH
    PARCHMENT PAPER

⅓ cup whole or lowfat milk

1½ tablespoons instant coffee powder

1 (18.25-ounce) package white cake mix

¼ cup (½ stick) butter, melted

1 large egg

1¼ cups toffee baking bits

½ cup sliced almonds

1. Mix the milk and coffee powder in a large bowl until dissolved. Add the cake mix, melted butter, and egg and mix with a wooden spoon until blended. Mix in the toffee bits and sliced almonds.
2. Drop the dough by tablespoonfuls, 2 inches apart, onto prepared cookie sheets.
3. Bake 9 to 12 minutes or until set at edges and just barely set at center when lightly touched. Cool 2 minutes on sheets, then remove cookies with spatula to wire racks to cool completely.

TOFFEE AND MILK CHOCOLATE CHUNKERS

Cake Mix
CHOCOLATE

Delicious in any state, these cookies are especially scrumptious when slightly warm, when the toffee is a touch melt-y—you can reheat them in the microwave for a few seconds for that just-baked goodness.

PREHEAT OVEN TO 350°F

MAKES 3½ DOZEN COOKIES

COOKIE SHEETS, UNGREASED OR LINED WITH
    PARCHMENT PAPER

1 (18.25-ounce) package chocolate cake
    mix

½ cup quick-cooking oats

½ cup (1 stick) butter, melted

2 large eggs

1 cup toffee baking bits

1 cup milk chocolate chunks or chips

1. Mix the cake mix, oats, melted butter, and eggs in a large bowl with wooden spoon until blended. Mix in the toffee bits and chocolate chunks or chips.

2. Drop the dough by tablespoonfuls, 2 inches apart, onto ungreased cookie sheets.
3. Bake 10 to 13 minutes or until set at edges and just barely set at center when lightly touched. Cool 1 minute on sheets, then remove cookies with spatula to wire racks to cool completely.

VARIATION *for Toffee and Milk Chocolate Chunkers*

TOFFEE AND WHITE CHOCOLATE CHUNKERS: Prepare as directed but use a white cake mix and white chocolate chunks or chips.

Cake Mix
WHITE

SHERBET MACAROONS

I know what you're thinking: sherbet? In a cookie recipe? Oh yes. Trust me; I've got a fabulous recipe here. The sherbet keeps these tender macaroons soft instead of crisp.

PREHEAT OVEN TO 350°F

MAKES 5½ DOZEN COOKIES

COOKIE SHEETS, GREASED OR LINED WITH PARCHMENT PAPER

1 (18.25-ounce) package white cake mix

1 pint pineapple, lemon, or orange sherbet, softened

1½ teaspoons almond extract

6 cups sweetened flake coconut

1. Mix the cake mix, sherbet, and almond extract in a large bowl with wooden spoon until blended. Mix in the coconut.
2. Drop the dough by tablespoonfuls, 2 inches apart, onto ungreased cookie sheets.
3. Bake 10 to 13 minutes or until set at edges and just barely set at center when lightly touched. Cool 1 minute on sheets, then remove cookies with spatula to wire racks to cool completely.

ICE CREAM MACAROONS

You're only four ingredients away from fantastic macaroons. And don't forget to try the variations; they are but the tip of the iceberg of options, so experiment to your heart's content with your favorite pint flavors.

PREHEAT OVEN TO 350°F

MAKES 5½ DOZEN COOKIES

COOKIE SHEETS, GREASED OR LINED WITH
   PARCHMENT PAPER

1 (18.25-ounce) package white cake mix

1 pint vanilla ice cream, softened

2 teaspoons vanilla extract

6 cups sweetened flake coconut

1. Mix the cake mix, ice cream, and vanilla in a large bowl with wooden spoon until blended. Mix in the coconut.
2. Drop the dough by tablespoonfuls, 2 inches apart, onto ungreased cookie sheets.
3. Bake 10 to 13 minutes or until set at edges and just barely set at center when lightly touched. Cool 1 minute on sheets, then remove cookies with spatula to wire racks to cool completely.

VARIATIONS *for Ice Cream Macaroons*

TRIPLE-CHOCOLATE ICE CREAM MACAROONS: Prepare as directed but use a devil's food cake mix, chocolate ice cream, and add 1 (12-ounce bag) miniature semisweet chocolate chips. Omit the vanilla.

STRAWBERRY ICE CREAM MACAROONS: Prepare as directed but use a strawberry cake mix and strawberry ice cream. Omit the vanilla.

PEPITA-CRANBERRY COOKIES

Pepitas are a great addition to a range of baked goods, especially cookies. Here they add a nutty crunch and pair beautifully—both in color and taste—with the tart-sweet dried cranberries. Look for them in the supermarket where nuts and seeds are sold.

PREHEAT OVEN TO 350°F

MAKES 3½ DOZEN COOKIES

COOKIE SHEETS, UNGREASED OR LINED WITH PARCHMENT PAPER

1 (18.25-ounce) package white cake mix

½ cup vegetable oil

½ cup quick-cooking oats

2 large eggs

2 teaspoons grated orange peel

¾ cup dried cranberries

½ cup roasted, lightly salted pepitas (green pumpkin seeds)

1. Mix the cake mix, oil, oats, eggs, and orange peel in a large bowl with a wooden spoon until blended. Mix in the cranberries and pepitas.
2. Drop by tablespoonfuls, 2 inches apart, onto ungreased cookie sheets.
3. Bake 10 to 13 minutes or until cracked in appearance and just barely set at center when lightly touched. Cool 1 minute on sheets, then remove cookies with spatula to wire racks to cool completely.

WHOLE WHEAT CHOCOLATE CHIP COOKIES

Here I've given chocolate chip cookies a healthy update with the additions of applesauce and whole wheat flour. I've opted for miniature chocolate chips because they disperse through the batter easily, allowing for chocolate in every bite (despite the smaller amount of chocolate overall). If you have regular chocolate chips on hand, use the same amount, but give the chips a quick chop before adding to the batter.

PREHEAT OVEN TO 350°F

MAKES 4 DOZEN COOKIES

COOKIE SHEETS, GREASED OR LINED WITH
    PARCHMENT PAPER

1 (18.25-ounce) package yellow cake mix

½ cup whole wheat flour

⅓ cup vegetable oil

½ cup applesauce

2 large eggs

1 teaspoon vanilla extract

1 cup miniature semisweet chocolate chips

Optional: 1 cup chopped walnuts or pecans

1. Mix the cake mix, flour, oil, applesauce, eggs, and vanilla in a large bowl with a wooden spoon until blended. Mix in the chocolate chips.
2. Drop by tablespoonfuls, 2 inches apart, onto prepared cookie sheets. If desired, sprinkle tops with chopped nuts.
3. Bake 10 to 13 minutes or until just barely set at center when lightly touched. Cool 1 minute on sheets, then remove cookies with spatula to wire racks to cool completely.

VARIATION *for Whole Wheat Chocolate Chip Cookies:*

WHOLE WHEAT RAISIN SPICE COOKIES: Prepare as directed, but use a spice cake mix, add 1½ teaspoons ground cinnamon, and use 1¼ cups raisins in place of the chocolate chips.

WHOLE WHEAT PUMPKIN BREAKFAST COOKIES

Forget the pop-up toaster tarts and super-sweet, overpriced muffins at the coffee shop—fill your thermos at home and grab one or two of these cookies instead. Packed with good things—whole grains, pumpkin, eggs, and dried fruit—they will start your day off on the right foot. Children love them too— what kid wouldn't love milk and cookies for breakfast?

PREHEAT OVEN TO 350°F

MAKES 2 DOZEN LARGE COOKIES

COOKIE SHEETS, GREASED OR LINED WITH
    PARCHMENT PAPER

1 (18.25-ounce) package spice cake mix

⅔ cup canned unsweetened pumpkin puree

½ cup whole wheat flour

⅓ cup vegetable oil

2 large eggs

1 cup dried cranberries, raisins, or other
    chopped dried fruit

Optional: 2 tablespoons ground flax seeds
    (flaxseed meal)

Optional: 1 cup chopped walnuts or pecans

1. Mix the cake mix, pumpkin, flour, oil, and eggs in a large bowl with a wooden spoon until all dry ingredients are moistened. Mix in the dried fruit and, if desired, ground flax seeds.
2. Drop by ¼-cupfuls, 3 inches apart, onto ungreased cookie sheets. If desired, sprinkle tops of cookies with nuts.
3. Bake 12 to 15 minutes or until just barely set at center when lightly touched. Cool 1 minute on sheets, then remove cookies with spatula to wire racks to cool completely.

FIBER-WONDERFUL COOKIES

These cookies are based on a popular morning breakfast bar of similar name. Mine are equally (if not more) delicious, full of healthy fiber, easy to make, and far less expensive.

PREHEAT OVEN TO 350°F

MAKES 4½ DOZEN COOKIES

COOKIE SHEETS, GREASED OR LINED WITH
    PARCHMENT PAPER

2 cups all-bran cereal

⅔ cup unsweetened applesauce

⅓ cup vegetable oil

2 large eggs

1 teaspoon ground cinnamon

1 (18.25-ounce) package white cake mix

¼ cup chopped dried cranberries or raisins

3 tablespoons miniature semisweet
    chocolate chips

1. Mix the bran cereal, applesauce, oil, eggs, and cinnamon in a large bowl with a wooden spoon until blended. Let stand 20 minutes, then stir in the cake mix, chopped cranberries, and chocolate chips.
2. Drop the dough by tablespoonfuls, 2 inches apart, onto prepared cookie sheets.
3. Bake 9 to 12 minutes or until just set at edges. Cool 1 minute on sheets, then remove cookies with spatula to wire racks to cool completely.

VARIATION *for Fiber-Wonderful Cookies*

DOUBLE-CHOCOLATE FIBER-WONDERFUL COOKIES: Prepare as directed, but use a devil's food cake mix, omit the cinnamon and cranberries, and increase the miniature chocolate chips to ⅓ cup.

GOOD-FOR-YOU DOUBLE-CHOCOLATE COOKIES

I love having good excuses to eat more chocolate. Not only is it delicious, but it's also chock-full of antioxidants. Here it's folded into a pumped-up dark chocolate batter—think pureed carrots, whole wheat flour, and egg whites—resulting in a soft, scrumptious, decadent treat.

PREHEAT OVEN TO 350°F

MAKES 3½ DOZEN COOKIES

COOKIE SHEETS, GREASED OR LINED WITH
　　PARCHMENT PAPER

1 (18.25-ounce) package devil's food cake mix

½ cup whole wheat flour

1 (4-ounce) jar strained carrots baby food

⅓ cup vegetable oil

2 large egg whites

1 large egg

¾ cup miniature semisweet chocolate chips

1. Mix the cake mix, flour, baby food, oil, egg whites, and egg in a large bowl with a wooden spoon until blended. Mix in the chocolate chips.
2. Drop by tablespoonfuls, 2 inches apart, onto ungreased cookie sheets.
3. Bake 10 to 13 minutes or until just barely set at center when lightly touched. Cool 1 minute on sheets, then remove cookies with spatula to wire racks to cool completely.

VEGAN CAKE MIX COOKIES

I have an increasing number of friends and acquaintances who cannot or do not eat milk and eggs, so I decided the time has come for a vegan (dairy- and egg-free) cake mix cookie. Be sure to check the cake mix package ingredients list for milk or egg products. Most do not have either, but it's a good idea to check each time.

PREHEAT OVEN TO 350°F

MAKES 4 DOZEN COOKIES

COOKIE SHEETS, GREASED OR LINED WITH
   PARCHMENT PAPER

1 (18.25-ounce) package cake mix (any flavor—check the label for egg or milk products)

1 teaspoon baking powder

⅔ cup vegetable oil or melted vegan margarine

⅔ cup applesauce

1¼ cups chocolate chips, chopped dried fruit, nuts, or a combination

1. Whisk the cake mix and baking powder in a large bowl. Add the oil and applesauce and mix with electric mixer set on low speed for 1 to 2 minutes until blended. Mix in the chocolate chips, dried fruit, or nuts with a wooden spoon.
2. Drop by tablespoonfuls, 2 inches apart, onto prepared cookie sheets.
3. Bake 9 to 12 minutes or until edges are firm and center is just barely set when lightly touched. Cool 1 minute on sheets, then remove cookies with spatula to wire racks to cool completely.

CHAPTER TWO

bar cookies

Think of the most decadent cookie ever to pass your palate. Chances are, it was a bar cookie. Silky cheesecake squares, intensely tart-sweet lemon bars, fudgy double dark-chocolate brownies, gooey coffeehouse carmelitas—bar cookies are magical in the world of home baking, able to highlight any sweet flavor combination, please any appetite, and match any occasion. What's more, bar cookies come together in a flash, are baked in one batch, and dirty but one pan. In short, bars are bliss!

BASIC BAR COOKIES

I love having "template" recipes in my cooking repertoire: single recipes that can be transformed in countless ways. This bar cookie recipe is just that. Use any cake mix flavor you like, then add any or all of your favorite mix-ins, from nuts to chocolate to dried fruit. Have fun, experiment, and come up with your signature combination.

PREHEAT OVEN TO 350°F

MAKES 3 DOZEN BARS

13 x 9-INCH BAKING PAN, GREASED OR LINED
   WITH FOIL (SEE PAGE 16)

1 (18.25-ounce) package cake mix

½ cup (1 stick) butter, softened

½ cup packed light brown sugar

1 large egg

2 tablespoons water

1½ cups chocolate or baking chips
(e.g., semisweet, butterscotch, white,
peanut butter, etc.)

1 cup chopped nuts (e.g., pecans, walnuts,
peanuts, macadamias, etc.) or chopped
dried fruit

1. Place the cake mix, butter, brown sugar, egg, and water in a large bowl. Beat with electric mixer on medium-high 1 to 2 minutes until light and fluffy. Mix in the chocolate chips and nuts. Spread the mixture into prepared pan.
2. Bake 30 to 35 minutes or until a toothpick inserted in center comes out clean. Transfer to wire rack and cool completely. Cut into bars.

PEANUT BUTTER AND JELLY BARS

The combination of peanut butter and jelly is nothing if not versatile. Here it is celebrated in an easy bar cookie that will be adored (and devoured) by one and all.

REHEAT OVEN TO 350°F

MAKES 3 DOZEN BARS

13 x 9-INCH BAKING PAN, GREASED OR LINED
  WITH FOIL (SEE PAGE 16)

1 (18.25-ounce) package white cake mix

1 cup quick-cooking oats

½ cup creamy-style peanut butter

1 large egg

2 tablespoons whole or lowfat milk

½ cup roasted, lightly salted peanuts,
  chopped

1 (12-ounce) jar seedless raspberry jam

1½ cups peanut butter baking chips

1. Mix the cake mix and oats in a large bowl. Add the peanut butter and, using fingers, mix until mixture resembles fine crumbs. Mix in the egg and milk with a wooden spoon until blended. Reserve 1 cup of oat mixture. Press remaining mixture into prepared pan.

2. Mix the peanuts into reserved oat mixture. Spoon the jam on top of prepared crust, then gently spread to cover. Sprinkle evenly with the peanut butter chips and reserved oat mixture.

3. Bake 28 to 30 minutes until topping is golden brown. Transfer to wire rack and cool completely. Cut into bars.

ORANGE, DATE, AND WALNUT BARS

Cake Mix
WHITE

To a traditional bar cookie, I've added Mediterranean touches: dates, for their honeylike sweetness, and fresh orange peel and walnuts to balance the flavors.

PREHEAT OVEN TO 350°F

MAKES 3 DOZEN BARS

13 x 9-INCH BAKING PAN, GREASED OR LINED
WITH FOIL (SEE PAGE 16)

1 (18.25 ounce) package white cake mix

¾ cup (1 stick) butter, melted

¾ cup packed light brown sugar

2 large eggs

1 tablespoon grated orange peel

2 cups chopped dates (from 2 8-ounce
packages)

2 cups chopped walnuts

1. Place the cake mix, melted butter, brown sugar, eggs, and orange peel in large bowl. Beat with electric mixer on medium-high 1 to 2 minutes until light and fluffy. Mix in the dates and walnuts. Spread evenly in prepared pan.
2. Bake 35 to 40 minutes or until a toothpick inserted in center comes out clean. Transfer to wire rack and cool completely. Cut into bars.

TOASTED COCONUT BARS

Cake Mix
WHITE

Enjoy these bars with caution—they are addictive!

PREHEAT OVEN TO 350°F

MAKES 3 DOZEN BARS

13 x 9-INCH BAKING PAN, GREASED OR LINED
WITH FOIL (SEE PAGE 16)

1 (18.25-ounce) package white cake mix

½ cup (1 stick) butter, melted

1⅔ cups packed light brown sugar

4 large eggs

¼ cup all-purpose flour

2 teaspoons baking powder

1 teaspoon vanilla extract

1½ cups sweetened flake coconut

1 cup chopped pecans

1. Mix the cake mix and melted butter in a large bowl with a wooden spoon until blended. Press mixture into prepared pan. Bake 15 minutes.
2. Meanwhile, whisk the brown sugar and eggs in a medium bowl until blended. Whisk in the flour, baking powder, and vanilla. Mix in the coconut and pecans. Pour and spread mixture over partially baked crust.
3. Bake 25 to 30 minutes longer until filling is just set. Transfer to wire rack and cool completely. Cut into bars.

Cake Mix WHITE — FRESH RASPBERRY BLONDIES

When raspberries are in season, these bars are a must-make. The brown sugar-y blondie batter is the perfect complement to the tart-sweet berries.

PREHEAT OVEN TO 350°F

MAKES 3 DOZEN BARS

13 x 9-INCH BAKING PAN, GREASED OR LINED WITH FOIL (SEE PAGE 16)

1 (18.25 ounce) package white cake mix

¾ cup (1 stick) butter, melted

¾ cup packed light brown sugar

2 large eggs

1 teaspoon vanilla extract

2 cups fresh raspberries

½ cups sliced almonds

1. Place the cake mix, melted butter, brown sugar, eggs, and vanilla in large bowl. Beat with electric mixer on medium-high 1 to 2 minutes until light and fluffy. Spread mixture into prepared pan. Scatter with the raspberries and almonds and gently press into dough.
2. Bake 35 to 40 minutes or until a toothpick inserted in center comes out clean. Transfer to wire rack and cool completely. Cut into bars.

APPLE BUTTER BARS

These home-style bars are loved by kids of all ages. Look for the apple butter in the supermarket where jams and jellies are shelved.

PREHEAT OVEN TO 350°F

MAKES 3 DOZEN BARS

13 x 9-INCH BAKING PAN, GREASED OR LINED WITH FOIL (SEE PAGE 16)

1 (18.25-ounce) package spice cake mix

1 cup apple butter

¼ cup (½ stick) butter, melted

2 large eggs

1 cup dried apples, chopped

1 cup chopped pecans or walnuts

1. Mix the cake mix, apple butter, melted butter, and eggs in a large bowl with a wooden spoon until blended. Stir in the dried apples. Spread into prepared pan and sprinkle with pecans or walnuts.
2. Bake 25 to 30 minutes or until a toothpick inserted in center comes out clean. Transfer to wire rack and cool completely. Cut into bars.

AMAZING DOUBLE-LEMON BARS

Cake Mix
WHITE

With lemon pie filling in the crust and a creamy, tart-sweet frosting, these bars are a lemon lover's dream come true.

PREHEAT OVEN TO 350°F

MAKES 2 DOZEN SQUARES

15 x 10 x 1-INCH JELLY ROLL PAN, GREASED OR LINED WITH FOIL (SEE PAGE 16)

1 (18.25-ounce) package white cake mix

1 (21-ounce) can lemon pie filling

1 cup sweetened flake coconut

Icing

2½ cups confectioners' sugar

1 (8-ounce) package cream cheese, softened

½ cup (1 stick) butter, softened

2 tablespoons lemon juice

1. Mix the cake mix, pie filling, and coconut in a large bowl with a wooden spoon until blended. Spread into prepared pan.

2. Bake 25 to 30 minutes or until edges are golden and toothpick inserted in center comes out clean. Transfer to wire rack and cool completely.
3. Place the confectioners' sugar, cream cheese, butter, and lemon juice in a large bowl. Beat with electric mixer on low speed 1 to 2 minutes on high speed until blended and smooth. Spread over cooled bars. Chill at least 2 hours. Cut into bars.

CHERRY CHEESECAKE BARS

Cake Mix
WHITE

My mother makes a to-die-for cherry cheesecake (it often appears—briefly!—at the Easter dinner table). These equally scrumptious bars capture the flavor, all in handheld form.

PREHEAT OVEN TO 350°F
MAKES 2 DOZEN SQUARES
9-INCH SQUARE BAKING PAN, GREASED OR LINED WITH FOIL (SEE PAGE 16)

1 (18.25-ounce) package white cake mix, divided
½ cup cornflake crumbs
3 large eggs
½ cup (1 stick) unsalted butter, melted, divided
2 (8-ounce packages) cream cheese, softened
¼ cup sugar
½ teaspoon almond extract
1 cup cherry preserves

1. Measure ½ cup cake mix and set aside. Mix the remaining cake mix, cornflake crumbs, 1 egg, and ¼ cup melted butter in large bowl with wooden spoon until blended. Press into prepared pan.
2. Beat the cream cheese, remaining 2 eggs, sugar, and almond extract in another large bowl with electric mixer on high speed until blended and smooth. Spread the mixture over crust. Spoon the cherry preserves over the cream cheese mixture, then spread gently to cover (need not cover perfectly).
3. Combine the reserved ½ cup cake mix and remaining ¼ cup melted butter in a small bowl until blended. Sprinkle over bars.
4. Bake 40 to 45 minutes or until topping is golden brown. Transfer to wire rack and cool completely. Cut into bars.

GET A GREAT SHAPE!

To give bars a fresh new appeal, skip the rectangles and squares and give diamonds and triangles a try.

To make diamonds, cut parallel lines 1 to 2 inches apart down the length of the pan. Next, cut diagonal lines the same distance apart across the pan, making diamond shapes.

To make triangles, cut bars into 2- or 2½-inch squares. Cut each square in half diagonally. Or, cut bars into rectangles and cut each diagonally into triangles.

Cake Mix
CHOCOLATE

BROWNIES

Good news: the box of chocolate cake mix in your cupboard not only makes great cakes and cookies but rich, dark chocolate brownies, too! Superb plain, they can be gussied up in numerous ways with chocolate chips, nuts, or a swath of frosting.

PREHEAT OVEN TO 350°F

MAKES 2 DOZEN SQUARES

9-INCH SQUARE BAKING PAN, GREASED OR LINED WITH FOIL (SEE PAGE 16)

1 (18.25-ounce) package chocolate cake mix
½ cup (1 stick) butter, softened
⅓ cup packed dark brown sugar
¼ cup whole or lowfat milk
2 large eggs
1 teaspoon vanilla
1 cup semisweet chocolate chips

1. Mix the cake mix, butter, brown sugar, milk, eggs, and vanilla in a large bowl with a wooden spoon until blended. Stir in the chocolate chips. Spread in pan with moistened fingers.

2. Bake 33 to 38 minutes or until edges are set. Transfer to wire rack and cool completely. Cut into bars.

JUST-RIGHT BROWNIES

Remove brownies from the oven while they are still slightly moist at the center. They will continue to firm up as they cool.

WALNUT BROWNIES: Prepare as directed but decrease chocolate chips to ½ cup and add 1 cup chopped, toasted walnuts.

Cake Mix DEVIL'S FOOD	# CHOCOLATE-MALLOW-PEANUT BUTTER BARS

Here's an over-the-top cookie bar that shows how a few simple addition from your pantry— peanut butter, marshmallow creme, and chocolate chips—can transform a cake mix from ordinary to extraordinary.

PREHEAT OVEN TO 350°F

MAKES 3 DOZEN BARS

13 x 9-INCH BAKING PAN, GREASED OR LINED WITH FOIL (SEE PAGE 16)

1 (18.25-ounce) package devil's food cake mix

⅔ cup whole or lowfat milk, divided

½ cup (1 stick) butter, melted

¾ cup creamy or chunky peanut butter

1 (7-ounce) jar marshmallow creme or fluff

1 cup semisweet or milk chocolate chips

1. Mix the cake mix, ⅓ cup milk, and melted butter in a large bowl with a wooden spoon until blended. Press ⅔ of dough in pan with moistened fingers. Bake 12 to 14 minutes until just set at edges.
2. Mix the peanut butter and remaining ⅓ cup milk in small bowl with wooden spoon until blended. Spread over partially baked crust. Dollop with small spoonfuls of the marshmallow creme and remaining cake mix, then sprinkle with chocolate chips.
3. Bake 17 to 20 minutes or until center is just set. Transfer to wire rack and cool completely. Cut into bars.

Cake Mix WHITE

BLACKBERRY CREAM CHEESE BARS

This is one of my go-to bar recipes. It always impresses, at gatherings fancy or informal, and the combination of berry and lemon (almost) beats chocolate in popularity.

PREHEAT OVEN TO 350°F

MAKES 3 DOZEN BARS

13 x 9-INCH BAKING PAN, GREASED OR LINED WITH FOIL (SEE PAGE 16)

1 (18.25-ounce) package white cake mix

½ cup (1 stick) butter, softened

3 large eggs

2 (8-ounce) packages cream cheese, softened

½ cup confectioners' sugar

2 tablespoons lemon juice

1 (21-ounce) can blackberry or blueberry pie filling

1. Place the cake mix, butter, and 1 egg in a large bowl. Beat with electric mixer on medium speed 1 to 2 minutes until blended. Press mixture into prepared pan.
2. Place the cream cheese, confectioners' sugar, lemon juice, and remaining 2 eggs in a separate large bowl. Beat with electric mixer on high speed 1 to 2 minutes until blended and smooth.
3. Spoon the cream cheese mixture evenly over crust, then spoon pie filling over. Cut through mixture with knife several times for marbled design.
4. Bake 35 to 40 minutes or until topping is crisp-looking and golden. Transfer to wire rack and cool completely. Chill at least 2 hours, then cut into bars.

VARIATION *for Blackberry Cream Cheese Bars*

CHOCOLATE-CHERRY CREAM CHEESE BARS: Prepare as directed but use a devil's food cake mix, omit the lemon juice, and use cherry pie filling.

CREAM CHEESE SWIRL BROWNIES

With the tang of vanilla-scented cream cheese swirled throughout a rich chocolate batter, this sweet treat is very special indeed. I love to make these for get-togethers with both adults and children in attendance because everyone thinks they are heavenly.

PREHEAT OVEN TO 350°F

MAKES 2 DOZEN SQUARES

9-INCH SQUARE BAKING PAN, GREASED OR LINED WITH FOIL (SEE PAGE 16)

1 (8-ounce) package cream cheese, softened

1 large egg

3 tablespoons sugar

½ teaspoon vanilla extract

1 (18.25-ounce) package chocolate fudge or chocolate cake mix

1 (5-ounce) can (⅔ cup) evaporated milk

½ cup (1 stick) butter, melted

Optional: ½ cup semisweet chocolate chips

1. Beat the cream cheese, egg, sugar, and vanilla in a medium bowl with electric mixer on medium speed 1 minute or until blended and smooth.

2. Mix the cake mix, evaporated milk, and melted butter in a medium bowl with a wooden spoon until blended. Spread ¾ cup dough in prepared pan. Spoon the cream cheese mixture over, then top with spoonfuls of the remaining dough. Cut through mixture with knife several times for marbled design. If desired, sprinkle with chocolate chips.

3. Bake 38 to 43 minutes or until toothpick inserted 1 inch from side of pan comes out clean. Transfer to wire rack and cool completely. Cut into squares. Store in refrigerator.

Cake Mix WHITE
WHITE CHOCOLATE CRANBERRY BARS

This lovely bar cookie combines two of my favorite cookie mix-ins: tart-sweet dried cranberries and white chocolate. They are particularly festive at holiday time.

PREHEAT OVEN TO 350°F

MAKES 3 DOZEN BARS

13 x 9-INCH BAKING PAN, GREASED OR LINED WITH FOIL (SEE PAGE 16)

1 (18.25-ounce) package white cake mix

⅓ cup (1 stick) butter, melted

2 large eggs

2 tablespoons whole or lowfat milk

1½ cups dried cranberries

1 cup white chocolate chips

1. Mix the cake mix, melted butter, eggs, and milk in a large bowl with a wooden spoon until blended. Mix in the cranberries and white chocolate chips. Spread evenly in prepared pan.

2. Bake 21 to 25 minutes or until edges are golden and toothpick inserted in center comes out clean. Transfer to wire rack and cool completely. Cut into bars.

Cake Mix SPICE
SOUR CREAM AND BLUEBERRY CRUMB BARS

A distinctive sour cream, orange, and dried blueberry filling nestles between layers of a spiced oat-crumble in these luscious bars. The combination of flavors and textures is extremely appealing.

PREHEAT OVEN TO 350°F

MAKES 3 DOZEN BARS

13 x 9-INCH BAKING PAN, GREASED OR LINED WITH FOIL (SEE PAGE 16)

1 (18.25-ounce) package spice cake mix

¾ cup (1½ sticks) butter, softened

2 large eggs

2 cups quick-cooking oats

1½ cups sour cream (not reduced fat)

3 tablespoons sugar

1 tablespoon grated orange peel

1¼ cups dried blueberries or cranberries

½ cup chopped pecans

1. Place the cake mix, butter, and 1 egg in a large bowl. Beat with electric mixer on medium speed 1 to 2 minutes until blended. Stir in the oats with a wooden spoon. Reserve 1½ cups cake mixture. Press remaining mixture into prepared pan.

2. Whisk the sour cream, sugar, orange peel, and remaining egg in small bowl until blended. Stir in the blueberries or cranberries.
3. Spread the sour cream mixture evenly over crust. Mix the pecans into reserved crumbs, then sprinkle over sour cream layer.
4. Bake 25 to 30 minutes or until topping is crisp-looking and golden. Run knife around sides of pan to loosen bars. Transfer to wire rack and cool completely. Chill at least 2 hours, then cut into bars.

Cake Mix SPICE — S'MORES BARS

A white cake mix makes campfire s'mores an anytime treat from your kitchen.

PREHEAT OVEN TO 350°F
MAKES 3 DOZEN BARS
13 x 9-INCH BAKING PAN, UNGREASED OR
   LINED WITH FOIL (SEE PAGE 16)

1 (18.25-ounce) package white cake mix
1¼ cups graham cracker crumbs
1 cup (2 sticks) butter, melted
3 cups milk chocolate chips
4½ cups miniature marshmallows

1. Mix the cake mix, graham cracker crumbs, and melted butter in a large bowl with a wooden spoon until blended. Press in ungreased pan with moistened fingers.
2. Bake 18 to 21 minutes or until just set. Immediately sprinkle with the chocolate chips. Let stand 5 minutes to soften chips, then spread evenly over bars.
3. Set oven to broil with rack positioned 6 inches from broiler element. Sprinkle the bars with marshmallows then broil 30 to 45 seconds until marshmallows are golden brown. Transfer to wire rack and cool 20 minutes. Cut into bars. Serve warm or cool completely.

CHOCOLATE MARBLE BANANA BARS

A package of cake mix makes quick work of the overripe bananas on your countertop, transforming them into decadent brownie-like bars.

PREHEAT OVEN TO 350°F

MAKES 1½ DOZEN BARS OR SQUARES

9-INCH SQUARE BAKING PAN, GREASED OR LINED WITH FOIL (SEE PAGE 16)

1 (18.25-ounce) package yellow cake mix

½ cup plus 2 tablespoons (1¼ sticks) butter, softened

1 large egg

¾ cup mashed, very ripe banana (about 2 small)

½ cup chopped pecans or peanuts

1¼ cups semisweet chocolate chips

1. Mix the cake mix, ½ stick butter, and egg in a large bowl with a wooden spoon until blended (dough will be thick). Measure out 1 cup of the dough and set aside. Mix the mashed banana and pecans into the remaining dough until blended, then spread into prepared pan.

2. Microwave ¾ cup of the chocolate chips and remaining 2 tablespoons butter in a medium microwaveable bowl on High 1 minute, stirring after 30 seconds, until melted and smooth. Mix in the reserved 1 cup dough with wooden spoon until blended. Drop by large spoonfuls over banana dough, then spread to almost cover. With tip of kitchen knife, lightly swirl the doughs. Sprinkle with remaining ½ cup chocolate chips.

3. Bake 35 to 40 minutes or until toothpick inserted in center comes out clean. Transfer to wire rack and cool completely. Cut into bars or squares.

CHOCOLATE CHIP CHEESECAKE BARS

Cheesecake is always a winning dessert choice in my book. These bars make it easy to enjoy in short order. You can vary the flavor by the cake mix and chocolate chips that you choose. Will you have classic chocolate chip, chocolate-butterscotch, or dark chocolate-white chocolate?

PREHEAT OVEN TO 350°F

MAKES 3 DOZEN BARS

13 x 9-INCH BAKING PAN, GREASED OR LINED
   WITH FOIL (SEE PAGE 16)

1 (18.25-ounce) package yellow cake mix

¾ cup (1½ sticks) butter, softened

3 large eggs

2 cups quick-cooking oats

2 (8-ounce) packages cream cheese, softened

½ cup sugar

1 teaspoon vanilla extract

1½ cups semisweet chocolate chips

1. Place the cake mix, butter, and 1 egg in a large bowl. Beat with electric mixer on medium speed 1 to 2 minutes until blended. Stir in the oats with a wooden spoon. Reserve 1½ cups cake mixture. Press remaining mixture into prepared pan.

2. Beat the cream cheese, sugar, and remaining 2 eggs with electric mixer on medium speed 1 to 2 minutes until smooth. Stir in 1 cup of the chocolate chips.

3. Spread the cream cheese mixture evenly over crust. Mix remaining ½ cup chocolate chips into reserved crumbs, then sprinkle over cheesecake layer.

4. Bake 35 to 40 minutes or until topping is crisp-looking and golden. Run knife around sides of pan to loosen bars. Transfer to wire rack and cool completely. Chill at least 2 hours, then cut into bars.

BLACK-BOTTOM BANANA CHEESECAKE BARS

Looking for a stylish dessert to wrap up a casual summer gathering? You can both cool things down and fire things up when you pull these pretty (and very chocolate) cheesecake bars out of the icebox.

PREHEAT OVEN TO 350°F

MAKES 3 DOZEN BARS

13 x 9-INCH BAKING PAN, GREASED OR LINED WITH FOIL (SEE PAGE 16)

1 (18.25-ounce) package devil's food cake mix

3 (8-ounce) packages cream cheese, softened, divided

½ cup (1 stick) butter, melted

3 large eggs

1 cup miniature semisweet chocolate chips

1 cup mashed ripe banana (about 2 large bananas)

1 cup confectioners' sugar

1½ teaspoons vanilla extract

1. Mix the cake mix, 4 ounces (half an 8-ounce package) cream cheese, melted butter, and 1 egg in large bowl with electric mixer on medium speed 2 minutes until blended. Stir in the chocolate chips, then press into prepared pan. Bake 15 minutes.
2. Meanwhile, beat the remaining cream cheese, banana, confectioners' sugar, and vanilla extract in a medium bowl with electric mixer on medium 1 to 2 minutes until smooth. Beat in the remaining 2 eggs until blended, then spread mixture evenly over partially baked crust.
3. Bake 25 to 28 minutes or until just set. Transfer to wire rack and cool completely. Chill at least 2 hours before serving. Cut into bars.

LAYERED PEANUT BUTTER BARS

These chocolate-topped peanut butter bars are decadence defined, yet their preparation is still a breeze.

PREHEAT OVEN TO 350°F

MAKES 3 DOZEN BARS

13 x 9-INCH BAKING PAN, GREASED OR LINED
   WITH FOIL (SEE PAGE 16)

Base:

1 (18.25-ounce) package white cake mix

⅓ cup butter, melted

2 large eggs

2 tablespoons whole or lowfat milk

1 cup chopped roasted, salted peanuts

Filling:

2 cups confectioners' sugar

½ cup creamy peanut butter

½ cup (1 stick) butter, softened

2 teaspoons vanilla extract

Topping:

1 cup semisweet chocolate chips

2 teaspoons vegetable shortening

1. Mix the cake mix, melted butter, eggs, and milk in a large bowl with a wooden spoon until blended. Spread evenly in prepared pan. Stir in the peanuts.

2. Bake 20 to 25 minutes or until toothpick inserted in center comes out clean. Transfer to wire rack and cool completely.

3. Mix the confectioners' sugar, peanut butter, softened butter, and vanilla in a medium bowl with electric mixer on medium speed 1 minute until blended. Spread over cooled bars.

4. In small microwaveable bowl, microwave chocolate chips and vegetable shortening uncovered on High 60 to 90 seconds, stirring every 30 seconds until melted and smooth. Spread over filling. Refrigerate uncovered until set, at least 1 hour. Cut into bars.

HOST A COOKIE SWAP!

A cookie swap is a great (and delicious) way to socialize with friends as well as save time in the kitchen during the holiday season. Plus, it's an easy party to put together:

Choose a date: Select a date and send out invitations about 3–4 weeks in advance. Weekday evenings or weekend afternoons work well because people may be less busy. Schedule the party to be about 2 hours long so guests will be able to schedule other events into their day.

Invite guests: Invite 8 to 12 guests (it gets complicated with more than 12). Make enough of one type of cookie to allow for ½ to 1 dozen for each person participating, plus an extra dozen for sampling at the party.

Ask for recipes: Gather a list of the type of cookie each person is making to avoid duplicates. Ask guests to email copies of the recipe ahead for printing, or have each guest bring printed copies of their recipes.

Request packaging: Have guests bring empty containers or resealable plastic bags to collect their goodies. Offer a variety of pretty ribbons and bows for adding flair to their boxes and bags.

Brew the coffee: On the day of the party, offer a few hot and cold appetizers.

Ready, set, swap: On the day of the party, offer plenty of coffee and tea, and clear a few tables for sampling and packaging cookies. Provide several platters and cake stands for displaying cookies, and smaller plates for sampling. Be sure to label each cookie type as it is set out for display.

Enjoy: Have fun sampling cookies and visiting with friends. Near the end of the party, have guests fill their containers with a ½ dozen or dozen of each kind of cookie.

CINNAMON-MOCHA BARS

Who wants an overpriced espresso drink from the local coffeehouse when you can bake a batch of these sophisticated coffee, cinnamon, and chocolate-flavored bars instead? I like to cut these into regular-size bars, but you can cut them into bite-size squares for a party (instant petits fours).

PREHEAT OVEN TO 350°F

MAKES 3 DOZEN BARS

13 x 9-INCH BAKING PAN, GREASED OR LINED WITH FOIL (SEE PAGE 16)

1 (18.25-ounce) package devil's food cake mix

½ cup (1 stick) butter, melted

2 large eggs

½ teaspoon ground cinnamon

2 teaspoons instant coffee powder

¼ cup hot water

3 cups confectioners' sugar

½ cup (1 stick) butter, softened

¼ cup unsweetened cocoa powder

1 teaspoon vanilla extract

1. Mix the cake mix, melted butter, eggs, and cinnamon in a large bowl with a wooden spoon until blended. Press dough in pan with moistened fingers.
2. Bake 18 to 23 minutes or until just barely set at center. Transfer to wire rack and cool completely.
3. Combine the coffee powder and hot water in medium bowl until dissolved. Add the confectioners' sugar, butter, cocoa powder, and vanilla. Beat with electric mixer on medium speed 1 to 2 minutes until blended and smooth. Spread over cooled bars. Chill at least 5 minutes, then cut into bars.

STRAWBERRY CHEESECAKE BARS

These pretty strawberry bars are perfect for welcoming in the beginning of spring, warmer weather, and the arrival of the first strawberries. For added strawberry goodness, serve with a slice of fresh strawberry atop each bar.

PREHEAT OVEN TO 350°F

MAKES 3 DOZEN BARS

13 x 9-INCH BAKING PAN, GREASED OR LINED WITH FOIL (SEE PAGE 16)

1 (18.25-ounce) package white cake mix

½ cup butter melted

3 large eggs

2 (8-ounce) packages cream cheese, softened

¼ cup sugar

1 teaspoon vanilla extract

¾ cup strawberry spreadable fruit

1. Mix the cake mix, butter, and 1 egg in a large bowl with a wooden spoon until blended and soft dough forms. Press evenly in prepared pan.
2. Bake 15 to 18 minutes or until light golden brown. Cool 15 minutes.
3. Meanwhile, beat the cream cheese, sugar, remaining 2 eggs, and vanilla with electric mixer on medium speed until blended and smooth. Spread evenly over crust in pan.
4. Place the spreadable fruit in small resealable plastic bag; seal bag. Cut off tiny corner of bag. Squeeze spreadable fruit in 3 lines the length of the pan. Use knife to pull spread from side to side through cream cheese mixture at 1-inch intervals.
5. Bake 25 to 30 minutes longer or until filling is set. Cool completely on wire rack, then chill at least 2 hours. Cut into bars.

PRALINE, CRUMB, AND CARAMEL SQUARES

Part cookie, part cheesecake, and 100 percent decadent, these luscious bars are praline perfection. Serve them up as a rich treat alongside a good cup of mid-afternoon coffee.

PREHEAT OVEN TO 350°F

MAKES 2 DOZEN SQUARES

9-INCH SQUARE BAKING PAN, GREASED OR LINED WITH FOIL (SEE PAGE 16)

1 (18.25-ounce) package white cake mix, divided

⅓ cup butter, softened

2 large eggs

1 (8-ounce) package cream cheese, softened

1 cup chopped pecans

½ cup toffee baking bits

½ cup caramel ice cream topping

1. Reserve 3 tablespoons cake mix. Beat the remaining cake mix, butter, and 1 egg in a large bowl with electric mixer on medium speed 1 minute or until blended and crumbly. Reserve 1 cup of crumb mixture. Firmly press remaining crumb mixture on prepared pan.
2. Beat the cream cheese, reserved 3 tablespoons cake mix, and remaining egg in a small bowl, then pour and spread over crust. Mix the pecans and toffee bits into reserved crumbs, then sprinkle over cream cheese layer.
3. Bake 25 to 28 minutes or until lightly browned. Transfer to wire rack and cool completely. Drizzle cooled bars with caramel. Chill at least 2 hours, then cut into squares.

NANAIMO BARS

Nanaimo bars are a treat from north of the border, specifically the West Coast city of Nanaimo, British Columbia. Their popularity extends across Canada, clearly because they are so delicious: a chocolate cookie-crumb crust, vanilla custard filling, and a chocolate glaze atop all. Although classic recipes for Nanaimo bars require no baking, I couldn't resist making a cake mix version. My Canadian mother approves!

PREHEAT OVEN TO 350°F

MAKES 3 DOZEN BARS

13 x 9-INCH BAKING PAN, LINED WITH FOIL
(SEE PAGE 16)

Base:

1 (18.25-ounce) package chocolate fudge cake mix

1 cup graham cracker crumbs

1 cup (2 sticks) butter, melted

½ cup chopped pecans or walnuts

½ cup sweetened flake coconut

1 large egg

Filling:

4 cups confectioners' sugar

⅓ cup butter, softened

¼ cup whole or lowfat milk

2 teaspoons vanilla extract

Topping:

1 (12-ounce) bag semisweet chocolate chips

¼ cup (½ stick) butter

1. Mix the cake mix, graham cracker crumbs, melted butter, nuts, coconut, and egg in large bowl with wooden spoon until blended. Spread and press into prepared pan. Bake 15 to 18 minutes or until just barely set (do not overbake). Transfer to wire rack and cool completely.
2. Place the confectioners' sugar, softened butter, milk, and vanilla in large bowl. Beat with electric mixer on medium speed until smooth (filling will be very thick). Spoon and spread over cooled cookie base. Chill while preparing topping.
3. Microwave the chocolate chips and ¼ cup butter, uncovered, in small microwaveable bowl on High for 60 to 90 seconds, stirring every 30 seconds until melted and smooth. Spread over filling. Refrigerate uncovered until set, at least 1 hour.
4. Use foil to lift bars from pan. Peel off foil and cut into bars. Store in refrigerator.

GRAHAM CRACKER BARS

How ironic is it that my wonderful husband—married to a recipe developer known for gussying up cookies, cakes, and sweets of all kinds—prefers simple desserts? So I created these cookies for him: old-fashioned and understated, they are the perfect accompaniment to his afternoon cup of coffee.

PREHEAT OVEN TO 350°F

MAKES 3 DOZEN BARS

13 x 9-INCH BAKING PAN, GREASED OR LINED
   WITH FOIL (SEE PAGE 16)

1 (18.25-ounce) package yellow cake mix

2 cups graham cracker crumbs

1 cup (2 sticks) butter, melted

1 large egg

1 cup semisweet chocolate chips

1. Mix the cake mix, graham cracker crumbs, melted butter, and egg in large bowl with wooden spoon until blended. Mix in 1 cup of the chocolate chips. Spread and press into prepared pan.
2. Bake 16 to 21 minutes until just set. Transfer to wire rack and cool completely. Cut into bars.

VARIATION *for Graham Cracker Bars*

CINNAMON GRAHAM BARS: Prepare as directed but add 1½ teaspoons ground cinnamon to dough. Replace the chocolate chips with 1 cup raisins, chopped pecans, or cinnamon baking chips.

APPLE CRUMBLE CHEESECAKE BARS

Apple pie, cheesecake, oatmeal cookies… I love them all, so why not combine them into one great bar? I couldn't think of a good answer, so I created these amazing bars.

PREHEAT OVEN TO 350°F

MAKES 3 DOZEN BARS

13 x 9-INCH BAKING PAN, GREASED OR LINED
   WITH FOIL (SEE PAGE 16)

1 (18.25-ounce) package spice cake mix

¾ cup (1½ sticks) butter, softened

2 large eggs

2 cups quick-cooking oats

2 (8-ounce) packages cream cheese, softened

¼ cup sugar

1 (21-ounce) can apple pie filling

Optional: ½ cup chopped pecans or walnuts

1. Place the cake mix, butter, and 1 egg in a large bowl. Beat with electric mixer on medium speed 1 to 2 minutes until blended. Stir in the oats with a wooden spoon. Reserve 1½ cups cake mixture. Press remaining mixture into prepared pan.

2. Beat the cream cheese, sugar, and remaining egg with electric mixer on medium speed 1 to 2 minutes until smooth.

3. Spread the cream cheese mixture evenly over crust. Spoon the apple pie filling over cream cheese layer. If desired, mix the nuts into reserved crumbs, then sprinkle over apple filling.

4. Bake 35 to 40 minutes or until topping is crisp-looking and golden. Run knife around sides of pan to loosen bars. Transfer to wire rack and cool completely. Chill at least 2 hours, then cut into bars.

TROPICAL PINEAPPLE AND CARAMEL BARS

Cake Mix
WHITE

For anyone who loves topical flavors, these bar cookies are the perfect combination. Eating one is a tropical escape in itself!

PREHEAT OVEN TO 350°F

MAKES 3 DOZEN BARS

13 x 9-INCH BAKING PAN, GREASED OR LINED WITH FOIL (SEE PAGE 16)

1 (18.25-ounce) package white cake mix

¾ cup (1½ sticks) butter, softened

1 large egg

2 cups quick-cooking oats

1 (14-ounce) bag caramels, unwrapped

1 (20-ounce) can crushed pineapple, well-drained, ¼ cup juice reserved

1 teaspoon ground ginger

1 cup sweetened flake coconut

1. Place the cake mix, butter, and egg in a large bowl. Beat with electric mixer on medium speed 1 to 2 minutes until blended. Stir in the oats with a wooden spoon. Reserve 1½ cups cake mixture. Press remaining mixture into prepared pan.

2. Heat the caramels and reserved ¼ cup juice in heavy medium saucepan over medium-low heat, stirring frequently, until melted. Stir in the drained pineapple and ginger, then pour over crust in pan. Add the coconut to the reserved cake mixture, then sprinkle over caramel.

3. Bake 23 to 28 minutes or until caramel bubbles along edges and topping is golden. Run knife around sides of pan to loosen bars. Transfer to wire rack and cool completely. Cut into bars.

RASPBERRY CRUMBLE BARS

These bars, made with a brown sugar-oat crumble and double-berry filling, are perfect for the summer when fresh raspberries are sweet, juicy, and readily available.

PREHEAT OVEN TO 350°F

MAKES 3 DOZEN BARS

13 x 9-INCH BAKING PAN, GREASED OR LINED
   WITH FOIL (SEE PAGE 16)

1 (18.25-ounce) package yellow cake mix

¾ cup (1½ sticks) butter, softened

1 large egg

2 cups quick-cooking oats

1 (12-ounce) jar seedless raspberry jam

1½ cups fresh raspberries

½ cup chopped pecans

⅓ cup packed light brown sugar

1. Mix the cake mix, butter, and egg in large bowl with electric mixer on low speed 1 minute or just until crumbly. Stir in the oats, using hands if necessary. Reserve 1½ cups oat mixture. Press the remaining oat mixture in pan. Bake 15 minutes.
2. Spoon the jam in dollops over hot crust. Let stand 1 minute to melt slightly (for easier spreading), then spread evenly. Top with the fresh raspberries.
3. Mix the pecans and brown sugar into reserved oat mixture, then sprinkle over raspberries and jam.
4. Bake 20 to 25 minutes or until golden brown. Transfer to wire rack and cool completely. Cut into bars.

DRIED BLUEBERRY AND LEMON BARS

I'm an avid tea drinker, so a constant thought as I develop my cookie recipes is "Will this go with tea?" The answer for this bar cookie is a resounding "yes." Bright with the flavor of fresh lemon, and enriched with a handful of dried blueberries, they are an excellent foil to a cup of Earl Grey.

PREHEAT OVEN TO 350°F

MAKES 3 DOZEN BARS

13 x 9-INCH BAKING PAN, GREASED OR LINED
   WITH FOIL (SEE PAGE 16)

1 (18.25-ounce) package white cake mix

½ cup sour cream (not reduced fat)

¼ cup (½ stick) butter, melted

2 large eggs

2 teaspoons finely grated lemon peel

1 cup dried blueberries

2 cups confectioners' sugar

1½ tablespoons fresh lemon juice

1. Mix the cake mix, sour cream, melted butter, eggs, and lemon peel in a large bowl with a wooden spoon until blended. Stir in the blueberries. Spread evenly in prepared pan.
2. Bake 20 to 25 minutes or until toothpick inserted in center comes out clean. Transfer to wire rack and cool completely.
3. Mix the confectioners' sugar and lemon juice in a small bowl until blended. Drizzle over cooled bars, then cut into bars.

COCONUT-RUM BROWNIE BARS

When you're desperate for a tropical escape, but haven't the time or the means, try one of these bars. They may not be quite the same, but the dark chocolate, coconut, and rum are undeniably transportive.

PREHEAT OVEN TO 350°F

MAKES 3 DOZEN BARS

13 x 9-INCH BAKING PAN, GREASED OR LINED WITH FOIL (SEE PAGE 16)

1 (18.25-ounce) package chocolate fudge or chocolate cake mix

½ cup (1 stick) butter, melted

1 large egg

1 (12-ounce) bag bittersweet or semisweet chocolate chips

1 (7-ounce) bag sweetened flake coconut

1 (14-ounce) can sweetened condensed milk (not evaporated)

3 tablespoons dark rum

1. Mix the cake mix, butter, and egg in a large bowl with a wooden spoon until blended. Press in prepared pan. Sprinkle evenly with the chocolate chips and coconut.
2. In a small bowl mix the condensed milk and rum until blended. Pour mixture evenly over the coconut and chocolate chips.
3. Bake 35 to 40 minutes or until edges and center are set. Transfer to wire rack and cool completely. Cut into bars.

RASPBERRY-ALMOND CHEESECAKE BARS

Topped with a creamy layer of cheesecake and tart raspberry jam, these bars offer a little taste of heaven. A hint of almond extract enhances the combination of cheesecake and raspberry. Try cutting them into tiny squares for perfect petits fours at a bridal or baby shower.

PREHEAT OVEN TO 350°F

MAKES 3 DOZEN BARS

13 x 9-INCH BAKING PAN, GREASED OR LINED WITH FOIL (SEE PAGE 16)

1 (18.25-ounce) package white cake mix

¼ cup (½ stick) butter, softened

3 (8-ounce) packages cream cheese, softened, divided

¼ cup sugar

2 tablespoons all-purpose flour

1 teaspoon almond extract

2 large eggs

1 (12-ounce) jar seedless raspberry jam

½ cup sliced almonds

1. Place the cake mix in large bowl. Cut in the butter and 4 ounces cream cheese with a pastry blender, fingers, or fork until mixture is crumbly. Reserve 1½ cups mixture for topping. Press remaining mixture in pan. Bake 12 minutes.

2. Place the remaining 2½ packages cream cheese, sugar, flour, almond extract, and eggs in a large bowl. Beat with electric mixer 1 to 2 minutes on medium speed until blended.

3. Spread the cream cheese mixture evenly over partially baked cookie base. Spoon the jam evenly over cream cheese mixture, then sprinkle with reserved topping and almonds.

4. Bake 40 to 45 minutes or until light golden brown. Transfer to wire rack and cool completely. Chill at least 2 hours, then cut into bars. Store covered in refrigerator.

FAVORITE FRUIT COBBLER BARS

Cake Mix WHITE

Forget rolling out pastry for cobbler. A box of dry cake mix makes fruit cobbler a snap to prepare. The most difficult task will be deciding which flavor fruit filling to use.

PREHEAT OVEN TO 350°F

MAKES 3 DOZEN BARS

13 x 9-INCH BAKING PAN, GREASED OR LINED
   WITH FOIL (SEE PAGE 16)

2 (18.25-ounce) packages white cake mix

1 cup (2 sticks) butter, softened

2 large eggs

1½ teaspoons almond extract, divided

1 (21-ounce) can fruit pie filling (e.g. cherry,
   apple, peach)

1½ cups confectioners' sugar

2 tablespoons whole or lowfat milk

1. Place the cake mixes, butter, eggs, and 1 teaspoon almond extract in a large bowl. Beat with electric mixer on medium speed 2 minutes until soft dough forms. Press half of dough in prepared pan.
2. Spread the pie filling over crust. Drop remaining dough by tablespoonfuls over filling.
3. Bake 45 to 50 minutes or until topping is set and golden brown. Transfer to wire rack and cool completely.
4. Mix the confectioners' sugar, milk, and remaining ½ teaspoon almond extract in small bowl until smooth. Drizzle over bars. Cut into bars.

HONEY-CASHEW BARS

Cake Mix WHITE

Cashews are an oft-overlooked nut in the baking world. They add a subtle sweetness as well as a buttery crunch, and they work in particularly sweet harmony paired with honey.

PREHEAT OVEN TO 350°F

MAKES 3 DOZEN BARS

13 x 9-INCH BAKING PAN, LINED WITH FOIL
   (SEE PAGE 16)

1 (18.25-ounce) package white cake mix

½ cup (1 stick) butter, softened

4 large eggs

¾ cup packed light brown sugar

¼ cup honey

1 teaspoon vanilla extract

2 cups honey-roasted cashews, coarsely
   chopped

1. Mix the cake mix, butter, and 1 egg in a large bowl with electric mixer on medium speed until blended. Spread evenly in prepared pan. Bake 15 minutes until golden.
2. Meanwhile, whisk the brown sugar, remaining 3 eggs, honey, and vanilla in a medium bowl until blended. Stir in the cashews, then pour over partially baked crust.
3. Bake 30 to 35 minutes or until center no longer jiggles when pan is gently shaken. Cool 20 minutes, then use foil to lift bars from pan to wire rack. Cool completely. Cut into bars.

Cake Mix WHITE — CANDY JUMBLE BARS

These cookies are a jumble of fun, and in case it needs to be said, kids love them!

PREHEAT OVEN TO 350°F

MAKES 3 DOZEN BARS

13 x 9-INCH BAKING PAN, GREASED OR LINED WITH FOIL (SEE PAGE 16)

1 (18.25-ounce) package white cake mix

½ cup packed light brown sugar

½ cup (1 stick) butter, softened

2 large eggs

3 tablespoons whole or lowfat milk

1 cup semisweet, milk, or white chocolate chips

1 cup miniature M&Ms

Optional: ½ cup chopped pecans or walnuts

1. Mix the cake mix, brown sugar, butter, eggs, and milk in large bowl with wooden spoon until blended. Mix in the chocolate chips and M&Ms. Spread and press into prepared pan. If desired, sprinkle with the nuts, gently pressing into dough.
2. Bake 25 to 30 minutes until just set. Transfer to wire rack and cool completely. Cut into bars.

VARIATION *for Candy Jumble Bars*

CHOCOLATE CANDY JUMBLE BARS: Prepare as directed, but use a devil's food or chocolate cake mix in place of the white cake mix. Omit the brown sugar.

PINK LEMONADE BARS

These bars are pretty in pink and delicious to boot. They make a perfect finale to a summer picnic.

PREHEAT OVEN TO 350°F

MAKES 3 DOZEN BARS

13 x 9-INCH BAKING PAN, GREASED OR LINED WITH FOIL (SEE PAGE 16)

1 (18.25-ounce) package white cake mix, divided

¼ cup (½ stick) butter, melted

4 large eggs

1 (12-ounce) container pink lemonade concentrate, thawed

1 (8-ounce) package cream cheese, softened

1 (8-ounce) container sour cream

Optional: 2–3 drops red food coloring

1. Measure out ½ cup of the cake mix and set aside. Mix the remaining cake mix, melted butter, and 1 egg in large bowl with electric mixer on medium speed 1 minute until blended. Press mixture into prepared pan.

2. Beat the pink lemonade concentrate, cream cheese, and sour cream with electric mixer on medium speed 1 minute. Add the reserved cake mix, remaining 3 eggs, and (optional) red food coloring (to tint darker pink). Beat on medium-high speed 1 minute longer until blended. Pour and spread evenly over prepared crust.

3. Bake 45 to 50 minutes or until center is just barely set when pan is jiggled (do not over-bake). Transfer to wire rack and cool completely. Refrigerate at least 4 hours or overnight. Cut into bars.

APPLE-CRANBERRY SNACK BARS

These sound like ideal autumn bars, and indeed they are. But don't wait until the leaves turn to give them a try—they are year-round winners.

PREHEAT OVEN TO 350°F

MAKES 4 DOZEN BARS

15 x 10 x 1-INCH JELLY ROLL PAN, GREASED OR LINED WITH FOIL (SEE PAGE 16)

1 (18.25-ounce) package spice cake mix

¾ cup sour cream (not reduced fat)

2 large eggs

1 cup coarsely grated tart apples (no need to peel)

1 cup dried cranberries or raisins

1 cup (½ a 16-ounce tub) ready-to-spread vanilla frosting

2 tablespoons pure maple syrup or maple-flavored pancake syrup

1. Mix the cake mix, sour cream, and eggs in large bowl with wooden spoon until blended. Mix in the apple and dried cranberries or raisins. Spread into prepared pan.
2. Bake 16 to 21 minutes until just set. Transfer to wire rack and cool 15 minutes.
3. Mix the frosting and maple syrup in a small bowl until blended. Spread over warm bars. Cool completely, then cut into bars.

Cake Mix YELLOW	# BAKLAVA BARS

The flavor of baklava—a butter-rich, many-layered Greek pastry, rich with spices, nuts, and lemon—is simplified here in an easy-to-prepare bar recipe.

PREHEAT OVEN TO 350°F

MAKES 3 DOZEN BARS

13 x 9-INCH BAKING PAN, GREASED OR LINED WITH FOIL (SEE PAGE 16)

1 (18.25-ounce) package yellow cake mix

¾ cup (1½ sticks) butter, melted, divided

4 large eggs

1½ cups packed light brown sugar

½ cup honey

2 teaspoons grated lemon peel

1 teaspoon vanilla extract

½ teaspoon ground cinnamon

1½ cups chopped walnuts

1. Mix the cake mix and ½ cup melted butter in a large bowl with a wooden spoon until blended. Press into the prepared pan. Bake 15 minutes until golden.
2. Meanwhile, whisk the eggs, brown sugar, honey, lemon peel, vanilla, and cinnamon in a large bowl until blended. Stir in the walnuts. Spread the mixture evenly over partially baked crust.
3. Bake an additional 40 to 45 minutes or until filling is just set when pan is gently shaken. Transfer to a wire rack and cool completely. Cut into bars.

Cake Mix YELLOW	# GOOEY BARS

When your kitchen is filled with the enticing aroma of vanilla and butter, you'll know that weekend baking will never be the same. These delectable treats are made with a buttery cake mix dough on the bottom and a generous layer of more butter, cream cheese, and vanilla on top—irresistible!

PREHEAT OVEN TO 350°F

MAKES 3 DOZEN BARS

13 x 9-INCH BAKING PAN, GREASED OR LINED WITH FOIL (SEE PAGE 16)

1 (18.25-ounce) package yellow cake mix

1 cup (2 sticks) butter, melted, divided

4 large eggs

1 (8-ounce) package cream cheese, softened

2 teaspoons vanilla extract

1 (16-ounce) package confectioners' sugar

1. Mix the cake mix, ½ cup (1 stick) melted butter, and 1 egg in large bowl with electric mixer on medium speed until blended (dough will be thick). Pat evenly into prepared pan.

2. Beat the cream cheese and vanilla in large bowl with electric mixer on high speed until blended and smooth. Beat in the remaining ½ cup (1 stick) melted butter and remaining 3 eggs. Beat in the confectioners' sugar until blended. Spread over prepared crust.

3. Bake 42 to 45 minutes until golden (do not overbake; bars should be slightly gooey). Transfer to a wire rack and cool completely. Cut into bars or squares. Cover and store in refrigerator.

Cake Mix CHOCOLATE or DEVIL'S FOOD | TRIPLE-CHOCOLATE GOOEY BARS

A chocolate lover's dream come true, these decadent bars are memorable after one bite. Their deep, rich flavor stems from chocolate times three: chocolate cake mix, cocoa powder in the filling, and miniature chocolate chips throughout.

PREHEAT OVEN TO 350°F

MAKES 3 DOZEN BARS

13 x 9-INCH BAKING PAN, GREASED OR LINED WITH FOIL (SEE PAGE 16)

1 (18.25-ounce) package chocolate or devil's food cake mix

1 cup (2 sticks) butter, melted, divided

4 large eggs

1 (8-ounce) package cream cheese, softened

⅓ cup unsweetened cocoa powder

2 teaspoons vanilla extract

1 (16-ounce) package confectioners' sugar

¾ cup miniature semisweet chocolate chips

1. Mix the cake mix, ½ cup (1 stick) melted butter, and 1 egg in large bowl with electric mixer on medium speed until blended (dough will be thick). Pat evenly into prepared pan.

2. Beat the cream cheese, cocoa powder, and vanilla in large bowl with electric mixer on high speed until blended and smooth. Beat in the remaining ½ cup (1 stick) melted butter and remaining 3 eggs. Beat in the confectioners' sugar until blended. Spread over prepared crust and sprinkle with chocolate chips.

3. Bake 42 to 45 minutes until just set at center (do not overbake; bars should be slightly gooey). Transfer to a wire rack and cool completely. Cut into bars or squares. Cover and store in refrigerator.

LEMON-BLUEBERRY GOOEY BARS

A box of lemon cake mix is transformed thanks to a little imagination and a handful of summer berries. You can substitute fresh or frozen (thawed) blackberries or raspberries in this recipe for an equally delicious, decadent result. An equal amount of diced fresh apricots or peaches is also excellent here at the height of the harvest.

PREHEAT OVEN TO 350°F

MAKES 3 DOZEN BARS

13 x 9-INCH BAKING PAN, GREASED OR LINED
   WITH FOIL (SEE PAGE 16)

1 (18.25-ounce) package lemon cake mix

1 cup (2 sticks) butter, melted, divided

4 large eggs

1 (8-ounce) package cream cheese, softened

⅓ cup lemon juice

1 (16-ounce) package confectioners' sugar

2 cups fresh blueberries or 2 cups frozen (thawed 10 minutes) blueberries

1. Mix the cake mix, ½ cup (1 stick) melted butter, and 1 egg in large bowl with electric mixer on medium speed until blended (dough will be thick). Pat evenly into prepared pan.

2. Beat the cream cheese and lemon juice in large bowl with electric mixer on high speed until blended and smooth. Beat in the remaining ½ cup (1 stick) melted butter and remaining 3 eggs. Beat in the confectioners' sugar until blended, then stir in blueberries. Spread over prepared crust.

3. Bake 42 to 45 minutes until golden (do not overbake; bars should be slightly gooey). Transfer to a wire rack and cool completely. Cut into bars or squares. Cover and store in refrigerator.

VARIATION *for Lemon-Blueberry Gooey Bars*

CRANBERRY-ORANGE GOOEY BARS: Prepare as directed but use an orange cake mix, substitute orange juice for the lemon juice, and fresh or frozen (thawed) cranberries for the blueberries.

RASPBERRY-VANILLA GOOEY BARS: Prepare as directed but substitute milk for the lemon juice, 1 teaspoon vanilla extract for the lemon peel, and fresh raspberries for the blueberries.

PEANUT BUTTER CHOCOLATE GOOEY BARS

Holy moly. Yes, the combination of chocolate and peanut butter is a match made in heaven, but it has never been quite as good as in these gooey bars. Part cake, part cookie, they are 100 percent scrumptious.

PREHEAT OVEN TO 350°F

MAKES 3 DOZEN BARS

13 x 9-INCH BAKING PAN, GREASED OR LINED WITH FOIL (SEE PAGE 16)

1 (18.25-ounce) package devil's food cake mix

1 cup (2 sticks) butter, melted, divided

4 large eggs

1 (8-ounce) package cream cheese, softened

1 cup creamy-style peanut butter

1 teaspoon vanilla extract

1 (16-ounce) package confectioners' sugar

1. Mix the cake mix, ½ cup (1 stick) melted butter, and 1 egg in large bowl with electric mixer on medium speed until blended (dough will be thick). Pat evenly into prepared pan.
2. Beat cream cheese, peanut butter, and vanilla in large bowl with electric mixer on high speed until blended and smooth. Beat in remaining ½ cup (1 stick) melted butter and remaining 3 eggs. Beat in confectioners' sugar until blended. Spread over prepared crust.
3. Bake 42 to 45 minutes until just set (do not overbake; bars should be slightly gooey). Transfer to a wire rack and cool completely. Cut into bars or squares. Cover and store in refrigerator.

VARIATION *for Peanut Butter Chocolate Gooey Bars*

PEANUT BUTTER GOOEY BARS: Prepare as directed, but use a white cake mix in place of the devil's food cake mix.

RUM-RAISIN GOOEY BARS

It was a sad day when ice cream parlors stopped carrying rum-raisin as a standard offering, because it's a fantastic flavor duo. It's better than ever in this gooey bar rendition.

PREHEAT OVEN TO 350°F

MAKES 3 DOZEN BARS

13 x 9-INCH BAKING PAN, GREASED OR LINED WITH FOIL (SEE PAGE 16)

1¼ cups golden or dark raisins

⅓ cup dark rum

1 (18.25-ounce) package white cake mix

1 cup (2 sticks) butter, divided

4 large eggs

1 (8-ounce) package cream cheese, softened

½ teaspoon ground nutmeg

1 (16-ounce) package confectioners' sugar

1. Combine the raisins and rum in a medium microwaveable bowl. Microwave on High 1 minute until hot. Let stand 10 minutes.

2. Mix the cake mix, ½ cup (1 stick) melted butter, and 1 egg in large bowl with electric mixer on medium speed until blended (dough will be thick). Pat evenly into prepared pan.

3. Beat the cream cheese in large bowl with electric mixer on high speed until blended and smooth. Beat in the remaining ½ cup (1 stick) melted butter, remaining 3 eggs, and nutmeg. Beat in the confectioners' sugar until blended. Stir in the rum-raisin mixture with a wooden spoon. Spread over prepared crust.

4. Bake 42 to 45 minutes until golden (do not overbake; bars should be slightly gooey). Transfer to a wire rack and cool completely. Cut into bars or squares. Cover and store in refrigerator.

PLUMP UP RAISINS

To plump up raisins—or any other dried fruits—that have become a bit dried out, soak them in hot water for about 10 minutes. Rinse with cool water, then squeeze dry and toss with a bit of flour (to prevent any extra water getting into the dough; shake off the excess flour) before adding to the dough.

VANILLA MALT GOOEY BARS

Inspired by malt shop confections, these gooey-licious bars are studded with crushed malt balls and infused with vanilla.

PREHEAT OVEN TO 350°F

MAKES 3 DOZEN BARS

13 x 9-INCH BAKING PAN, GREASED OR LINED WITH FOIL (SEE PAGE 16)

1 (18.25-ounce) package vanilla cake mix

1 cup (2 sticks) butter, melted, divided

4 large eggs

1 (8-ounce) package cream cheese, softened

2 teaspoons vanilla extract

1 (16-ounce) package confectioners' sugar

2 cups chocolate-covered malt balls (e.g., Whoppers or Maltesers), coarsely crushed

1. Mix the cake mix, ½ cup (1 stick) melted butter, and 1 egg in large bowl with electric mixer on medium speed until blended (dough will be thick). Pat evenly into prepared pan.

2. Beat the cream cheese and vanilla in large bowl with electric mixer on high speed until blended and smooth. Beat in the remaining ½ cup (1 stick) melted butter and remaining 3 eggs. Beat in the confectioners' sugar until blended. Stir in the malt balls with a wooden spoon. Spread over prepared crust.

3. Bake 42 to 45 minutes until golden (do not overbake; bars should be slightly gooey). Transfer to a wire rack and cool completely. Cut into bars or squares. Cover and store in refrigerator.

VARIATION *for Vanilla Malt Gooey Bars*

CHOCOLATE MALT GOOEY BARS: Prepare as directed, but use a chocolate cake mix in place of the vanilla cake mix.

PINEAPPLE GOOEY BARS

These sunny, golden bars are chock-full of fruits and flavor: chunks of moist, naturally sweet Hawaiian pineapple, zesty lime, and peppery ginger—all baked to perfection in a rich, buttery dough.

PREHEAT OVEN TO 350°F

MAKES 3 DOZEN BARS

13 x 9-INCH BAKING PAN, GREASED OR LINED
   WITH FOIL (SEE PAGE 16)

1 (18.25-ounce) package yellow cake mix

1 cup (2 sticks) butter, melted, divided

4 large eggs

1 (8-ounce) package cream cheese, softened

1 (20-ounce) can crushed pineapple, well drained

2 tablespoons fresh lime juice

1 teaspoon ground ginger

1 (16-ounce) package confectioners' sugar

1. Mix the cake mix, ½ cup (1 stick) melted butter, and 1 egg in large bowl with electric mixer on medium speed until blended (dough will be thick). Pat evenly into prepared pan.
2. Beat the cream cheese, pineapple, lime juice, and ginger in large bowl with electric mixer on high speed until blended and smooth. Beat in the remaining ½ cup (1 stick) melted butter and remaining 3 eggs. Beat in the confectioners' sugar until blended. Spread over prepared crust.
3. Bake 42 to 45 minutes until golden (do not overbake; bars should be slightly gooey). Transfer to a wire rack and cool completely. Cut into bars or squares. Cover and store in refrigerator.

VARIATION *for Pineapple Gooey Bars*

MANDARIN ORANGE GOOEY BARS: Prepare as directed but use 2 (11-ounce) cans mandarin oranges (drained and roughly chopped) in place of the pineapple, an equal amount of orange juice for the lime juice, and omit the ginger.

PUMPKIN GOOEY BARS

Bye-bye, pumpkin pie—that's what you'll likely croon once you try these out-of-this-world gooey bars. Be sure to use pure pumpkin in the filling, not pumpkin pie mix. Both come in a can, but the latter is pre-spiced and presweetened, which will lead to an overly sweet bar with the wrong consistency.

PREHEAT OVEN TO 350°F

MAKES 3 DOZEN BARS

13 x 9-INCH BAKING PAN, GREASED OR LINED WITH FOIL (SEE PAGE 16)

1 (18.25-ounce) package spice or yellow cake mix

1 cup (2 sticks) butter, melted, divided

4 large eggs

1 (8-ounce) package cream cheese, softened

1 (15-ounce) can pumpkin purée

2 teaspoons pumpkin pie spice or ground cinnamon

2 teaspoons vanilla extract

1 (16-ounce) package confectioners' sugar

1. Mix the cake mix, ½ cup (1 stick) melted butter, and 1 egg in large bowl with electric mixer on medium speed until blended (dough will be thick). Pat evenly into prepared pan.

2. Beat the cream cheese, pumpkin, pumpkin pie spice, and vanilla in large bowl with electric mixer on high speed until blended and smooth. Beat in the remaining ½ cup (1 stick) melted butter and remaining 3 eggs. Beat in the confectioners' sugar until blended. Spread over prepared crust.

3. Bake 42 to 45 minutes until just set (do not overbake; bars should be slightly gooey). Transfer to a wire rack and cool completely. Cut into bars or squares. Cover and store in refrigerator.

COOKIES-AND-CREAM GOOEY BARS

Life moves quickly these days, but here's a delicious reason to slow down: rich and gooey and oh-so-comforting bar cookies, filled with more chopped creme-filled cookies. They'll bring everyone to the kitchen.

PREHEAT OVEN TO 350°F

MAKES 3 DOZEN BARS

13 x 9-INCH BAKING PAN, GREASED OR LINED
   WITH FOIL (SEE PAGE 16)

1 (18.25-ounce) package chocolate cake
   mix

1 cup (2 sticks) butter, melted, divided

4 large eggs

1 (8-ounce) package cream cheese,
   softened

1 teaspoon vanilla extract

1 (16-ounce) package confectioners' sugar

12 creme-filled chocolate sandwich cookies
   (e.g., Oreos), coarsely crumbled

1. Mix the cake mix, ½ cup (1 stick) melted butter, and 1 egg in large bowl with electric mixer on medium speed until blended (dough will be thick). Pat evenly into prepared pan.

2. Beat the cream cheese and vanilla in large bowl with electric mixer on high speed until blended and smooth. Beat in the remaining ½ cup (1 stick) melted butter and remaining 3 eggs. Beat in the confectioners' sugar until blended, then stir in the cookies. Spread over prepared crust.

3. Bake 42 to 45 minutes until just set (do not overbake; bars should be slightly gooey). Transfer to a wire rack and cool completely. Cut into bars or squares. Cover and store in refrigerator.

CINNAMON MACCHIATO GOOEY BARS

Infused with coffee and cinnamon and studded with white chocolate, these wickedly good bars are the only choice for coffee lovers. Expecting friends round for a visit? Surprise them by brewing some coffee and whipping up a batch of these scrumptious treats.

PREHEAT OVEN TO 350°F

MAKES 3 DOZEN BARS

13 x 9-INCH BAKING PAN, GREASED OR LINED WITH FOIL (SEE PAGE 16)

1 (18.25-ounce) package white cake mix

1 cup (2 sticks) butter, divided

1 teaspoon ground cinnamon

4 large eggs

1 (8-ounce) package cream cheese, softened

1½ tablespoons instant coffee powder, dissolved in 1 tablespoon water

2 teaspoons vanilla extract

1 (16-ounce) package confectioners' sugar

1 cup white chocolate chips

1. Mix the cake mix, ½ cup (1 stick) melted butter, cinnamon, and 1 egg in large bowl with electric mixer on medium speed until blended (dough will be thick). Pat evenly into prepared pan.
2. Beat the cream cheese, coffee mixture, and vanilla in large bowl with electric mixer on high speed until blended and smooth. Beat in the remaining ½ cup (1 stick) melted butter and remaining 3 eggs. Beat in the confectioners' sugar until blended. Spread over prepared crust and sprinkle with white chocolate chips.
3. Bake 42 to 45 minutes until just set (do not overbake; bars should be slightly gooey). Transfer to a wire rack and cool completely. Cut into bars or squares. Cover and store in refrigerator.

VARIATION *for Cinnamon Macchiato Gooey Bars*

MOCHA LATTE GOOEY BARS: Prepare as directed but use a chocolate or devil's food cake mix and semisweet chocolate chips, and omit the cinnamon.

MAPLE-PECAN GOOEY BARS

Maple and pecan is a classic combination in these lusciously simple gooey bars. You might even convince yourself that one of these can stand in for pancakes and syrup for breakfast!

PREHEAT OVEN TO 350°F

MAKES 3 DOZEN BARS

13 x 9-INCH BAKING PAN, GREASED OR LINED WITH FOIL (SEE PAGE 16)

1 (18.25-ounce) package butter pecan cake mix

1 cup (2 sticks) butter, divided

4 large eggs

1 (8-ounce) package cream cheese, softened

¼ cup pure maple syrup

2 teaspoons maple-flavored extract

1 (16-ounce) package confectioners' sugar

1 cup chopped pecans

1. Mix the cake mix, ½ cup (1 stick) melted butter, and 1 egg in large bowl with electric mixer on medium speed until blended (dough will be thick). Pat evenly into prepared pan.

2. Beat the cream cheese, maple syrup, and maple extract in large bowl with electric mixer on high speed until blended and smooth. Beat in the remaining ½ cup (1 stick) melted butter and remaining 3 eggs. Beat in the confectioners' sugar until blended. Spread over the prepared crust and sprinkle with pecans.

3. Bake 42 to 45 minutes until golden (do not overbake; bars should be slightly gooey). Transfer to a wire rack and cool completely. Cut into bars or squares. Cover and store in refrigerator.

NONSTICK SYRUP MEASUREMENT

To prevent syrup or honey from sticking to the sides of a measuring cup, lightly spray the inside of the cup first with nonstick cooking spray.

CHOCOLATE BANANA GOOEY BARS

Who would have guessed that such commonly available, reasonably priced ingredients—a cake mix, a few bananas, and a package of cream cheese—could lead to such a supreme treat, with such little effort to boot? Kids of all ages will line up for seconds (and thirds!).

PREHEAT OVEN TO 350°F

MAKES 3 DOZEN BARS

13 x 9-INCH BAKING PAN, GREASED OR LINED WITH FOIL (SEE PAGE 16)

1 (18.25-ounce) package yellow or chocolate cake mix

1 cup (2 sticks) butter, melted, divided

4 large eggs

1 (8-ounce) package cream cheese, softened

1½ cups mashed banana (about 3 large bananas)

2 teaspoons vanilla extract

1 (16-ounce) package confectioners' sugar

½ teaspoon ground nutmeg

1. Mix the cake mix, ½ cup (1 stick) melted butter, and 1 egg in large bowl with electric mixer on medium speed until blended (dough will be thick). Pat evenly into prepared pan.

2. Beat the cream cheese and mashed banana in large bowl with electric mixer on high speed until blended and smooth. Beat in the remaining ½ cup (1 stick) melted butter, remaining 3 eggs, and vanilla extract. Beat in the confectioners' sugar and nutmeg until blended. Spread over prepared crust.

3. Bake 42 to 45 minutes until golden (do not overbake; bars should be slightly gooey). Transfer to a wire rack and cool completely. Cut into bars or squares. Cover and store in refrigerator.

BLUEBERRY KUCHEN BARS

As the name implies, these easily assembled bars are inspired by German kuchen (pronounced KOO-khehn), which is a cheese- or fruit-filled bread that can be eaten for breakfast or dessert. The blueberries can be substituted for with your favorite fruit of choice, from apricots to apples to fresh or frozen peaches.

PREHEAT OVEN TO 350°F

MAKES 3 DOZEN BARS

13 x 9-INCH BAKING PAN, GREASED OR LINED WITH FOIL (SEE PAGE 16)

1 (18.25-ounce) package yellow cake mix

½ cup (1 stick) butter, softened

1 (3-ounce) package cream cheese, softened

2 large eggs

2 cups sour cream (not reduced fat)

¼ cup sugar

½ teaspoon cinnamon

2 cups fresh or frozen (thawed) blueberries

1. Place the cake mix, butter, cream cheese, and 1 egg in a large bowl. Blend with electric mixer for 1 to 2 minutes on medium speed until dough forms. Press into prepared pan. Bake 15 minutes.

2. Whisk the sour cream, sugar, cinnamon, and remaining egg in a medium bowl until blended. Stir in the blueberries. Spread mixture over partially baked crust.

3. Bake 13 to 15 minutes, until the sour cream layer is just set. Transfer to a wire rack and cool completely. Cut into bars. Store, covered, in refrigerator.

BROWN SUGAR AND MILK CHOCOLATE MERINGUE BARS

Growing up, I loved lemon meringue pie, but only the lemon filling and crust—I thought the puffy meringue was some sort of penance for an otherwise heavenly dessert. Some years later, I had my first crisp meringue at a neighborhood bakery. Crisp and crunchy—it was nothing like the soft and seepy version I was accustomed to, and I was instantly hooked. These bars have the same crispy meringue, made even better with brown sugar, wrapped around a milk chocolate and almond filling.

PREHEAT OVEN TO 375°F

MAKES 3 DOZEN BARS

13 x 9-INCH BAKING PAN, GREASED OR LINED WITH FOIL (SEE PAGE 16)

1 (18.25-ounce) package German chocolate or chocolate cake mix

½ cup (1 stick) butter, melted

2 large egg yolks

1 (12-ounce) package (2 cups) milk chocolate chips

1 cup sliced almonds, divided

4 large egg whites, room temperature

1 cup packed dark brown sugar

1. Place the cake mix, melted butter, and egg yolks in a large bowl. Blend for 1 to 2 minutes with electric mixer on low speed until blended. Press mixture evenly into prepared pan. Bake 15 minutes. Remove pan from oven and sprinkle with the chocolate chips and ½ cup of the almonds. Transfer to wire rack while preparing meringue.

2. Beat the egg whites in a large bowl with electric mixer on high until frothy. Gradually add the brown sugar, beating until stiff peaks form. Carefully spread the meringue over chips and nuts. Sprinkle with the remaining ½ cup almonds.

3. Bake an additional 13 to 15 minutes or until meringue is golden brown. Transfer to a wire rack and cool completely. Cut into bars.

VARIATION *for Brown Sugar and Milk Chocolate Meringue Bars*

DARK CHOCOLATE AND RASPBERRY MERINGUE BARS: Prepare as directed but use semisweet chocolate chips in place of the milk chocolate chips and omit the almonds. After sprinkling crust with chocolate chips, dollop ½ cup seedless raspberry preserves, by teaspoons, over the chips. Use plain white granulated sugar in place of the brown sugar in the meringue.

COCONUT-MACADAMIA BARS

Cake Mix
YELLOW

Conclude your next summer BBQ on a sweet note with these easy, island-inspired bars.

PREHEAT OVEN TO 350°F

MAKES 3 DOZEN BARS

13 x 9-INCH BAKING PAN, GREASED OR LINED
WITH FOIL (SEE PAGE 16)

1 (18.25-ounce) package yellow cake mix

½ cup (1 stick) butter, melted

1 (14-ounce) can sweetened condensed
milk (not evaporated)

2 large eggs

2 tablespoons dark rum (or 2 teaspoons
rum-flavored extract)

1½ cups sweetened shredded coconut

1 cup chopped macadamia nuts

1 cup milk or white chocolate chips

1. Blend the cake mix and melted butter in a large bowl with electric mixer on medium speed until blended and crumbly. Press mixture into prepared pan. Bake 15 minutes.
2. While crust bakes, whisk the condensed milk, eggs, and rum in a medium bowl until blended. Stir in the coconut and macadamia nuts. Pour mixture over partially baked crust and sprinkle with chocolate chips.
3. Bake 18 to 20 minutes longer or until golden at edges and just set at the center. Transfer to a wire rack and cool completely. Cut into bars.

BUTTERSCOTCH BLONDIES

The brownie has legions of loyal fans, but the blondie has a multitude of equally steadfast enthusiasts. *The reasons are clear: a rich and chewy butterscotch bar, studded with more butterscotch or a contrast of chocolate chips—highly transportable to boot.*

PREHEAT OVEN TO 350°F

MAKES 3 DOZEN BARS

13 x 9-INCH BAKING PAN, GREASED OR LINED WITH FOIL (SEE PAGE 16)

1 (18.25-ounce) package yellow cake mix

2 large eggs

½ cup (1 stick) butter, melted

¼ cup packed dark brown sugar

1 teaspoon vanilla extract

1 cup semisweet chocolate chips or butterscotch baking chips

Optional: 1 cup chopped pecans

1. Blend the cake mix, eggs, melted butter, brown sugar, and vanilla in a large bowl with electric mixer on medium speed 1 to 2 minutes until all dry ingredients are moistened. Mix in the chocolate chips.
2. Press dough into prepared pan. If desired, sprinkle with pecans, gently pressing into dough.
3. Bake 22 to 25 minutes or until the bars are golden brown and just barely set at center. Transfer pan to a wire rack and cool completely. Cut into bars or squares.

VARIATIONS *for Butterscotch Blondies*

TOFFEE-APPLE BLONDIES: Prepare as directed but substitute 1 cup chopped dried apples and ½ cup toffee baking bits for the chocolate chips (pecans are still optional).

WHITE CHOCOLATE BLONDIES: Prepare as directed but omit the brown sugar, substitute vanilla cake mix for the yellow cake mix, use white chocolate chips in place of semisweet chocolate chips, and use ½ teaspoon almond extract in place of the vanilla extract. If nuts are desired, substitute an equal amount of sliced or slivered almonds for the pecans.

ALMOND-BUTTERCRUNCH BARS

I made these bars extra-special by lacing the dough with a trifecta of deliciousness: almonds, toffee, and chocolate chips.

PREHEAT OVEN TO 350°F

MAKES 3 DOZEN BARS

13 x 9-INCH BAKING PAN, GREASED OR LINED WITH FOIL (SEE PAGE 16)

1 (18.25-ounce) package butter recipe yellow cake mix

2 large eggs

½ cup (1 stick) butter, melted

¼ cup packed light brown sugar

1 teaspoon almond extract

1 cup toffee baking bits

1 cup miniature semisweet chocolate chips

1 cup slivered almonds

1. Blend the cake mix, eggs, melted butter, brown sugar, and almond extract in a large bowl with electric mixer on medium speed for 1 to 2 minutes until blended. Stir in the toffee bits and chocolate chips.
2. Press dough into prepared pan. Sprinkle with the almonds, gently pressing into dough.
3. Bake 22 to 25 minutes or until the bars are just barely set at center. Transfer pan to a wire rack and cool completely. Cut into bars or squares.

CARAMEL CHOCOLATE CHIP BARS

Who doesn't love the combination of caramel and chocolate? By adding brown sugar to caramel cake mix, these simple-to-prepare bars become richly flavored treats.

PREHEAT OVEN TO 375°F

MAKES 3 DOZEN BARS

13 x 9-INCH BAKING PAN, GREASED OR LINED WITH FOIL (SEE PAGE 16)

1 (18.25-ounce) package caramel cake mix

2 large eggs

¼ cup (½ stick) butter, melted

¼ cup firmly packed dark brown sugar

¼ cup whole or lowfat milk

1 cup semisweet chocolate chips

1. Mix the cake mix, eggs, melted butter, brown sugar, and milk in a large bowl with a wooden

spoon until blended. Press dough into prepared pan. Sprinkle with the chocolate chips, gently pressing into dough.

2. Bake 22 to 25 minutes or until the bars are just barely set at center. Transfer pan to a wire rack and cool completely. Cut into bars or squares.

RASPBERRY ROCKY ROAD BARS

Rocky road is a favorite flavor combination, but I love to tweak the classics. Hence, these newfangled bars, which have become one of my most requested cookies.

PREHEAT OVEN TO 350°F

MAKES 3 DOZEN BARS

13 x 9-INCH BAKING PAN, GREASED OR LINED WITH FOIL (SEE PAGE 16)

1½ cups pecans, divided

1 (18.25-ounce) package white cake mix

1 cup (2 sticks) butter, melted

2¼ cups quick-cooking oats

1 (12-ounce) jar seedless raspberry jam

4 cups miniature marshmallows

1½ cups semisweet chocolate chips

1. Coarsely chop ½ cup of the pecans. Place the chopped pecans, cake mix, and melted butter in a large bowl. Blend for 1 to 2 minutes with electric mixer on medium speed until blended. Stir in the oats with wooden spoon. Press half of mixture into prepared pan.

2. Spoon the jam over crust, carefully spreading to cover. Sprinkle with the marshmallows, remaining 1 cup pecans, and chocolate chips. Top with the reserved oat mixture, pressing down gently.

3. Bake 30 to 34 minutes or until topping is set and firm to the touch. Transfer to wire rack and cool completely. Cut into bars.

CARMELITAS

Pick up a good book, brew a pot of coffee, and head to your favorite easy chair with one of these carmelita bars in hand. Don't forget the napkin as these treats are definitely on the (deliciously) gooey side.

PREHEAT OVEN TO 350°F

MAKES 3 DOZEN BARS

13 x 9-INCH BAKING PAN, GREASED OR LINED
  WITH FOIL (SEE PAGE 16)

1 (18.25-ounce) package yellow cake mix

1 cup (2 sticks) butter, melted

2 cups quick-cooking oats

1 (16-ounce) tub caramel apple dip

1 (12-ounce) bag semisweet chocolate chips

1. Mix the cake mix and melted butter in a large bowl with electric mixer on low speed 1 to 2 minutes until blended. Stir in the oats with a wooden spoon. Press half of the mixture into prepared pan.
2. Pour and spread the caramel over prepared crust. Sprinkle with the chocolate chips, then top with the reserved oat mixture, gently pressing down.
3. Bake 28 to 30 minutes or until topping is firm to the touch. Transfer to a wire rack and cool completely. Cut into bars.

Tip: Caramel apple dip can typically be found in the produce department of the supermarket.

CARROT CAKE BARS WITH ORANGE AND CREAM CHEESE FROSTING

I like to convince myself that eating one of these moist, cream-cheese-frosted bars is not an exercise in indulgence but rather good health. After all, carrots have been revered for their nutritional benefits for more than 2,000 years. You might just have to eat two to be on the safe side.

PREHEAT OVEN TO 350°F

MAKES 3 DOZEN BARS

13 x 9-INCH BAKING PAN, GREASED OR LINED WITH FOIL (SEE PAGE 16)

1 (18.25-ounce) package carrot cake or spice cake mix

⅔ cup vegetable oil

3 large eggs

1 cup peeled, shredded carrots

1 cup raisins or dried cranberries

1 cup chopped pecans

1 cup (½ a 16-ounce tub) ready-to-spread cream cheese frosting

1 tablespoon fresh orange juice

1 teaspoon grated orange peel

1. Mix the cake mix, oil, and eggs in a large bowl with electric mixer on low speed 1 to 2 minutes until blended. Stir in the carrots and raisins or cranberries. Spread into the prepared pan. Sprinkle with the pecans, gently pressing into dough.
2. Bake 22 to 25 minutes or until just barely set at center. Transfer to a wire rack and cool completely.
3. Mix the frosting, orange juice, and orange peel in a small bowl with a wooden spoon until blended. Spread over cooled bars. Cut into bars.

CHERRY CRUMB PIE BARS

It's hard to escape the allure of plump, red cherries. But if the notion of baking a pie seems like too much work, consider these simple bars, which offer the pleasure of pie with a lot less effort.

PREHEAT OVEN TO 350°F

MAKES 3 DOZEN BARS

13 x 9-INCH BAKING PAN, GREASED OR LINED
   WITH FOIL (SEE PAGE 16)

1 (18.25-ounce) package white cake mix

1¼ cups quick-cooking oats, divided

8 tablespoons (1 stick) butter, melted,
   divided

1 large egg

1 (21-ounce) can cherry pie filling

½ cup chopped pecans

¼ cup packed light brown sugar

1. Mix the cake mix, 1 cup oats, and 6 tablespoons melted butter in a large bowl with a wooden spoon until blended (mixture will be crumbly). Reserve 1 cup of the crumb mixture. Stir the egg into the remaining mixture until blended and press into prepared pan.

2. Spread the cherry pie filling over crust. Combine the reserved crumb mixture, pecans, brown sugar, remaining ¼ cup oats, and remaining 2 tablespoons melted butter in small bowl until blended. Sprinkle evenly over cherry filling.

3. Bake 30 to 35 minutes or until filling is bubbly and topping is golden. Transfer to wire rack and cool completely. Cut into bars.

VARIATION *for Cherry Crumb Pie Bars*

CHOCOLATE-CHERRY PIE BARS: Prepare as directed but use chocolate cake mix and use 1 cup miniature semisweet chocolate chips in place of the pecans.

CHOCOLATE, CARAMEL, AND PEANUT BUTTER BARS

If ever there was a pull-out-all-the-stops bar cookie, this is it. Caramel, chocolate, cream cheese, peanut butter—on a scale of 1 to 10, these are an 11.

PREHEAT OVEN TO 350°F

MAKES 3 DOZEN BARS

13 x 9-INCH BAKING PAN, GREASED OR LINED WITH FOIL (SEE PAGE 16)

1 (18.25-ounce) package white cake mix

1 cup quick-cooking oats

½ cup creamy-style peanut butter

1 large egg

2 tablespoons whole or lowfat milk

1 (12-ounce) jar caramel ice cream topping

1 (8-ounce) package cream cheese, softened

2 cups milk or semisweet chocolate chips

1 cup roasted, lightly salted peanuts

1. Mix the cake mix and oats in a large bowl. Add the peanut butter and, using fingers, mix in until mixture resembles fine crumbs. Add the egg and milk, stirring until blended. Reserve 1 cup of oat mixture. Press remaining mixture into prepared pan.
2. Beat the caramel topping and cream cheese in a medium bowl with electric mixer on medium speed 1 to 2 minutes until blended and smooth. Spread on top of prepared crust. Sprinkle evenly with the chocolate chips, peanuts, and reserved oat mixture.
3. Bake 28 to 30 minutes until topping is golden brown. Transfer to wire rack and cool completely. Cut into bars.

CHOCOLATE CHEESECAKE BARS

Guaranteed to make chocoholic hearts beat faster, these enticing confections combine a velvet cheesecake and chocolate filling with even more chocolate in the base. In a word, irresistible.

PREHEAT OVEN TO 350°F

MAKES 3 DOZEN BARS

13 x 9-INCH BAKING PAN, GREASED OR LINED
WITH FOIL (SEE PAGE 16)

1 (18.25-ounce) package chocolate cake mix, divided

3 large eggs

⅓ cup butter, melted

2 (8-ounce) packages cream cheese

1 cup sour cream

1½ cups semisweet chocolate chips

1. Reserve 1 cup of cake mix. Mix the remaining cake mix, 1 egg, and melted butter in a medium bowl with electric mixer on medium speed until blended. Press into prepared pan. Bake 10 minutes.

2. Meanwhile, beat the cream cheese, reserved cake mix, sour cream, and remaining 2 eggs in a medium bowl with electric mixer on medium speed until blended and smooth. Stir in the chocolate chips then spread over crust.

3. Bake 30 to 35 minutes or until center is just barely set. Transfer to wire rack and cool completely. Refrigerate at least 2 hours before serving. Cut into bars.

VARIATIONS *for Chocolate Cheesecake Bars*

CHOCOLATE-RASPBERRY CHEESECAKE BARS: Prepare as directed but dollop ⅔ cup seedless raspberry preserves in teaspoons over surface of cheesecake dough. Swirl dough and preserves with tip of a kitchen knife before baking.

WHITE CHOCOLATE AND LEMON CHEESECAKE BARS: Prepare as directed but use a lemon cake mix. Reduce sour cream to ¾ cup and add ¼ cup fresh lemon juice to cream cheese dough. Use white chocolate chips in place of semisweet.

WHITE CHOCOLATE LATTE CHEESECAKE BARS: Prepare as directed but use a white cake mix. Add 1 tablespoon instant coffee powder dissolved in 2 teaspoons vanilla extract to the cream cheese dough. Use white chocolate chips in place of semisweet.

IRISH CREAM AND MILK CHOCOLATE CHEESECAKE BARS: Prepare as directed but use a white cake mix. Replace ½ cup of the sour cream with ½ cup Irish cream liqueur or Irish cream coffee creamer. Use milk chocolate chips in place of semisweet.

TOFFEE BARS

Toffee bar recipes are relatively easy to come by. Exceptional toffee bars, this recipe for example, on the other hand, are an entirely different matter. Decadent with nuts, toffee, and chocolate but still easy to assemble—one bite and I think you'll decide this is the only toffee bar recipe you'll need from now on.

PREHEAT OVEN TO 350°F

MAKES 3 DOZEN BARS

13 x 9-INCH BAKING PAN, GREASED OR LINED
  WITH FOIL (SEE PAGE 16)

1 (18.25-ounce) package yellow cake mix

½ cup (1 stick) butter, softened

1 large egg

2 cups semisweet chocolate chips, divided

1 cup coarsely chopped nuts (e.g., walnuts, pecans, or peanuts)

1 (14-ounce) can sweetened condensed milk (not evaporated)

1¼ cups toffee baking bits, divided

1. Mix the cake mix, butter, and egg in a large bowl with electric mixer on medium speed until blended and crumbly. Stir in 1½ cups chocolate chips and nuts with a wooden spoon. Set aside 1½ cups of the crumb mixture. Firmly press the remaining crumb mixture into prepared pan. Bake 15 minutes.
2. Pour the condensed milk evenly over partially baked crust. Sprinkle with 1 cup of the toffee bits. Sprinkle with the reserved crumb mixture and remaining ½ cup chocolate chips.
3. Bake 25 to 28 minutes or until golden brown. Immediately sprinkle with the remaining ¼ cup toffee bits. Transfer to wire rack and cool completely. Cut into bars.

VARIATIONS *for Toffee Bars*

DOUBLE-CHOCOLATE TOFFEE BARS: Prepare as directed but use a chocolate or devil's food cake mix.

TOFFEE-BUTTERSCOTCH BARS: Prepare as directed but use pecans for the nuts and use butterscotch baking chips in place of the chocolate chips.

CHOCOLATE PRETZEL CANDY BARS

Cake Mix
CHOCOLATE
or YELLOW

Everyone who loves the combination of salty and sweet will think these bars are brilliant.

PREHEAT OVEN TO 350°F

MAKES 3 DOZEN BARS

13 x 9-INCH BAKING PAN, GREASED OR LINED WITH FOIL (SEE PAGE 16)

1 (18.25-ounce) package chocolate or yellow cake mix

½ cup (1 stick) butter, melted

1 large egg

1 cup crushed pretzels

1 cup semisweet chocolate chips

1 cup butterscotch baking chips

1 cup flaked coconut

1 cup coarsely chopped lightly salted mixed nuts

1 (14-ounce) can sweetened condensed milk

1. Mix the cake mix, melted butter, and egg in a large bowl with electric mixer on medium-low speed 1 to 2 minutes until blended. Stir in the pretzels with a wooden spoon. Press into prepared pan. Bake 15 minutes.
2. Layer the chocolate chips, butterscotch chips, coconut, and nuts over partially baked crust, then evenly drizzle with condensed milk.
3. Bake 25 to 28 minutes or until edges are golden brown. Transfer to wire rack and cool completely before cutting into bars.

RASPBERRY-HAZELNUT LINZER BARS

Cake Mix
WHITE

These sophisticated bars are a long way from their Austrian forebears, marrying traditional sense with modern sensibility.

PREHEAT OVEN TO 350°F

MAKES 3 DOZEN BARS

13 x 9-INCH BAKING PAN, GREASED OR LINED WITH FOIL (SEE PAGE 16)

1 (18.25-ounce) package white cake mix

1½ cups chopped hazelnuts or almonds

⅓ cup vegetable oil

1 large egg

¾ teaspoon almond extract

1 (12-ounce) jar seedless raspberry jam

1. Place the cake mix, 1 cup hazelnuts, oil, egg, and almond extract in a large bowl. Blend with electric mixer on medium speed until blended and crumbly. Set aside 1½ cups of the crumb mixture. Firmly press the remaining crumb mixture into prepared pan.
2. Spread the raspberry jam evenly over crust. Stir the remaining ½ cup hazelnuts into reserved crumb mixture, then sprinkle over jam.
3. Bake 25 to 28 minutes or until topping is firm to the touch. Transfer to wire rack and cool completely. Cut into bars.

VARIATIONS *for Raspberry-Hazelnut Linzer Bars*

CHOCOLATE LINZER BARS: Prepare as directed but use a chocolate cake mix in place of white cake mix and sprinkle bars with 1 cup miniature semisweet chocolate chips before baking.

APRICOT SACHER TORTE BARS: Prepare as directed but use a chocolate cake mix and apricot preserves in place of the raspberry preserves.

Cake Mix
YELLOW

CHOCOLATE FUDGE CRUMBLE BARS

They shouldn't be this easy. They shouldn't be this delicious. But oh, how they are.

PREHEAT OVEN TO 350°F

MAKES 3 DOZEN BARS

13 x 9-INCH BAKING PAN, GREASED OR LINED WITH FOIL (SEE PAGE 16)

1 (18.25-ounce) package yellow cake mix

1 cup (2 sticks) butter, melted

¼ cup packed dark brown sugar

2 large eggs

2½ cups quick-cooking oats

2 cups semisweet chocolate chips

1 (14-ounce) can sweetened condensed milk (not evaporated)

1 teaspoon vanilla extract

½ cup chopped pecans or walnuts

1. Mix the cake mix, melted butter, brown sugar, and eggs in a large bowl with electric mixer on medium speed 1 to 2 minutes until blended. Stir in the oats with a wooden spoon. Reserve 2 cups of the oat mixture. Press remaining mixture into prepared pan.
2. Melt the chocolate chips with the condensed milk in a medium saucepan set over low heat, stirring until smooth. Remove from heat and stir in the vanilla extract. Spread the chocolate filling evenly over the oat crust. Stir the pecans into remaining oat mixture, then sprinkle over filling.

3. Bake 24 to 27 minutes or until topping looks crisp and golden (filling will still look slightly wet). Transfer to wire rack and cool completely. Cut into bars.

Cake Mix
CHOCOLATE or
DEVIL'S FOOD

CHOCOLATE TRUFFLE BARS

An opulent treat for chocolate lovers, this recipe involves a rich chocolate truffle filling sandwiched between two layers of chocolate streusel to create a uniquely delicious chocolate treat.

PREHEAT OVEN TO 350°F

MAKES 3 DOZEN BARS

13 x 9-INCH BAKING PAN, GREASED OR LINED WITH FOIL (SEE PAGE 16)

1 (18.25-ounce) package chocolate or devil's food cake mix

⅓ cup butter, melted

1 large egg

1 (14-ounce) can sweetened condensed milk (not evaporated)

2 cups semisweet chocolate chips, divided

2 teaspoons vanilla extract

1 cup chopped walnuts

1. Mix the cake mix, melted butter, and egg in a large bowl. Blend with electric mixer on medium speed until crumbly. Set aside 1 cup of the crumb mixture. Firmly press remaining crumb mixture into prepared baking pan. Bake 15 minutes.
2. Combine the condensed milk and 1 cup chocolate chips in a medium saucepan. Melt over low heat, stirring until smooth. Remove from heat and stir in the vanilla, then spread over partially baked crust. Stir the walnuts and remaining 1 cup chocolate chips into reserved crumb mixture, then sprinkle over chocolate filling.
3. Bake 25 to 28 minutes or until topping is firm to the touch. Transfer to wire rack and cool completely. Cut into bars.

CARAMEL APPLE STREUSEL BARS

Surprise your favorite apple aficionado with these caramel apple bars to convey the extent of your good wishes.

PREHEAT OVEN TO 350°F

MAKES 3 DOZEN BARS

13 x 9-INCH BAKING PAN, GREASED OR LINED
    WITH FOIL (SEE PAGE 16)

1 (18.25-ounce) package yellow cake mix

1 cup (2 sticks) butter, melted

2¼ cups quick-cooking oats

4 cups coarsely chopped, peeled, and cored
    tart apples (about 4 large apples)

1 (16-ounce) container caramel apple dip

1. Reserve 3 tablespoons cake mix. Mix the remaining cake mix and melted butter in a large bowl with a wooden spoon until blended. Stir in the oats. Press half the mixture evenly into prepared pan.
2. Combine the apples and reserved 3 tablespoons cake mix in large bowl, then spread over prepared crust. Pour the caramel dip evenly over apples, then top with reserved crumb mixture.
3. Bake 30 to 34 minutes or until topping is set and firm to the touch. Transfer to wire rack and cool completely. Cut into bars.

VARIATION *for Caramel Apple Streusel Bars*

PEACH STREUSEL BARS: Prepare as directed but substitute chopped fresh, canned, or frozen (thawed) peaches for the apples and 1 (12-ounce) jar of peach preserves or jam for the caramel apple dip.

SPICED RAISIN-NUT CRUMB BARS

Brown sugar and spice are extra nice when accompanied by crunchy nuts and plump raisins in a quick cookie bar. For a tart contrast of flavors, substitute dried cranberries or tart dried cherries for the raisins.

PREHEAT OVEN TO 350°F

MAKES 3 DOZEN BARS

13 x 9-INCH BAKING PAN, GREASED OR LINED
   WITH FOIL (SEE PAGE 16)

1 (18.25-ounce) package spice cake mix

¾ cup (1½ sticks) butter, softened

2 large eggs

2 cups quick-cooking oats

1½ cups sour cream (not reduced fat)

¼ cup packed dark brown sugar

1¼ cups raisins

1 cup chopped walnuts or pecans

1. Place the cake mix, butter, and 1 egg in a large bowl. Beat with electric mixer on medium speed 1 to 2 minutes until blended. Stir in the oats with a wooden spoon. Reserve 1½ cups crumb mixture. Press remaining mixture into prepared pan.

2. Whisk the sour cream, brown sugar, and remaining egg in small bowl until blended. Stir in the raisins, then spread over crust. Mix the walnuts or pecans into reserved crumbs, then sprinkle over sour cream layer.

3. Bake 25 to 30 minutes or until topping is crisp-looking and golden. Run knife around sides of pan to loosen bars. Transfer to wire rack and cool completely. Chill at least 2 hours before serving. Cut into bars.

COCONUT-PECAN CHOCOLATE BARS

These bars walk a fine line between cookie and candy.

PREHEAT OVEN TO 350°F

MAKES 3 DOZEN BARS

13 x 9-INCH BAKING PAN, GREASED OR LINED
WITH FOIL (SEE PAGE 16)

1 (18.25-ounce) package chocolate cake mix

¾ cup butter, melted

1 large egg

2½ cups quick-cooking oats

1 (16-ounce) tub ready-to-spread coconut
pecan frosting

1 (12-ounce) bag (2 cups) semisweet
chocolate chips

1 cup chopped pecans

1. Reserve 3 tablespoons of cake mix. Mix the remaining cake mix, melted butter, and egg in a large bowl with electric mixer on low speed 1 to 2 minutes until blended. Stir in the oats with wooden spoon. Reserve 1½ cups crumb mixture. Press remaining mixture into prepared pan.
2. Microwave the frosting in medium microwave-safe bowl 1 minute. Mix in reserved 3 table-spoons cake mix until blended. Drizzle half of the frosting mixture over crust, spreading evenly. Sprinkle with the chocolate chips and pecans. Drizzle with the remaining frosting mixture, then sprinkle with reserved crumb mixture.
3. Bake 25 to 30 minutes or until top is golden brown and edges are bubbly. Transfer to wire rack and cool completely. Cut into bars.

CRANBERRY-CREAM CRUMBLE BARS

Spectacular but easy, thanks to boxed cake mix and cranberry sauce.

PREHEAT OVEN TO 350°F

MAKES 3 DOZEN BARS

13 x 9-INCH BAKING PAN, GREASED OR LINED
WITH FOIL (SEE PAGE 16)

1 (18.25-ounce) package white cake mix

⅓ cup whole or lowfat milk

¼ cup (½ stick) butter, melted

1 (16-ounce) container sour cream

1 large egg

1 (16-ounce) can whole cranberry sauce,
stirred to loosen

½ cup chopped pecans

1. Mix the cake mix, milk, and melted butter in a large bowl with electric mixer on medium speed 1 to 2 minutes until blended. Press half of dough into prepared pan. Bake 10 minutes.
2. Whisk the sour cream and egg in a medium bowl until blended, then spoon and spread over crust. Spoon the cranberry sauce in teaspoonfuls over sour cream layer. Crumble the remaining dough over cranberry layer and sprinkle with pecans.
3. Bake 25 to 27 minutes or until topping is firm and deep golden. Transfer to wire rack and cool completely. Chill at least 2 hours before serving. Cut into bars.

Cake Mix DEVIL'S FOOD
WHITE CHOCOLATE AND RASPBERRY TRUFFLE BARS

Scrumptious. These decadent, double-chocolate, raspberry-rich bars answer the question of what to make when you want to impress a crowd.

PREHEAT OVEN TO 350°F

MAKES 3 DOZEN BARS

13 x 9-INCH BAKING PAN, GREASED OR LINED WITH FOIL (SEE PAGE 16)

1 (18.25-ounce) package devil's food cake mix

¼ cup (½ stick) butter, melted

1 large egg

1 (14-ounce) can sweetened condensed milk (not evaporated)

1 (12-ounce) package (2 cups) white chocolate chips, divided

½ teaspoon almond extract

½ cup chopped almonds

½ cup seedless raspberry jam

1. Mix the cake mix, melted butter, and egg in a large bowl with electric mixer on medium speed until crumbly. Set aside 1 cup of crumb mixture. Press remaining crumb mixture into prepared pan. Bake 15 minutes.
2. Combine the condensed milk and 1 cup white chocolate chips in a medium saucepan. Warm over low heat, stirring until smooth. Remove from heat and stir in the almond extract, then spread over partially baked crust.
3. Stir the almonds into reserved crumb mixture, then sprinkle over chocolate filling. Drop teaspoonfuls of the raspberry jam over crumb mixture. Sprinkle with the remaining 1 cup white chocolate chips.
4. Bake 25 to 28 minutes or until topping is firm to the touch. Transfer to wire rack and cool completely. Cut into bars.

DATE BARS DELUXE

As a child I painstakingly picked out every date from the granola, trail mix, and gorp my mother offered up as snacks. I'm unsure of my reason, but I think it was because I did not like the look of them. So it came as a surprise to everyone when I went crazy for the date bars delivered on a neighbor's cookie plate one Christmas. Most likely my instant love affair stemmed from my failure to recognize that dates were involved. Date bars remain one of my favorite curl-up-with-a-cup-of-tea cookie options. Although simplified with cake mix, this version tastes nothing short of deluxe.

PREHEAT OVEN TO 350°F

MAKES 3 DOZEN BARS

13 x 9-INCH BAKING PAN, GREASED OR LINED WITH FOIL (SEE PAGE 16)

3 cups chopped dates (about 2 8-ounce packages)

2½ cups water

½ cup fresh lemon juice

1 (18.25-ounce) package yellow cake mix

1 cup (2 sticks) butter, melted

1 teaspoon ground cinnamon

2¼ cups quick-cooking oats

1. Combine the dates, water, and lemon juice in a medium saucepan. Bring to a boil over medium heat. Reduce heat to low and simmer until very soft and thick, stirring occasionally, about 10 minutes. Cool to room temperature.

2. Mix the cake mix, melted butter, and cinnamon in a large bowl with electric mixer on medium speed 1 to 2 minutes until blended. Stir in the oats with wooden spoon.

3. Press half of the oat mixture evenly into prepared pan. Spoon and spread the date mixture over prepared crust, then sprinkle with remaining oat mixture, pressing down gently.

4. Bake 30 to 34 minutes or until topping is firm to the touch. Transfer to wire rack and cool completely. Cut into bars.

CHOCOLATE AND SOUR CREAM BARS

Surrender to the sublime. Smooth and deeply chocolate, chocoholics will be hard-pressed to find a more opulent option.

PREHEAT OVEN TO 350°F

MAKES 3 DOZEN BARS

13 x 9-INCH BAKING PAN, GREASED OR LINED
WITH FOIL (SEE PAGE 16)

1 (18.25-ounce) package chocolate cake mix

¾ cup (1½ sticks) butter, melted, divided

4 large eggs

1 cup sour cream (not reduced fat)

⅓ cup packed light brown sugar

2 cups semisweet chocolate chips

1. Reserve 1 cup of the cake mix; set aside. Mix the remaining cake mix, ¼ cup (½ stick) melted butter, and 1 egg in a large bowl with electric mixer on low speed 1 to 2 minutes until blended. Press into prepared pan.

2. Whisk the sour cream, reserved 1 cup cake mix, remaining ½ cup (1 stick) melted butter, brown sugar, and remaining 3 eggs in medium bowl until blended. Stir in the chocolate chips, then pour over prepared crust.

3. Bake 35 to 38 minutes, until just set at center. Transfer to wire rack and cool completely. Chill 1 hour before serving. Cut into bars.

DELUXE CHOCOLATE CARAMEL CANDY BARS

These luscious treats are a cross between a cookie and a candy bar. In other words, to die for. For a birthday treat, serve them warm, topped with a scoop of ice cream, sliced bananas, and fudge sauce for a brownie banana split. Don't forget the whipped cream, cherries, and nuts!

PREHEAT OVEN TO 350°F

MAKES 3 DOZEN BARS

13 x 9-INCH BAKING PAN, GREASED OR LINED
   WITH FOIL (SEE PAGE 16)

1 (18.25-ounce) package white cake mix

½ cup (1 stick) butter, melted

1 large egg

1½ cups coarsely chopped pecans, divided

1½ cups sweetened flaked coconut, divided

2 cups quartered chocolate-covered
   caramel candies (e.g., about 1 12-ounce
   bag Rolos)

1 (14-ounce) can sweetened condensed
   milk (not evaporated)

1. Mix the cake mix, melted butter, and egg in a large bowl with a wooden spoon until blended and crumbly. Mix in the ½ cup pecans and ½ cup coconut, then press into prepared pan. Bake 10 minutes.
2. Sprinkle the caramel candies, remaining 1 cup pecans, and 1 cup coconut over partially baked crust, then drizzle with condensed milk.
3. Bake an additional 25 to 28 minutes or until filling is set and golden brown. Transfer to a wire rack and cool completely. Cut into bars.

Cake Mix
WHITE

DOUBLE-BERRY STREUSEL BARS

Looking for the perfect picnic bar cookie? The search is over. Loaded with the flavor of blueberries, raspberries, and the zing of fresh lemon peel, they taste like summer.

PREHEAT OVEN TO 350°F

MAKES 3 DOZEN BARS

13 x 9-INCH BAKING PAN, GREASED OR LINED WITH FOIL (SEE PAGE 16)

1 (18.25-ounce) package white cake mix

1 cup (2 sticks) butter, melted

2¼ cups quick-cooking oats

1 (12-ounce) package frozen (thawed) blueberries

¾ cup seedless raspberry jam

2 teaspoons grated lemon peel

1. Set aside 3 tablespoons of the cake mix. Mix the remaining cake mix and melted butter in a large bowl with electric mixer on low speed 1 to 2 minutes until blended. Stir in the oats with wooden spoon. Press half of mixture evenly into prepared pan.
2. Mix the blueberries, jam, reserved 3 tablespoons cake mix, and lemon peel in a medium bowl. Spoon and spread the berry mixture over prepared crust, then sprinkle with reserved crumb mixture. Press down gently.
3. Bake 30 to 34 minutes or until topping is set and firm to the touch. Transfer to wire rack and cool completely. Cut into bars.

Cake Mix
LEMON

BLACKBERRY-LEMON CRUMB BARS

Think summer, then think refreshing and sweet. Lemons come to mind? Let this easy lemon bar cookie, bursting with blackberries, celebrate the picnics, parties, and barbecues to come. Raspberries or blueberries may be used in place of the blackberries for equally delicious variations.

PREHEAT OVEN TO 350°F

MAKES 3 DOZEN BARS

13 x 9-INCH BAKING PAN, GREASED OR LINED WITH FOIL (SEE PAGE 16)

1 (18.25-ounce) package lemon cake mix

½ cup (1 stick) butter, softened

1 large egg

1 (14-ounce) can sweetened condensed milk (not evaporated)

½ cup lemon juice

2 cups fresh or frozen (thawed) blackberries

1. Mix the cake mix, butter, and egg in a large bowl with electric mixer on low speed 1 to 2 minutes until blended and crumbly. Press half of mixture into prepared pan. Bake 15 minutes.
2. Meanwhile, whisk the condensed milk and lemon juice in a medium bowl until blended.
3. Arrange the blackberries evenly over surface of partially baked crust. Pour condensed milk over blackberries as evenly as possible. Sprinkle with reserved crumb mixture.
4. Bake 20 to 24 minutes or until topping is golden brown. Transfer to wire rack and cool completely. Cut into bars.

BANANA MONKEY BARS

Cake Mix
YELLOW

What are you waiting for? Any time is a good time to get together with friends and family—and bring along a great recipe you can share and soon be known for. Like these quick and delicious banana bars that are made with ingredients likely in your pantry already.

PREHEAT OVEN TO 350°F

MAKES 3 DOZEN BARS

13 x 9-INCH BAKING PAN, GREASED OR LINED
   WITH FOIL (SEE PAGE 16)

1 (18.25-ounce) package yellow cake mix

⅓ cup vegetable oil

1 large egg

1 cup chopped nuts (e.g., peanuts, walnuts, or pecans)

1 (14-ounce) can sweetened condensed milk (not evaporated)

1 cup mashed banana (about 2 large bananas)

1⅓ cups sweetened flaked coconut

1 cup butterscotch baking chips or milk chocolate chips

1. Mix the cake mix, oil, and egg in a large bowl with electric mixer on medium speed 1 minute or until blended and crumbly. Stir in the nuts with wooden spoon. Reserve 1 cup of crumb mixture. Firmly press remaining mixture into prepared pan.
2. Combine the condensed milk and mashed banana in a small bowl, then pour and spread over crust. Top with the coconut, butterscotch chips, and reserved crumb mixture, pressing down gently.
3. Bake 25 to 28 minutes or until lightly browned. Transfer to wire rack and cool completely. Cut into bars.

CRANBERRY STREUSEL BARS

You know that cookie on the Christmas cookie plate that everyone fights over? This is it. You may not have considered the combination of cranberry and caramel before now, but you'll never forget it after tasting these rich treats. They are definitely holiday fare, but if you stow a few bags of fresh cranberries in the freezer, you can make and enjoy them year-round.

PREHEAT OVEN TO 350°F

MAKES 3 DOZEN BARS

13 x 9-INCH BAKING PAN, GREASED OR LINED
   WITH FOIL (SEE PAGE 16)

1 (18.25-ounce) package yellow or spice
   cake mix

1 cup (2 sticks) butter, melted

2⅓ cups quick-cooking oats

1 (12-ounce) jar caramel ice cream topping

1½ cups chopped fresh cranberries

1 (8-ounce) package chopped dates

¾ cup chopped pecans

1. Set aside ⅓ cup cake mix. Mix the remaining cake mix and melted butter in a large bowl with electric mixer on medium speed 1 to 2 minutes until blended. Stir in the oats with wooden spoon. Press half of mixture evenly into prepared pan.
2. Whisk the caramel topping and reserved ⅓ cup cake mix in a medium bowl until blended, then stir in the cranberries and dates. Spoon and spread the caramel mixture over prepared crust and top with reserved crumb mixture and pecans. Press down gently.
3. Bake 30 to 34 minutes or until topping is firm to the touch. Transfer to wire rack and cool completely. Cut into bars.

GERMAN CHOCOLATE BARS

Delight chocolate aficionados with this gooey cookie bar that showcases chocolate in all its decadent glory.

PREHEAT OVEN TO 350°F

MAKES 3 DOZEN BARS

13 x 9-INCH BAKING PAN, GREASED OR LINED
   WITH FOIL (SEE PAGE 16)

1 (18.25-ounce) package German chocolate
   cake mix

⅓ cup butter, softened

2 large eggs

1 (14-ounce) can sweetened condensed milk

1⅓ cups flaked sweetened coconut, divided

1 cup chopped pecans

1½ cups milk chocolate chips, divided

1. Mix the cake mix, butter, and 1 egg in a large bowl with electric mixer on low speed until blended. Press mixture into prepared pan.
2. Whisk the condensed milk and remaining egg in a medium bowl until blended. Stir in 1 cup of the coconut, the pecans, and ¾ cup chocolate chips. Spread mixture evenly over crust. Sprinkle with the remaining coconut and chocolate chips, lightly pressing into condensed milk layer.
3. Bake 30 to 32 minutes or until center is almost set. Center will firm when cool. Transfer to wire rack and cool completely. Cut into bars.

CARAMEL-MALLOW-BUTTERSCOTCH BARS

We all know about the great matches that chocolate and peanut butter, lemon and ginger, and cinnamon and vanilla make. Well, here's another made-for-each-other combination: caramel and marshmallow. Prepare to hoot and holler when you take a bite.

PREHEAT OVEN TO 350°F

MAKES 3 DOZEN BARS

13 x 9-INCH BAKING PAN, GREASED OR LINED
   WITH FOIL (SEE PAGE 16)

1 (18.25-ounce) package yellow cake mix

¼ cup (1 stick) butter, melted

¼ cup water

¼ cup packed light brown sugar

2 large eggs

3 cups miniature marshmallows

1 cup butterscotch baking chips

¾ cup caramel ice cream topping

1. Blend the cake mix, butter, water, brown sugar, and eggs in a large bowl with electric mixer on medium speed for 1 to 2 minutes until blended. Press into prepared pan.
2. Bake 15 to 18 minutes or until golden. Remove from oven and sprinkle with the marshmallows and butterscotch baking chips.
3. Bake 5 to 8 minutes longer or until the marshmallows are puffed and golden. Transfer to wire rack and cool completely. Drizzle with the caramel topping. Cut into bars.

Cake Mix
WHITE

IRISH CREAM SWIRL BARS

Not only are these rich bars incredible and incredibly rich, the recipe can be used as a template for countless variations, depending on the cake mix, frosting, and flavor of coffee creamer used.

PREHEAT OVEN TO 350°F

MAKES 4 DOZEN BARS

15 x 10 x 1-INCH JELLY ROLL PAN, GREASED OR LINED WITH FOIL (SEE PAGE 16)

1 (18.25-ounce) package white cake mix

3 large eggs

1 cup Irish Cream coffee creamer, divided

⅓ cup vegetable oil

2 (8-ounce) packages cream cheese, softened

1½ cups white chocolate chips

1. Mix the cake mix, eggs, ⅔ cup creamer, and oil in a large bowl with electric mixer on low speed 1 to 2 minutes until blended. Spread all but ½ cup dough into prepared pan.
2. Beat the cream cheese, reserved cake mix dough, and remaining ⅓ cup creamer with electric mixer on low speed 1 to 2 minutes until blended. Stir in the white chocolate chips. Drop in large spoonfuls over the cake dough. Swirl with tip of knife to marble.
3. Bake 24 to 27 minutes, or until the bars are just set and golden. Transfer pan to a wire rack and cool completely. Chill 1 hour before serving. Cut into bars.

VARIATION *for Irish Cream Swirl Bars*

AMARETTO-CHOCOLATE SWIRL BARS: Prepare as directed but use chocolate cake mix, chocolate cream cheese frosting in place of cream cheese frosting, Amaretto creamer in place of Irish Cream creamer, and semisweet chocolate chips in place of white chocolate chips.

ORANGE CREAMSICLE SWIRL BARS

Cake Mix
WHITE

Reminiscent of the orange sherbet-vanilla ice cream bars from your childhood, these bars are perfect for summertime, when the baking should be easy.

PREHEAT OVEN TO 350°F

MAKES 4 DOZEN BARS

15 x 10 x 1-INCH JELLY ROLL PAN, GREASED OR LINED WITH FOIL (SEE PAGE 16)

1 (18.25-ounce) package white cake mix

3 large eggs

1 (12-ounce) container orange juice concentrate, thawed

⅓ cup vegetable oil

2 (8-ounce) packages cream cheese, softened

1½ cups white chocolate chips

1. Mix the cake mix, eggs, ⅔ cup thawed concentrate, and oil in a large bowl with electric mixer on low speed 1 to 2 minutes until blended. Spread all but ½ cup dough into prepared pan.
2. Beat the reserved cake mix dough, cream cheese, and remaining ⅓ cup concentrate with electric mixer on low speed 1 to 2 minutes until blended. Stir in the white chocolate chips. Drop in large spoonfuls over the cake dough. Swirl with tip of knife to marble.
3. Bake 24 to 27 minutes, or until the bars are just set and golden. Transfer pan to a wire rack and cool completely. Chill 1 hour before serving. Cut into bars.

LEMON CURD SWIRL CHEESECAKE BARS

Cake Mix
LEMON

A swirl of purchased lemon curd makes all the difference in these simple-to-make, elegant bars. Serve them at your next summertime get-together and let the kudos resound.

PREHEAT OVEN TO 350°F

MAKES 3 DOZEN BARS

13 x 9-INCH BAKING PAN, GREASED OR LINED WITH FOIL (SEE PAGE 16)

1 (18.25-ounce) package lemon cake mix

½ cup (1 stick) butter, melted

3 large eggs

2 (8-ounce) packages cream cheese, softened

¼ cup sugar

1 tablespoon fresh lemon juice

1 (12-ounce) jar lemon curd, room temperature

1. Reserve 2 tablespoons cake mix. Mix the remaining cake mix, melted butter, and 1 egg in a large bowl with electric mixer on medium speed 1 to 2 minutes until blended. Press into prepared pan. Bake 15 minutes.
2. Meanwhile, beat the cream cheese, sugar, lemon juice, and reserved cake mix in large bowl with electric mixer on medium-high speed 1 to 2 minutes until light and fluffy. Scrape down bowl, then beat in remaining 2 eggs, one at a time, until blended.
3. Spread the cream cheese mixture evenly over partially baked crust. Drop the lemon curd in spoonfuls evenly over the cream cheese layer. Swirl the lemon curd and cream cheese dough with tip of a knife.
4. Bake 23 to 26 minutes or until topping is just barely set when the pan is jiggled (do not over-bake). Transfer to a wire rack and cool completely. Chill 2 hours before serving. Cut into bars.

Cake Mix
VANILLA

KEY LIME BARS

Whether the weather is already warm or just heating up, these chilled, tart, creamy bars have immense appeal. And even though they are excellent served cold on a sultry day, they are not exclusively hot-weather fare. It would be a shame to limit such pleasures to only one season of the year!

PREHEAT OVEN TO 350°F

MAKES 3 DOZEN BARS

13 x 9-INCH BAKING PAN, GREASED OR LINED WITH FOIL (SEE PAGE 16)

1 (18.25-ounce) package vanilla cake mix

⅓ cup butter, melted

5 large eggs

1 (14-ounce) can sweetened condensed milk (not evaporated)

⅔ cup lime juice

1 tablespoon grated lime peel

1. Reserve 1 tablespoon cake mix. Mix the remaining cake mix, melted butter, and 1 egg in a large bowl with electric mixer on low speed 1 to 2 minutes until blended and crumbly. Press mixture into prepared pan. Bake 15 minutes.
2. While crust bakes, whisk the condensed milk, remaining 4 eggs, lime juice, lime peel, and reserved tablespoon of cake mix in a large bowl until smooth. Carefully spread over partially baked crust.
3. Bake an additional 20 to 24 minutes or until topping is just set. Transfer to a wire rack and cool completely. Refrigerate 2 to 3 hours before serving. Cut into bars.

VARIATIONS *for Key Lime Bars*

CREAMY LEMON BARS: Prepare as directed but use lemon juice in place of the lime juice and lemon peel in place of the lime peel.

ORANGE BURST BARS: Prepare as directed but use ½ cup orange juice plus 2½ tablespoons lemon juice in place of the lime juice and orange peel in place of the lime peel.

Cake Mix
LEMON

LEMON BUTTERMILK BARS

I'm a firm believer in making the most of the summer months. The living, as an old song suggests, should be easy, the food, light. With that said, these treats are indispensable. The buttermilk brightens the lemon for a very citrusy, very summery bar (plain yogurt can be used in place of the buttermilk for equally good results). The only other items needed are a glass of iced tea, a good book, and a few hours of nothing else to do.

PREHEAT OVEN TO 350°F

MAKES 3 DOZEN BARS

13 x 9-INCH BAKING PAN, GREASED OR LINED
    WITH FOIL (SEE PAGE 16)

1 (18.25-ounce) package lemon cake mix, divided

4 large eggs

¾ cup (1½ sticks) butter, melted, divided

¾ cup buttermilk

⅓ cup sugar

¼ cup fresh lemon juice

1 tablespoon grated lemon peel

1–2 tablespoons confectioners' sugar

1. Reserve 1 cup cake mix. Mix the remaining cake mix, 1 egg, and ¼ cup (½ stick) melted butter in a large bowl with electric mixer on low speed until blended and crumbly. Press mixture into prepared pan. Bake 15 minutes.
2. Meanwhile, beat the buttermilk, sugar, lemon juice, lemon peel, reserved 1 cup cake mix, remaining 3 eggs, and remaining ½ cup melted butter in a large bowl with electric mixer on low speed 1 to 2 minutes until blended. Pour over partially baked crust.
3. Bake 35 to 38 minutes, until just set and light golden on top. Transfer to wire rack and cool completely. Cut into bars and sift with confectioners' sugar.

LEMON MACAROON BARS

A memorable dessert is something to be proud of, whether hosting a fancy dinner party or just throwing something together for the family some weeknight or weekend. No matter what the occasion, this is an easy option that will make any home baker beam and blush from all of the kudos.

PREHEAT OVEN TO 350°F

MAKES 3 DOZEN BARS

13 x 9-INCH BAKING PAN, GREASED OR LINED WITH FOIL (SEE PAGE 16)

1 (18.25-ounce) package lemon cake mix

⅓ cup butter, softened

2 large eggs

1 (14-ounce) can sweetened condensed milk (not evaporated)

3 tablespoons lemon juice

2-⅔ cups (7-ounce bag) sweetened flake coconut, divided

1. Mix the cake mix, butter, and 1 egg in a large bowl with electric mixer on medium speed 1 to 2 minutes until blended. Press mixture into prepared pan.
2. Whisk the condensed milk, remaining egg, and lemon juice in a medium bowl until blended. Stir in 1⅓ cups coconut, then spread evenly over crust. Sprinkle with the remaining coconut, lightly pressing into condensed milk layer.
3. Bake 28 to 30 minutes or until filling is just barely set (it will firm as it cools). Transfer to wire rack and cool completely. Cut into bars.

VARIATION *for Lemon Macaroon Bars*

MACAROON BARS: Prepare as directed but use white cake mix, use 3 tablespoons whole or lowfat milk in place of the lemon juice, and add 1 teaspoon almond extract to condensed milk mixture.

CHOCOLATE MACAROON BARS: Prepare as directed but use devil's food cake mix, use 3 tablespoons whole or lowfat milk in place of the lemon juice, and sprinkle 1 cup miniature semisweet chocolate chips over bars along with the coconut.

MAGIC COOKIE BARS

Call them hello dollies, 7-layer bars, or magic cookie bars—an incredible cookie, no matter the name, tastes just as sweet. A bit of crispy from the toasted coconut and pecans, a touch of buttery from the quick crust, and a good dose of gooey from the condensed milk and chocolate chips guarantee that these will magically disappear from the cookie jar.

PREHEAT OVEN TO 350°F

MAKES 4 DOZEN BARS

15 x 10 x 1-INCH BAKING PAN, UNGREASED OR LINED WITH FOIL (SEE PAGE 16)

1 (18.25-ounce) package yellow cake mix

½ cup (1 stick) butter, melted

1 large egg

2 cups semisweet chocolate chips

1½ cups sweetened flaked coconut

1 cup chopped walnuts or pecans

1 (14-ounce) can sweetened condensed milk (not evaporated)

1. Mix the cake mix, melted butter, and egg in a large bowl with a wooden spoon until blended. Press in ungreased pan with moistened fingers.
2. Sprinkle the crust with the chocolate chips, coconut, and nuts. Pour the condensed milk evenly over crust and ingredients.
3. Bake 25 to 28 minutes or until lightly browned. Transfer to a wire rack and cool completely. Cut into bars.

VARIATIONS *for Magic Cookie Bars*

BUTTERSCOTCH MAGIC COOKIE BARS: Prepare as directed but use butterscotch baking chips in place of the chocolate chips.

DOUBLE-CHOCOLATE MAGIC COOKIE BARS: Prepare as directed but use chocolate cake mix in place of the yellow cake mix.

WHITE MAGIC COOKIE BARS: Prepare as directed but use white cake mix in place of the yellow cake mix, vanilla baking chips or white chocolate chips in place of the semisweet chocolate chips, and macadamia nuts in place of the chopped walnuts or pecans.

MANDARIN ORANGE CHEESECAKE BARS

Mandarin oranges and cheesecake? Oh yes. This is the kind of recipe home bakers dream about: so simple, so beautiful, and so delicious that everyone will want to linger to have a second or third helping. The fresh flavors of this bar make it a great choice for spring and summer get-togethers.

PREHEAT OVEN TO 350°F

MAKES 3 DOZEN BARS

13 x 9-INCH BAKING PAN, GREASED OR LINED
   WITH FOIL (SEE PAGE 16)

1 (18.25-ounce) package white cake mix

3 large eggs

⅓ cup butter, melted

2 (8-ounce) packages of cream cheese

⅔ cup sour cream

⅓ cup orange marmalade

1 (11-ounce) can mandarin oranges,
   drained, roughly chopped

1. Reserve 1 cup of cake mix. Mix the remaining cake mix, 1 egg, and melted butter in a large bowl with electric mixer on medium speed 1 to 2 minutes until blended. Press into prepared pan. Bake 10 minutes.

2. Meanwhile, beat the cream cheese, sour cream, marmalade, reserved cake mix, and remaining 2 eggs in a medium bowl with electric mixer on medium-high speed 1 to 2 minutes until blended and smooth. Stir in the mandarin oranges. Spread the cream cheese mixture over crust.

3. Bake 30 to 35 minutes or until just barely set at center. Transfer to wire rack and cool completely. Chill at least 2 hours before serving. Cut into bars.

VARIATION *for Mandarin Orange Cheesecake Bars*

GINGER-LIME CHEESECAKE BARS: Prepare as directed but add 2 teaspoons ground ginger to the cake mix-egg-butter mixture, use lime juice in place of the marmalade, and omit the mandarin oranges.

TROPICAL FRUIT AND CASHEW BARS

For an imaginative cookie, try this tropics-inspired cookie bar. They are definitely summer barbecue fare, so invite the guests and fire up the grill.

PREHEAT OVEN TO 350°F

MAKES 3 DOZEN BARS

13 x 9-INCH BAKING PAN, GREASED OR LINED
    WITH FOIL (SEE PAGE 16)

1 (18.25-ounce) package yellow cake mix

½ cup (1 stick) butter, melted

1 large egg

1 (14-ounce) can sweetened condensed
    milk (not evaporated)

2 tablespoons lime juice

1½ cups white chocolate chips

1½ cups sweetened flake coconut

1 (7-ounce) bag dried tropical fruit bits

1 cup roasted, lightly salted cashew pieces

1. Mix the cake mix, melted butter, and egg in a large bowl with a wooden spoon until blended. Press mixture into prepared pan.
2. Whisk the condensed milk and lime juice in a small bowl until blended. Sprinkle the crust with the white chocolate chips, coconut, dried fruit, and cashews. Pour the condensed milk mixture evenly over crust and ingredients.
3. Bake 35 to 40 minutes or until lightly browned. Cool completely. Cut into bars.

MOTHER LODE CHOCOLATE CARAMEL BARS

It seems that something chocolate is nearly everyone's favorite dessert. These quick and easy bars, loaded with caramel, toffee, and even more chocolate, qualify as one such something, effortlessly.

PREHEAT OVEN TO 350°F

MAKES 3 DOZEN BARS

13 x 9-INCH BAKING PAN, GREASED OR LINED WITH FOIL (SEE PAGE 16)

1 (18.25-ounce) package yellow cake mix

⅓ cup vegetable oil

2 large eggs

1 cup semisweet chocolate chips

1 cup white chocolate chips

3 (1.4-ounce) chocolate-covered toffee candy bars, coarsely chopped

32 caramels, unwrapped

1 (14-ounce) can sweetened condensed milk (not evaporated)

½ cup (1 stick) butter

1. Mix the cake mix, oil, and eggs in a large bowl with a wooden spoon until blended. Stir in the semisweet chocolate chips and white chocolate chips. Press half of dough into prepared pan. Bake 10 minutes.
2. Stir the toffee into remaining cake mix mixture.
3. Melt the caramels, condensed milk, and butter in a medium heavy saucepan, stirring over medium-low heat until blended and smooth. Pour evenly over the partially baked crust and sprinkle with the remaining cake mix mixture.
4. Bake 25 to 28 minutes or until the topping is golden and firm to the touch. Transfer to wire rack. Run knife around edges of pan to loosen. Cool completely, then cut into bars.

NEW YORK CHEESECAKE BARS

Forget the springform pan—you can make an incredible, New York-style cheesecake in a plain 13 x 9-inch baking pan. Not only is it a breeze to make, it is much easier to cut and serve to a crowd—or a small army. Because this silky-rich cheesecake is skyscraper-high, one square will go a long way. For a dressed-up dessert, serve the squares plated with a drizzle of chocolate or caramel sauce, fresh fruit, or a quick berry compote. And for an easy flavor variation, vary the cake mix for the crust. Lemon, chocolate, and spice cake are particularly delicious.

PREHEAT OVEN TO 350°F

MAKES 3 DOZEN BARS

13 x 9-INCH BAKING PAN, GREASED OR LINED
    WITH FOIL (SEE PAGE 16)

1 (18.25-ounce) package white cake mix

½ cup (1 stick) butter, melted

4 large eggs

3 (8-ounce) packages cream cheese, softened

1¾ cups confectioners' sugar, divided

3 teaspoons vanilla extract, divided

1 (16-ounce) container sour cream

1. Mix the cake mix, melted butter, and 1 egg in a large bowl with electric mixer on medium speed 1 to 2 minutes until blended. Press into prepared pan. Bake 15 minutes.

2. Meanwhile, beat the cream cheese, 1¼ cups of the confectioners' sugar, and 2 teaspoons of the vanilla with electric mixer on high speed until blended and smooth, scraping down bowl several times. Add the remaining 3 eggs, one at a time, mixing on low speed after each addition just until blended. Pour over hot crust.

3. Bake 23 to 26 minutes or until center is just barely set when pan is jiggled (do not overbake).

4. Whisk the sour cream, remaining ½ cup confectioners' sugar, and 1 teaspoon vanilla in small bowl until blended. Spread evenly over bars. Return bars to oven for 5 minutes. Transfer to wire rack and cool completely. Chill at least 4 hours or overnight. Cut into bars.

VARIATION *for New York Cheesecake Bars*

FRESH BERRY CHEESECAKE BARS: Prepare as directed but omit the final sour cream topping steps. Instead, distribute 2 cups fresh raspberries, blackberries, or blueberries over the cheesecake dough before baking. Sprinkle the cooled, chilled bars with confectioners' sugar.

PEANUT BRITTLE BARS

Cake Mix
YELLOW

This satisfying, candy-like finale features all the flavors of homemade peanut brittle. With a few simple steps, you'll impress any dessert lover.

PREHEAT OVEN TO 350°F

MAKES 3 DOZEN BARS

13 x 9-INCH BAKING PAN, GREASED OR LINED
WITH FOIL (SEE PAGE 16)

1 (18.25-ounce) package yellow cake mix

1⅓ cups creamy peanut butter, divided

1 large egg

½ cup vegetable oil

1 (14-ounce) can sweetened condensed
milk (not evaporated)

2 teaspoons vanilla extract

2 cups lightly salted roasted peanuts

1 cup toffee baking bits

1. Mix the cake mix, 1 cup peanut butter, egg, and oil in a large bowl with electric mixer on medium speed 1 to 2 minutes until blended and crumbly. Reserve 1½ cups dough. Press remaining dough into prepared pan. Bake 10 minutes.

2. Meanwhile, whisk the condensed milk, remaining ⅓ cup peanut butter, and vanilla in a medium bowl until blended. Spread over partially baked crust. Sprinkle with the peanuts, remaining dough, and toffee bits.

3. Bake 20 to 25 minutes or until golden brown and topping is firm to the touch. Transfer to wire rack and cool completely. Cut into bars.

PEANUT BUTTER BLONDIES

Can the butterscotch blondie be made better? For peanut butter fiends, the answer is a resounding yes and is as simple as stirring some peanut butter into the dough. Delicious!

PREHEAT OVEN TO 350°F

MAKES 3 DOZEN BARS

13 x 9-INCH BAKING PAN, GREASED OR LINED
   WITH FOIL (SEE PAGE 16)

1 (18.25-ounce) package yellow cake mix

⅓ cup butter, melted

2 large eggs

2 teaspoons vanilla extract, divided

⅔ cup plus 1 tablespoon creamy peanut
   butter (not natural style), divided

1 cup confectioners' sugar

2–3 tablespoons whole or lowfat milk

1. Mix the cake mix, melted butter, eggs, and 1 teaspoon vanilla extract in a large bowl with electric mixer on medium speed 1 to 2 minutes until blended. Stir in ⅔ cup peanut butter with a wooden spoon (need not be perfectly blended). Press into ungreased pan.
2. Bake 22 to 25 minutes until just barely set at center (do not overbake). Transfer to a wire rack and cool completely.
3. Whisk the confectioners' sugar, remaining 1 teaspoon vanilla, and remaining 1 tablespoon peanut butter in a small bowl until blended, adding enough milk to make drizzling consistency. Drizzle icing over cooled bars. Cut into bars.

VARIATIONS *for Peanut Butter Blondies*

CHOCOLATE CHIP PEANUT BUTTER BLONDIES: Prepare as directed but add 1 cup semi-sweet or milk chocolate chips to the dough along with the peanut butter.

PEANUT BUTTER BLONDIES DELUXE: Prepare as directed but add 1 cup peanut butter baking chips to the dough along with the peanut butter. After drizzling blondies with icing, sprinkle with ⅔ cup chopped roasted, lightly salted peanuts.

PEANUT BUTTER CUP BARS

Cake Mix CHOCOLATE or YELLOW

Peanut butter, chocolate, caramel, cake, and frosting in one bar cookie? Gooey-licious.

PREHEAT OVEN TO 350°F

MAKES 3 DOZEN BARS

13 x 9-INCH BAKING PAN, GREASED OR LINED
WITH FOIL (SEE PAGE 16)

1 (18.25-ounce) package yellow or
   chocolate cake mix

⅓ cup butter, melted

¼ cup creamy peanut butter

2 large eggs

20 miniature peanut butter cups,
   unwrapped, coarsely chopped

1 cup lightly salted, roasted peanuts, chopped

1. Mix the cake mix, melted butter, peanut butter, and eggs in a large bowl with a wooden spoon until blended. Stir in the peanut butter cups and peanuts. Spread mixture evenly into the prepared pan.
2. Bake 18 to 22 minutes or until golden brown. Transfer to wire rack and cool completely. Cut into bars.

PEANUT BUTTER FUDGE BARS

Cake Mix YELLOW

Just like politics, dessert preferences are local. Maybe you're partial to Georgia peach cobbler. Or perhaps California coconut-lime ice cream or a New England cranberry betty is your style. But one thing's for certain: these over-the-top peanut butter chocolate fudge bars bridge all boundaries.

PREHEAT OVEN TO 350°F

MAKES 3 DOZEN BARS

13 x 9-INCH BAKING PAN, GREASED OR LINED
WITH FOIL (SEE PAGE 16)

1 (18.25-ounce) package yellow cake mix

1 cup creamy peanut butter

2 large eggs

½ cup vegetable oil

2 cups semisweet chocolate chips

1 (14-ounce) can sweetened condensed
   milk (not evaporated)

2 tablespoons butter

1 teaspoon vanilla extract

1. Mix the cake mix, peanut butter, eggs, and oil in a large bowl. Blend for 1 to 2 minutes with electric mixer on low speed until blended. Reserve 1½ cups of the dough. Press remaining dough into prepared pan.
2. Melt the chocolate chips, condensed milk, and butter in a heavy saucepan set over low heat, stirring until smooth. Remove from heat and stir in the vanilla extract, then pour over crust. Sprinkle with remaining dough.
2. Bake 20 to 25 minutes or until golden brown and topping is firm to the touch. Transfer to wire rack and cool completely. Cut into bars.

VARIATIONS *for Peanut Butter Fudge Bars*

DOUBLE-PEANUT BUTTER FUDGE BARS: Prepare as directed but substitute 2 cups peanut butter-flavored baking chips for the chocolate chips.

DOUBLE-CHOCOLATE PEANUT BUTTER FUDGE BARS: Prepare as directed but use a chocolate cake mix instead of yellow cake mix.

CHOCOLATE-HAZELNUT FUDGE BARS: Prepare as directed but use a chocolate cake mix instead of yellow cake mix and use chocolate-hazelnut spread in place of the peanut butter.

Cake Mix
YELLOW

PECAN PIE BARS

These decadent dessert bars are dedicated to all my fellow cookie aficionados who cannot resist the pecan pie bars in the coffeehouse pastry case. Great with a cup of coffee at any time of the year, they can also replace traditional pecan pie when you need to serve a crowd.

PREHEAT OVEN TO 350°F

MAKES 3 DOZEN BARS

13 x 9-INCH BAKING PAN, GREASED OR LINED WITH FOIL (SEE PAGE 16)

1 (18.25-ounce) package yellow cake mix
⅓ cup butter, softened
4 large eggs
1½ cups dark corn syrup
½ cup firmly packed dark brown sugar
1½ teaspoons vanilla extract
1¼ cups chopped pecans, divided

1. Reserve ⅔ cup of the cake mix. Mix the remaining cake mix, butter, and 1 egg in a large bowl with electric mixer 1 to 2 minutes on medium speed until blended and crumbly. Press mixture into prepared pan. Bake 15 minutes.
2. Meanwhile, mix the reserved ⅔ cup cake mix, corn syrup, brown sugar, vanilla, and remaining 3 eggs in large bowl with electric mixer on medium speed for 1 to 2 minutes until

blended. Stir in the ¾ cup chopped pecans. Pour mixture over hot crust and sprinkle with remaining pecans.

3. Bake an additional 30 to 35 minutes or until filling is set. Transfer to wire rack and cool completely. Cut into bars.

VARIATION *for Pecan Pie Bars*

CHOCOLATE CHIP AND PECAN PIE BARS: Prepare as directed but use chocolate cake mix and add 1 cup miniature semisweet chocolate chips to the filling.

Cake Mix
WHITE

PEPPERMINT AND WHITE CHOCOLATE CHEESECAKE BARS

The weather outside may be frightful, but your kitchen will be delightful if you bake up these cool mint-y bars come holiday-time. To crush the candies, place in a heavy-duty zippered plastic bag and bang with a rolling pin or can (it doubles as holiday stress relief).

PREHEAT OVEN TO 350°F

MAKES 3 DOZEN BARS

13 x 9-INCH BAKING PAN, GREASED OR LINED WITH FOIL (SEE PAGE 16)

1 (18.25-ounce) package white cake mix

½ cup (1 stick) butter, melted

3 large eggs

2 (8-ounce) packages cream cheese, softened

¼ cup sugar

1 teaspoon peppermint extract

2 cups white chocolate chips, divided

2 teaspoons vegetable shortening

1 cup coarsely crushed red and white striped peppermint candies or candy canes

1. Mix the cake mix, melted butter, and 1 egg in a large bowl with electric mixer on medium speed 1 to 2 minutes until blended. Press into prepared pan. Bake 15 minutes.

2. Meanwhile, beat the cream cheese, sugar, remaining 2 eggs, and peppermint extract in large bowl with electric mixer on high speed 1 to 2 minutes until smooth. Stir in 1 cup white chocolate chips. Pour over partially baked crust.

3. Bake 23 to 26 minutes until just barely set at center. Transfer to a wire rack and cool completely.

4. Microwave the remaining 1 cup chocolate chips and shortening in a medium microwaveable bowl on High 1 minute, stirring after 30 seconds, until melted and smooth. Drizzle over

cooled bars and then immediately sprinkle with crushed peppermint candies. Chill at least 3 hours before serving. Cut into bars.

__VARIATION__ *for Peppermint and White Chocolate Cheesecake Bars*

PEPPERMINT AND DARK CHOCOLATE CHEESECAKE BARS: Prepare as directed but use chocolate or devil's food cake mix in place of the white cake mix and semisweet chocolate chips in place of the white chocolate chips.

Cake Mix SPICE
CRANBERRY CREAM CHEESE BARS

Dazzle those dear to you with these easy-to-make, beautiful-to-behold bars.

PREHEAT OVEN TO 350°F

MAKES 3 DOZEN BARS

13 x 9-INCH BAKING PAN, GREASED OR LINED WITH FOIL (SEE PAGE 16)

1 (18.25-ounce) package spice cake mix

1 cup (2 sticks) butter, melted

2¼ cups quick-cooking oats

1 cup white chocolate chips

1 (14-ounce) can sweetened condensed milk (not evaporated)

1 (8-ounce) package cream cheese, softened

¼ cup fresh lemon juice

1 (16-ounce) can whole cranberry sauce

1. Mix the cake mix and melted butter in a large bowl with a wooden spoon until blended. Stir in the oats. Press half of mixture evenly into prepared pan. Add the white chocolate chips to remaining oat mixture.
2. Beat the condensed milk, cream cheese, and lemon juice in large bowl with electric mixer on medium speed 1 to 2 minutes until smooth. Spread over prepared crust.
3. Spoon the cranberry sauce by teaspoonfuls over cream cheese mixture. Top with the reserved crumb mixture and press down gently.
4. Bake 35 to 38 minutes or until topping is set and firm to the touch. Transfer to wire rack and cool completely. Chill 1 hour before serving. Cut into bars.

RASPBERRY SWIRL BARS

Spring is a season of celebrations. Start the party planning with these quick-to-prepare, but oh-so-impressive bars, perfect for receptions, showers, and graduation parties. Other jams and preserves can be substituted for the raspberry preserves. Consider apricot preserves, orange marmalade, or lemon curd.

PREHEAT OVEN TO 350°F

MAKES 3 DOZEN BARS

13 x 9-INCH BAKING PAN, GREASED OR LINED WITH FOIL (SEE PAGE 16)

1 (18.25-ounce) package white cake mix

½ cup sour cream

⅓ cup butter, melted

1 teaspoon vanilla extract

2 large eggs

1 cup seedless raspberry jam

1. Mix the cake mix, sour cream, melted butter, vanilla extract, and eggs in a large bowl with electric mixer on medium speed 1 to 2 minutes until blended. Reserve 1 cup of dough. Spread remaining dough into prepared pan.
2. Spread the raspberry jam evenly over dough. Drop the remaining cake dough by tablespoonfuls over preserves. Swirl the dough and jam with tip of knife.
3. Bake 23 to 26 minutes or until toothpick inserted near center comes out clean. Transfer to wire rack and cool completely. Cut into bars.

ROCKY ROAD BARS

A lumpy-bumpy cookie made of marshmallow, chocolate, and nuts? Who wouldn't want to take a stroll down this rocky road?

PREHEAT OVEN TO 350°F

MAKES 3 DOZEN BARS

13 x 9-INCH BAKING PAN, GREASED OR LINED WITH FOIL (SEE PAGE 16)

1 (18.25-ounce) package chocolate or devil's food cake mix

½ cup (1 stick) butter, melted

2 large eggs

3 cups miniature marshmallows

1 cup roasted, lightly salted cashew pieces or peanuts

1 cup semisweet or milk chocolate chips

1. Mix the cake mix, melted butter, and eggs in a large bowl with electric mixer on medium speed for 1 to 2 minutes until blended. Spread evenly in prepared pan.
2. Bake 22 to 25 minutes until just set at center. Immediately sprinkle with the marshmallows, nuts, and chocolate chips.
3. Bake 5 to 8 minutes longer or until the marshmallows are puffed and golden. Transfer to wire rack and cool completely. Cut into bars.

VARIATION *for Rocky Road Bars*

BUTTERSCOTCH BUMPY BARS: Prepare as directed but use a white cake mix, and butterscotch chips in place of chocolate chips.

Cake Mix
WHITE

SHORTBREAD SQUARES

Begin brewing the Earl Grey and Darjeeling—this is one sophisticated tea-time nibble. Be sure to use white cake mix here—it has less fat than other cake mixes, producing just the right consistency.

PREHEAT OVEN TO 350°F

MAKES 4 DOZEN BARS

15 x 10 x 1-INCH BAKING PAN, GREASED OR LINED WITH FOIL (SEE PAGE 16)

1 (18.25-ounce) package white cake mix

½ cup (1 stick) butter, softened

1 (3-ounce) package cream cheese, softened

1 large egg white, room temperature

½ teaspoon vanilla extract

2 tablespoons confectioners' sugar

1 cup finely chopped nuts (e.g., pecans, walnuts, or slivered almonds)

1. Mix the cake mix, butter, and cream cheese in a large bowl with electric mixer on medium speed 1 to 2 minutes until crumbly dough forms. Press into prepared pan.
2. Beat the egg white, vanilla, and confectioners' sugar in medium bowl with electric mixer on high speed until stiff peaks form. Spread over prepared crust and sprinkle with nuts.
3. Bake 15 to 18 minutes until golden brown and firm to the touch. Transfer to wire rack and cool completely. Cut into bars.

VARIATIONS *for Shortbread Squares*

LEMON-MACADAMIA SHORTBREAD: Prepare as directed but add 1 tablespoon grated lemon peel to the dough, omit the vanilla, and use 1 cup chopped macadamias for the nuts.

BROWN SUGAR-PECAN SHORTBREAD: Prepare as directed but add 3 tablespoons packed dark brown sugar to the dough, use 1 tablespoon dark brown sugar in place of confectioners' sugar, and use 1 cup finely chopped pecans for the nuts.

SALTY-SWEET CHEWY PEANUT BARS

These easy and very delicious bars bear a strong resemblance to one of my favorite candy bars: *PayDay. Have fun playing around with the cake and chip flavors. Consider chocolate cake mix and chocolate chips or caramel cake mix (harder to find, but worth the hunt) combined with butterscotch or white chocolate chips.*

PREHEAT OVEN TO 350°F

MAKES 3 DOZEN BARS

13 x 9-INCH BAKING PAN, GREASED OR LINED WITH FOIL (SEE PAGE 16)

1 (18.25-ounce) package yellow cake mix

10 tablespoons (1¼ sticks) butter, softened, divided

1 large egg

3 cups miniature marshmallows

⅔ cup light corn syrup

1 (10-ounce) package peanut butter baking chips

2 cups crisp rice cereal

2 cups salted, roasted peanuts

1. Mix the cake mix, 6 tablespoons butter, and egg in a large bowl with electric mixer on medium speed 1 to 2 minutes until blended and crumbly. Press into prepared pan. Bake 15 minutes.
2. Remove the crust from oven and sprinkle with marshmallows. Bake 2 minutes longer until marshmallows begin to puff. Transfer to wire cooling rack.
3. Meanwhile, combine the corn syrup, peanut butter chips, and remaining 4 tablespoons (¼ cup) butter in a heavy saucepan set over medium heat, stirring until melted and smooth. Stir in the cereal and peanuts, then immediately spread over marshmallows. Chill at least 1 hour. Cut into bars.

PUMPKIN PIE BARS

This extra-easy take on everybody's Thanksgiving favorite brings easy entertaining up to date.

PREHEAT OVEN TO 350°F

MAKES 3 DOZEN BARS

13 x 9-INCH BAKING PAN, GREASED OR LINED
WITH FOIL (SEE PAGE 16)

1 (18.25-ounce) package yellow cake mix

¼ cup vegetable oil

4 large eggs

½ cup chopped pecans

1 (15-ounce) can pumpkin purée

1 (14-ounce) can sweetened condensed
milk (not evaporated)

2 teaspoons vanilla extract

1½ teaspoons pumpkin pie spice

1. Reserve ½ cup cake mix. Mix the remaining cake mix, oil, and 1 egg in a large bowl with electric mixer on medium speed 1 to 2 minutes until blended and crumbly. Stir in the pecans with a wooden spoon. Press mixture into prepared pan.

2. Mix the pumpkin, condensed milk, vanilla, pumpkin pie spice, remaining 3 eggs, and ½ cup reserved cake mix in large bowl with electric mixer on medium speed 1 to 2 minutes until blended. Spread over crust.

3. Bake 40 to 45 minutes or until filling is just set. Transfer to a wire rack and cool completely. Cut into bars.

Cake Mix
SPICE

SPICED AND ICED PUMPKIN SNACK BARS

Solid pack pumpkin is available year-round in the baking aisle of grocery stores, which means these moist and delicious bars can be made any season.

PREHEAT OVEN TO 350°F

MAKES 4 DOZEN BARS

15 x 10 x 1-INCH BAKING PAN, GREASED OR LINED WITH FOIL (SEE PAGE 16)

1 (18.25-ounce) package spice cake mix

1 (15-ounce) can pumpkin purée

¾ cup sour cream (not reduced fat)

3 large eggs

¼ cup vegetable oil

2 teaspoons ground cinnamon, divided

Optional: 1 cup dried cranberries or raisins

1½ cups (from a 16-ounce tub) ready-to-spread cream cheese frosting

1. Mix the cake mix, pumpkin, sour cream, eggs, oil, and 1 teaspoon cinnamon in a large bowl with electric mixer 1 to 2 minutes on medium speed until blended. If desired, stir in dried cranberries or raisins. Spread into prepared pan.
2. Bake 18 to 20 minutes or until toothpick inserted in center comes out clean. Transfer to wire rack and cool completely.
3. Combine the frosting and remaining 1 teaspoon cinnamon in a small bowl until blended. Spread over cooled bars.

Cake Mix
SPICE

SPICED APPLE BUTTER BARS

After-school snacks have never been better than with this home-style bar. The Apple Butter-Cream Cheese Frosting adds a luxurious smoothness to these moist bars, which happen to keep extremely well.

PREHEAT OVEN TO 350°F

MAKES 3 DOZEN BARS

13 x 9-INCH BAKING PAN, GREASED OR LINED WITH FOIL (SEE PAGE 16)

1 (18.25-ounce) package spice cake mix

¾ cup apple butter, divided

1 large egg

¼ cup vegetable oil

1 cup chopped walnuts

1¼ cups (from a 16-ounce tub) ready-to-spread cream cheese frosting

1. Mix the cake mix, ½ cup of the apple butter, egg, and oil in a large bowl with electric mixer on low speed 1 to 2 minutes until blended. Spread into prepared pan. Sprinkle with walnuts.
2. Bake 30 to 35 minutes until lightly browned and firm to the touch. Transfer to wire rack and cool completely.
3. Combine the frosting and remaining ¼ cup apple butter in a small bowl until blended. Spread over cooled bars.

Cake Mix DEVIL'S FOOD

MEXICAN CHOCOLATE BARS

Kicked up with cinnamon, orange peel, and a hint of heat, these very rich, dark chocolate bars have gone south of the border.

PREHEAT OVEN TO 350°F
MAKES 3 DOZEN BARS
13 x 9-INCH BAKING PAN, GREASED OR LINED WITH FOIL (SEE PAGE 16)

1 (18.25-ounce) package devil's food cake mix

1 cup chopped nuts (almonds, pecans, or walnuts)

½ cup (1 stick) butter, melted

1 teaspoon grated orange peel

1 teaspoon ground cinnamon

⅛ teaspoon cayenne pepper

1 (14-ounce) can sweetened condensed milk (not evaporated)

1½ cups semisweet chocolate chips

1. Mix the cake mix, nuts, melted butter, orange peel, cinnamon, and cayenne in a large bowl with a wooden spoon. Press into prepared pan. Bake 15 minutes.
2. Meanwhile, melt the condensed milk and chocolate chips in a medium saucepan set over low heat, stirring until smooth. Pour over partially baked crust.
3. Bake an additional 15 minutes. Transfer to a wire rack and cool completely. Cut into bars.

TENNESSEE JAM CAKE BARS

Tennessee Jam Cake is a classic Southern dessert made with layers of spice cake, and blackberry jam (sometimes stirred into the dough, sometimes spread between the layers of cake) and finished with penuche (caramel fudge) frosting. Heaven. Here the same flavor is captured in an impressive, but still easy, streusel bar.

PREHEAT OVEN TO 350°F

MAKES 3 DOZEN BARS

13 x 9-INCH BAKING PAN, GREASED OR LINED WITH FOIL (SEE PAGE 16)

1 (18.25-ounce) package spice cake mix

1 cup (2 sticks) butter, melted

1 teaspoon pumpkin pie spice or ground cinnamon

2 cups quick-cooking oats

1 (12-ounce) jar seedless blackberry jam

1 cup butterscotch baking chips

½ cup chopped pecans (or walnuts)

1. Mix the cake mix, melted butter, and pumpkin pie spice in a large bowl with electric mixer on medium speed 1 to 2 minutes until blended. Mix in the oats with a wooden spoon. Press half of the mixture into prepared pan.
2. Spoon and spread the blackberry jam over prepared crust. Sprinkle with the butterscotch chips, pecans, and remaining oat mixture. Gently press into jam layer.
3. Bake 30 to 34 minutes or until topping is golden brown and firm to the touch. Transfer to wire rack and cool completely. Cut into bars.

Cake Mix
WHITE

TIRAMISU BARS

Tiramisu was a nineties hit, appearing on most every dessert menu around. But while the fad has faded, the popularity of the ambrosial Italian concoction of cream and cake has not. Here it finds new life as inspiration for an easily assembled bar cookie. Buon appetito!

PREHEAT OVEN TO 350°F

MAKES 3 DOZEN BARS

13 x 9-INCH BAKING PAN, GREASED OR LINED WITH FOIL (SEE PAGE 16)

2½ tablespoons dark rum

1½ tablespoons instant coffee powder

1 (18.25-ounce) package white cake mix, divided

¼ cup (½ stick) butter, melted

4 large eggs

2 cups ricotta cheese

1 (14-ounce) can sweetened condensed milk (not evaporated)

1 cup chocolate-covered toffee baking bits, divided

Optional: 1 tablespoon unsweetened cocoa powder

1. Combine the dark rum and coffee powder in small cup, stirring until dissolved.
2. Reserve ½ cup cake mix. Mix the remaining cake mix, melted butter, and 1 egg in a large bowl with electric mixer on medium speed 1 to 2 minutes until blended. Press into prepared pan.
3. Mix the ricotta cheese, condensed milk, and rum-coffee mixture in a large bowl with electric mixer on medium speed for 1 minute until blended. Mix in the reserved ½ cup cake mix and remaining 3 eggs on medium speed for 1 to 2 minutes until blended. Stir in the toffee bits with a wooden spoon. Spread evenly over prepared crust.
4. Bake 45 to 50 minutes or until center is just barely set when pan is jiggled (do not overbake). Transfer to wire rack and cool completely. Chill at least 4 hours or overnight. If desired, dust bars with cocoa powder. Cut into bars.

TOASTED ALMOND BUTTERMILK BARS

The toasted almonds are a delicious, crunchy counterpoint to the creamy buttermilk custard in these home-style bars.

PREHEAT OVEN TO 350°F

MAKES 3 DOZEN BARS

15 x 10 x 1-INCH BAKING PAN, GREASED OR
LINED WITH FOIL (SEE PAGE 16)

1 (18.25-ounce) package white cake mix

½ cup (1 stick) butter, softened

1 (3-ounce) package cream cheese, softened

2 cups packed light brown sugar

1½ cups buttermilk (not nonfat)

4 large eggs

½ cup (1 stick) butter, melted

⅓ cup all-purpose flour

2 teaspoons vanilla extract

2 cups sliced almonds

1 to 2 tablespoons confectioners' sugar

1. Mix the cake mix, softened butter, and cream cheese in a large bowl. Blend with electric mixer on low speed 1 to 2 minutes until blended and crumbly in texture. Press into prepared pan and bake 10 minutes.
2. Meanwhile, place the brown sugar, buttermilk, eggs, melted butter, flour, and vanilla extract in a large bowl and mix with electric mixer on low speed until blended. Stir in the almonds. Pour mixture over partially baked crust.
3. Bake 25 to 28 minutes or until golden brown and firm to the touch. Transfer to wire rack and cool completely before cutting into squares. Dust cooled squares with confectioners' sugar.

TOFFEE CHEESECAKE STREUSEL BARS

I do not trust myself alone with these bars. Loaded with brown sugar, cream cheese, and toffee, they are everything a favorite bar cookie should be: simple to make and splendid to eat.

PREHEAT OVEN TO 350°F

MAKES 3 DOZEN BARS

13 x 9-INCH BAKING PAN, GREASED OR LINED WITH FOIL (SEE PAGE 16)

1 (18.25-ounce) package white cake mix

¾ cup packed light brown sugar, divided

1 cup (2 sticks) butter, melted

2¼ cups quick-cooking oats

2 (8-ounce) packages cream cheese, softened

2 large eggs

1 teaspoon vanilla extract

1 cup toffee baking bits, divided

1. Mix the cake mix, ¼ cup dark brown sugar, and melted butter in a large bowl. Blend for 1 to 2 minutes with electric mixer on medium speed until smooth. Stir in the oats. Press half of mixture evenly into prepared pan.

2. Beat the cream cheese and remaining ½ cup brown sugar in a large bowl with electric mixer on high speed 1 to 2 minutes until smooth. Add the eggs and vanilla, beating on medium speed until just blended. Stir in ½ cup toffee bits. Spoon and spread the cream cheese mixture over base layer. Sprinkle the remaining toffee bits and remaining crumb mixture over cream cheese layer, pressing down gently.

3. Bake 30 to 34 minutes or until topping is golden and firm to the touch. Transfer to wire rack and cool completely. Chill at least 2 hours before serving. Cut into bars.

MOCHA-CAPPUCCINO CHEESECAKE BARS

As luscious proof that decadent desserts can be quick and easy too, these delectable coffee-chocolate treats come together in no time. A chocolate lover's delight, they will satisfy even the most intense chocolate cravings.

PREHEAT OVEN TO 350°F

MAKES 3 DOZEN BARS

13 x 9-INCH BAKING PAN, GREASED OR LINED
   WITH FOIL (SEE PAGE 16)

1 (18.25-ounce) package chocolate cake mix

½ cup (1 stick) butter, melted

3 large eggs

2 (8-ounce) packages cream cheese, softened

¾ cup confectioners' sugar, divided

1½ tablespoons instant coffee powder, dissolved in 1 tablespoon water

1 (16-ounce) container (2 cups) sour cream (not reduced fat)

1. Mix the cake mix, butter, and 1 egg with electric mixer on low speed until blended. Press into prepared pan. Bake 10 minutes.
2. Beat the cream cheese and ½ cup of the confectioners' sugar in large bowl with electric mixer on high speed until blended and smooth. Add the remaining 2 eggs mixing on medium-low speed until just blended. Spread over hot crust.
3. Bake 22 to 25 minutes or until center is just barely set when pan is jiggled (do not overbake).
4. Whisk the sour cream and remaining ¼ cup confectioners' sugar in a medium bowl until smooth. Spread evenly over bars. Return bars to oven for 5 minutes. Transfer to wire rack and cool completely. Chill at least 4 hours or overnight. Cut into bars.

VIENNESE ALMOND TEACAKES

Cake Mix
WHITE

My favorite coffeehouse back home in Berkeley, California, serves a moist, dense almond cake that I love. This very easy version comes very close to replicating the original. An added bonus is that these bars keep and travel extremely well. The almond filling (not to be confused with almond paste or marzipan) can be found in the baking section of most supermarkets, alongside the fruit pie fillings.

PREHEAT OVEN TO 350°F

MAKES 3 DOZEN BARS

13 x 9-INCH BAKING PAN, GREASED OR LINED
   WITH FOIL (SEE PAGE 16)

1 (18.25-ounce) package white cake mix

1 (12.5-ounce) can almond filling

⅓ cup butter, melted

2 large eggs

1 to 2 tablespoons confectioners' sugar

1. Mix the cake mix, almond filling, melted butter, and eggs in a large bowl with electric mixer on medium-high speed for 1 to 2 minutes until blended. Press into prepared pan.
2. Bake 22 to 25 minutes or until just set at center. Transfer to wire rack and cool completely. Cut into bars. Dust with confectioners' sugar.

VARIATION *for Viennese Almond Teacakes*

CHOCOLATE, CHOCOLATE CHIP, AND ALMOND TEACAKES: Prepare as directed but use a chocolate cake mix and add 1 cup miniature semisweet chocolate chips to the dough.

CHOCOLATE CARAMEL BARS

Cake Mix
CHOCOLATE

A voluptuous combination of caramel and chocolate comprise these mouthwatering brownies. Share them—it's certain they will create countless new friendships and memories.

PREHEAT OVEN TO 350°F

MAKES 3 DOZEN BARS

13 x 9-INCH BAKING PAN, GREASED OR LINED
   WITH FOIL (SEE PAGE 16)

1 (18.25-ounce) package chocolate cake mix

1 (5-ounce) can (⅔ cup) evaporated milk,
   divided

½ cup (1 stick) butter, melted

1 (14-ounce) bag caramels, unwrapped

1½ cups semisweet chocolate chips

1 cup chopped pecans or walnuts

1. Place the cake mix, ⅓ cup milk, and melted butter in a large bowl. Blend with electric mixer on medium speed 1 to 2 minutes until blended (dough will be thick). Press half of the dough into prepared pan. Bake 10 minutes.
2. Meanwhile, melt the caramels with remaining ⅓ cup milk in small saucepan over low heat, stirring constantly. Sprinkle the chocolate chips over partially baked crust; drizzle with caramel mixture. Sprinkle with nuts, then drop remaining dough by heaping spoonfuls over caramel mixture.
3. Bake 17 to 20 minutes longer or until topping is crisp-looking. Transfer to wire rack and cool completely. Cut into bars.

Cake Mix
WHITE

CANDIED GINGER BARS

A great last-minute choice for Christmas cookie giving—everyone will ask for the recipe (you're welcome to share it)!

PREHEAT OVEN TO 350°F
MAKES 3 DOZEN BARS
13 x 9-INCH BAKING PAN, GREASED OR LINED
    WITH FOIL (SEE PAGE 16)

1 (18.25-ounce) package white cake mix
½ cup (1 stick) butter, melted
¼ cup packed light brown sugar
2 large eggs
2 teaspoons ground ginger
½ cup finely chopped crystallized ginger

1. Mix the cake mix, melted butter, brown sugar, eggs, and ground ginger in a large bowl with a wooden spoon until blended. Stir in the crystallized ginger. Press dough in pan with moistened fingers.
2. Bake 18 to 23 minutes or until edges are light golden brown. Transfer to wire rack and cool completely. Cut into bars.

HERMIT BARS

Hermit cookies are a New England classic, redolent with spices and rich with brown sugar and dried fruit. They are made even easier here with the help of a cake mix and by making them in bar cookie form.

PREHEAT OVEN TO 350°F

MAKES 3 DOZEN BARS

13 x 9-INCH BAKING PAN, GREASED OR LINED WITH FOIL (SEE PAGE 16)

1 (18.25-ounce) package spice cake mix

½ cup (1 stick) butter, melted

¼ cup packed light brown sugar

2 large eggs

2 teaspoons ground ginger

1½ teaspoons ground cinnamon

½ teaspoon ground cloves

1 cup raisins or chopped dates

1. Mix the cake mix, melted butter, brown sugar, eggs, ginger, cinnamon, and cloves in a large bowl with a wooden spoon until blended. Stir in the raisins or dates. Press dough in pan with moistened fingers.
2. Bake 18 to 23 minutes or until edges are light golden brown. Transfer to wire rack and cool completely. Cut into bars.

HONEY-FIG BARS

Honey and figs have been a favorite since Ancient Greek times. But here they are thoroughly modern in a sophisticated cookie that is further enhanced with a bright lemon glaze.

PREHEAT OVEN TO 350°F

MAKES 3 DOZEN BARS

13 x 9-INCH BAKING PAN, GREASED OR LINED WITH FOIL (SEE PAGE 16)

8 ounces dried figs, stems removed

1 (18.25-ounce) package spice cake mix

½ cup (1 stick) butter, melted

¼ cup honey

2 large eggs

2 teaspoons finely grated lemon peel

Icing

2 cups confectioners' sugar

2 tablespoons lemon juice

1. Place the figs in a small bowl. Add enough boiling water to cover. Let stand 10 minutes, then drain and chop.
2. Mix the cake mix, melted butter, honey, eggs, and lemon peel in a large bowl with a wooden spoon until blended. Stir in the drained figs. Press dough in prepared pan.
3. Bake 19 to 24 minutes or until edges are light golden brown. Transfer to wire rack and cool completely.
4. Mix the confectioners' sugar and lemon juice in a small bowl until blended. Drizzle or spread icing over cooled bars. Cut into bars.

Cake Mix WHITE
STRAWBERRY AND WHITE CHOCOLATE BARS

A stunning bar cookie that will fast become a fail-safe option for any event. You can change out the strawberry jam for any flavor of jam or preserves, such as raspberry, blackberry, or blueberry, or orange marmalade.

PREHEAT OVEN TO 350°F
MAKES 3 DOZEN BARS
13 x 9-INCH BAKING PAN, GREASED OR LINED
    WITH FOIL (SEE PAGE 16)

1 (18.25-ounce) package white cake mix
½ cup (1 stick) butter, softened
2 large eggs
1 cup strawberry jam
1 (8-ounce) package cream cheese, softened
2 tablespoons whole or lowfat milk
1 (11-ounce) package white chocolate chips

1. Mix the cake mix, butter, and eggs in a large bowl with a wooden spoon until blended. Press into prepared pan.
2. Bake 15 to 20 minutes or until edges are golden brown and a toothpick inserted in center comes out clean. Cool 5 minutes on wire rack. Spread evenly with the jam. Cool 30 minutes.
3. Beat the cream cheese and milk in a medium bowl with electric mixer on medium speed until smooth.
4. Microwave the chocolate chips in a medium microwaveable bowl on High 60 to 90 seconds, stirring after 30 seconds, until melted and smooth. Add the warm melted white chocolate to cream cheese mixture. Beat on medium speed until creamy (mixture may look slightly curdled). Carefully spread over jam. Refrigerate at least 2 hours or until set. Cut into bars.

CARAMEL-MOCHA LATTE BARS

The rich flavors of coffee, caramel, and chocolate, with discreet undertones of vanilla.

PREHEAT OVEN TO 350°F

MAKES 3 DOZEN BARS

13 x 9-INCH BAKING PAN, GREASED OR LINED
WITH FOIL (SEE PAGE 16)

1 (18.25-ounce) package vanilla cake mix

¾ cup (1½ sticks) butter, softened

1 large egg

2 cups quick-cooking or old-fashioned oats

1 (14-ounce) package caramels, unwrapped

¼ cup whole or lowfat milk

1½ tablespoons instant coffee powder

1 cup milk chocolate chips

½ cup chopped pecans

1. Mix the cake mix, butter, and egg in a large bowl with electric mixer on low speed 1 to 2 minutes until blended. Stir in the oats with a wooden spoon. Reserve 1½ cups crumb mixture. Press remaining mixture into pan.
2. Melt the caramels, milk, and coffee powder in a medium saucepan set over medium-low heat, stirring frequently, until melted. Pour over crust in pan. Sprinkle with the chocolate chips and pecans. Sprinkle reserved cake mixture over top.
3. Bake 22 to 28 minutes until caramel bubbles along edges and topping appears crisp and dry. Transfer to wire rack and cool completely. Cut into bars.

APPLE BUTTER CRUMB BARS

Old-fashioned and fruity, and especially delicious in the fall and winter, these bars are winners with adults and children alike. They also travel well, making them good lunch box and picnic fare.

PREHEAT OVEN TO 350°F

MAKES 3 DOZEN BARS

13 x 9-INCH BAKING PAN, GREASED OR LINED
WITH FOIL (SEE PAGE 16)

1 (18.25-ounce) package white cake mix

¾ cup (1½ sticks) butter, melted

1 large egg

1 teaspoon ground cinnamon

2 cups quick-cooking or old-fashioned oats

1 (16-ounce) jar apple butter

½ cup chopped pecans

1. Mix the cake mix, melted butter, egg, and cinnamon in a large bowl with a wooden spoon until blended. Stir in the oats (mixture will be crumbly). Reserve 1½ cups of crumb mixture. Press remaining mixture into prepared pan.
2. Spoon and spread the apple butter over crust. Add the pecans to the reserved cake mix mixture and sprinkle evenly over apple butter.
3. Bake 30 to 35 minutes or until topping is golden. Transfer to wire rack and cool completely. Cut into bars.

CHOCOLATE CREAM CHEESE BARS

Chocolate flavor is well suited to these rich, cheesecake-like bars. Take care not to overbake them; the cheese filling should remain creamy.

PREHEAT OVEN TO 325°F

MAKES 3 DOZEN BARS

15 x 10 x 1-INCH BAKING PAN, GREASED OR LINED WITH FOIL (SEE PAGE 16)

1 (18.25-ounce) package chocolate cake mix

½ cup (1 stick) butter, softened

2 (8-ounce) packages cream cheese, softened

1 (16-ounce) tub ready-to-spread chocolate frosting

3 large eggs

1. Mix the cake mix and butter in a large bowl with electric mixer on medium speed 1 to 2 minutes until blended and crumbly. Reserve 1 cup of mixture. Press remaining mixture into prepared pan.
2. Beat the cream cheese and frosting in a medium bowl with electric mixer 1 to 2 minutes on high speed until smooth. Beat in the eggs until blended. Spread over crust and sprinkle with reserved cake mix mixture.
3. Bake 40 to 45 minutes or until just set. Transfer to wire rack and cool completely. Cut into bars. Cut into bars.

VARIATION *for Chocolate Cream Cheese Bars*

VANILLA CREAM CHEESE BARS: Prepare as directed, but use a vanilla cake mix and vanilla frosting.

SOUTHERN SWEET POTATO BARS

I love to make these bars at Thanksgiving time. Even die-hard pumpkin pie fans tend to make them their first pick at the holiday dessert table.

PREHEAT OVEN TO 350°F

MAKES 3 DOZEN BARS

13 x 9-INCH BAKING PAN, GREASED OR LINED
   WITH FOIL (SEE PAGE 16)

1 (18.25-ounce) package yellow cake mix

½ cup (1 stick) butter, softened

2 large eggs

1 (15-ounce) can sweet potatoes, drained

1 (8-ounce) package cream cheese, softened

2 teaspoons pumpkin pie spice

¾ cup sugar, divided

1 cup sour cream

½ teaspoon vanilla extract

1. Mix the cake mix, butter, and 1 egg in a large bowl with electric mixer 1 to 2 minutes on low speed until crumbly. Press evenly into prepared pan.
2. Blend the sweet potatoes, cream cheese, pumpkin pie spice, ½ cup sugar, and remaining egg in a food processor until smooth. Spread evenly over crust.
3. Bake 34 to 36 minutes or until filling is just set.
4. While cheesecake bakes, whisk the sour cream, remaining ¼ cup sugar, and vanilla in a small bowl. Spread over hot bars and return to oven.
5. Bake 5 minutes longer. Transfer to wire rack and cool completely. Chill at least 3 hours before serving. Cut into bars.

PISTACHIO-LEMON BARS

This recipe carries a double dose of lemon: grated peel and fresh lemon juice in both the crust and the filling. The pistachios add buttery flavor and texture—as well as beautiful green color.

PREHEAT OVEN TO 350°F

MAKES 3 DOZEN BARS

13 x 9-INCH BAKING PAN, GREASED OR LINED
   WITH FOIL (SEE PAGE 16)

1 (18.25-ounce) package lemon cake mix

3 large eggs

4 tablespoons butter, melted, divided

¾ cup fresh lemon juice, divided

4 large egg yolks

1 (14-ounce) can sweetened condensed
   milk (not evaporated)

½ cup lightly salted shelled pistachios,
   coarsely chopped

1. Reserve ¾ cup cake mix. Mix the remaining cake mix, 1 egg, 2 tablespoons melted butter, and 2 tablespoons lemon juice until coarse crumbs form. Press into prepared pan. Bake 15 minutes.
2. Whisk the remaining 2 eggs in a medium bowl until blended. Whisk in the condensed milk and remaining lemon juice until blended. Spread over crust.
3. Combine the reserved ¾ cup cake mix and pistachios in a small bowl. Mix in the remaining 2 tablespoons butter until coarse crumbs form. Sprinkle mixture evenly with pistachio mixture.
4. Bake 15 to 18 minutes until filling is just set. Transfer to wire rack and cool completely. Cut into bars.

CHOCOLATE-COVERED RAISIN BARS

Here I've transformed my favorite movie theater candy choice into an oh-so-easy, buttery bar cookie.

PREHEAT OVEN TO 350°F

MAKES 3 DOZEN BARS

13 x 9-INCH BAKING PAN, GREASED OR LINED
   WITH FOIL (SEE PAGE 16)

1 (18.25-ounce) package white cake mix

¾ cup packed light brown sugar

¾ cup (1½ stick) butter, melted

2 large eggs

1 teaspoon vanilla extract

1½ cups raisins

1½ cups semisweet chocolate chips

1. Mix the cake mix, brown sugar, melted butter, eggs, and vanilla in a large bowl with electric mixer on medium speed 1 to 2 minutes until blended. Stir in the raisins and chocolate chips. Press into prepared pan.
2. Bake 35 to 40 minutes until edges are golden brown and center is just set. Transfer to wire rack and cool completely. Cut into bars.

FLUFFERNUT BARS

Peanut butter and toasted marshmallows on a peanut-y cookie crust? Hello, delicious.

PREHEAT OVEN TO 350°F

MAKES 3 DOZEN BARS

13 x 9-INCH BAKING PAN, GREASED OR LINED
   WITH FOIL (SEE PAGE 16)

1 (18.25-ounce) package yellow cake mix

½ cup (1 stick) butter, melted

⅓ cup whole or lowfat milk

¼ cup packed brown sugar

2 large eggs

1 cup chopped dry-roasted peanuts

1 cup creamy peanut butter

3 cups miniature marshmallows

1. Mix the cake mix, melted butter, milk, brown sugar, and eggs in a large bowl with a wooden spoon until blended. Stir in the peanuts. Press into prepared pan. Bake 20 minutes.

2. Microwave the peanut butter in a small microwaveable bowl for 15 to 30 seconds until melted. Drizzle over partially baked bars in pan, then sprinkle with the marshmallows.

3. Bake 10 to 12 minutes longer or until marshmallows are puffed and golden. Transfer to wire rack and cool completely. Cut into bars.

Cake Mix WHITE — TANGERINE BARS

Tangerines are slightly tarter than oranges, making them a fine choice to contrast with a butter cookie crust.

PREHEAT OVEN TO 350°F

MAKES 3 DOZEN BARS

13 x 9-INCH BAKING PAN, GREASED OR LINED WITH FOIL (SEE PAGE 16)

1 (18.25-ounce) package white cake mix

½ cup (1 stick) butter, melted

3 large eggs

1 tablespoon grated tangerine or orange peel

2 cups graham cracker crumbs

1 (14-ounce) can sweetened condensed milk (not evaporated)

⅔ cup tangerine or orange juice

1. Mix the cake mix, melted butter, 1 egg, and tangerine peel in a large bowl with electric mixer on medium speed until blended and crumbly. Mix in the graham cracker crumbs with a wooden spoon. Reserve 2 cups crumb mixture. Press remaining crumb mixture into prepared pan. Bake 15 minutes.

2. Whisk the sweetened condensed milk, tangerine juice, and remaining 2 eggs in a medium bowl until blended and smooth. Spread evenly over prepared crust. Sprinkle with reserved crumb mixture.

3. Bake 16 to 20 minutes longer until golden and filling is just barely set (it will form as it cools). Transfer to wire rack and cool completely. Chill at least 2 hours before serving. Cut into bars.

SALTY-SWEET MIXED NUT BARS

The combination of brown sugar and butter is my sweet-tooth nirvana. I've taken the pairing to new heights in this easy, salty sweet bar cookie. Choose a deluxe nut blend (that is, peanut-free) for the best flavor here.

PREHEAT OVEN TO 350°F

MAKES 3 DOZEN BARS

13 x 9-INCH BAKING PAN, GREASED OR LINED WITH FOIL (SEE PAGE 16)

1 (18.25-ounce) package white cake mix

1¼ cups (2½ sticks) butter, softened

1 large egg

½ cup packed dark brown sugar

2 cups milk chocolate chips

2 cups lightly salted deluxe mixed nuts, roughly chopped

1. Mix the cake mix, ½ cup (1 stick) butter, and egg in large bowl with electric mixer on medium speed until blended and crumbly. Press into prepared pan. Bake 15 minutes.
2. Meanwhile, cook and stir the brown sugar and remaining ¾ cup (1½ sticks) butter in a small saucepan set over medium heat 4 to 5 minutes until brown sugar is melted and mixture is bubbly.
3. Sprinkle the partially baked crust with chocolate chips and nuts. Pour brown sugar mixture evenly over all.
4. Bake 15 minutes longer. Transfer to wire rack and cool completely. Cut into bars.

ITALIAN CHOCOLATE-HAZELNUT BARS

These rich chocolate bars—studded with chips and nuts—offer an astonishing abundance of tastiness.

PREHEAT OVEN TO 350°F

MAKES 3 DOZEN BARS

13 x 9-INCH BAKING PAN, GREASED OR LINED WITH FOIL (SEE PAGE 16)

1 (18.25-ounce) package chocolate cake mix

½ cup (1 stick) butter, softened

1 large egg

1 cup chopped hazelnuts

1 cup miniature semisweet chocolate chips

1 (13-ounce) jar chocolate-hazelnut spread (e.g., Nutella)

1. Mix the cake mix, butter, and egg in a large bowl with a wooden spoon until blended and crumbly. Press half of dough into prepared pan. Bake 10 minutes.
2. Mix the hazelnuts and chocolate chips into reserved cake mix mixture. Spoon the chocolate-hazelnut spread over warm, partially baked crust. Let stand 1 minute to melt slightly, then evenly spread over crust. Sprinkle with remaining dough.
3. Bake 18 to 21 minutes until just set. Transfer to wire rack and cool completely. Cut into bars.

Cake Mix
YELLOW

TRAIL MIX BARS

Hit the trail in great taste with a few of these yummy bars in tow. Your fellow trekkers will thank you!

PREHEAT OVEN TO 350°F

MAKES 3 DOZEN BARS

13 x 9-INCH BAKING PAN, GREASED OR LINED WITH FOIL (SEE PAGE 16)

1 (18.25-ounce) package yellow cake mix

3 large eggs

½ cup (1 stick) butter, melted

1 cup candy-coated chocolate pieces (e.g., M&Ms)

1 cup salted mixed nuts, roughly chopped

1 cup dried fruit bits

¾ cup quick-cooking oats

1. Mix the cake mix, eggs, and butter in a large bowl with a wooden spoon until blended. Stir in the candy, nuts, dried fruit, and oats. Press into prepared pan.
2. Bake 24 to 27 minutes or until golden brown and just set at center. Transfer to wire rack and cool completely. Cut into bars.

MAPLE-CRANBERRY OAT BARS

The simple addition of sweet maple syrup into buttery dough gives these cookies their signature flavor.

PREHEAT OVEN TO 350°F

MAKES 3 DOZEN BARS

13 x 9-INCH BAKING PAN, GREASED OR LINED WITH FOIL (SEE PAGE 16)

⅔ cup butter

½ cup packed light brown sugar

⅓ cup pure maple syrup

1 (18.25-ounce) package white cake mix

2 cups quick cooking oats

¾ cup dried cranberries

1 large egg

Optional: 1 cup chopped pecans or walnuts

1. Combine the butter, brown sugar, and maple syrup in a small saucepan over medium heat. Bring to a boil and cook for 3 minutes. Remove from heat.
2. Mix the cake mix, oats, cranberries, egg, and (optional) nuts in a large bowl with a wooden spoon until blended. Mix in the brown sugar mixture, stirring until blended.
3. Bake 30 to 35 minutes or until golden brown. Transfer to wire rack and cool completely. Cut into bars.

HONEY BEAR BARS

The floral notes of honey accentuate the toasty flavor of almonds in these sweet bars.

PREHEAT OVEN TO 350°F

MAKES 3 DOZEN BARS

13 x 9-INCH BAKING PAN, GREASED OR LINED WITH FOIL (SEE PAGE 16)

1 (18.25-ounce) package white cake mix

⅓ cup butter, melted

4 large eggs

1 cup honey

⅔ cup packed light brown sugar

1 teaspoon vanilla extract

1 cup sliced almonds

1. Reserve ⅔ cup cake mix. Mix the remaining cake mix, melted butter, and 1 egg in large bowl with a wooden spoon until blended and crumbly. Press into prepared pan. Bake 15 minutes.

2. Mix the honey, brown sugar, vanilla, reserved cake mix, and remaining 3 eggs in a large bowl with electric mixer on medium speed 1 to 2 minutes until blended. Spread mixture over prepared crust. Sprinkle with the almonds.
3. Bake 30 to 35 minutes or until filling is just set. Transfer to wire rack and cool completely. Cut into bars.

Cake Mix
CHOCOLATE

BUCKEYE BARS

The famous Ohio Buckeye candies—peanut butter chocolate heaven—are reinvented here with my easy-to-make bars. Just try to limit yourself to one!

PREHEAT OVEN TO 350°F
MAKES 3 DOZEN BARS
13 x 9-INCH BAKING PAN, GREASED OR LINED
    WITH FOIL (SEE PAGE 16)

1 (18.25-ounce) package chocolate cake mix
½ cup (1 stick) butter, softened
2 large eggs
1 cup roasted, salted peanuts, coarsely chopped
1 (14-ounce) can sweetened condensed milk (not evaporated)
⅔ cup creamy peanut butter

1. Mix the cake mix, butter, and eggs in a large bowl with a wooden spoon until blended and crumbly. Stir in the peanuts. Press half the dough into prepared pan.
2. Whisk the sweetened condensed milk and peanut butter in a medium bowl until smooth. Spread peanut butter mixture evenly over prepared crust. Crumble remaining dough on top of peanut butter mixture.
3. Bake 25 to 30 minutes until top is set and edges are lightly browned. Transfer to wire rack and cool completely. Cut into bars.

COCONUT-CREAM BARS

The rich, indulgent flavor of these coconut bars belies their short list of ingredients.

PREHEAT OVEN TO 350°F

MAKES 3 DOZEN BARS

13 x 9-INCH BAKING PAN, GREASED OR LINED WITH FOIL (SEE PAGE 16)

1 (18.25-ounce) package white cake mix

4 large eggs

¾ cup (1½ sticks) butter, melted, divided

1 (8-ounce) container sour cream (not reduced fat)

1½ cups sweetened flake coconut

1 cup white chocolate chips

1. Reserve 1 cup cake mix. Mix the remaining cake mix, 1 egg, and ¼ cup (½ stick) melted butter in a large bowl. Blend for 1 to 2 minutes with electric mixer on low speed until blended. Press mixture into prepared pan.
2. Mix the sour cream, reserved cake mix, remaining 3 eggs, and remaining ½ cup (1 stick) melted butter in medium bowl with electric mixer on low speed 1 to 2 minutes until blended. Stir in the coconut and white chocolate chips. Pour over prepared crust.
3. Bake 35 to 38 minutes, until just set. Transfer to wire rack and cool completely. Cut into bars.

MARGARITA BARS

Spoil the over-twenty-one set at your next cookout with these intensely flavored cocktail cookies— spiked with tequila, lime, and orange—made expressly for them.

PREHEAT OVEN TO 350°F

MAKES 3 DOZEN BARS

13 x 9-INCH BAKING PAN, GREASED OR LINED WITH FOIL (SEE PAGE 16)

1 (18.25-ounce) package white cake mix

4 large eggs

¾ cup (1½ sticks) butter, melted, divided

1 (8-ounce) container sour cream (not reduced fat)

3 tablespoons tequila

2 tablespoons lime juice

1 teaspoon grated orange peel

1. Reserve 1 cup cake mix. Mix the remaining cake mix, 1 egg, and ¼ cup (½ stick) melted butter

in a large bowl. Blend for 1 to 2 minutes with electric mixer on low speed until blended. Press mixture into prepared pan.

2. Mix the sour cream, remaining ½ cup (1 stick) melted butter, remaining 3 eggs, reserved cake mix, tequila, lime juice, and orange peel in medium bowl with electric mixer on low speed 1 to 2 minutes until blended. Pour over prepared crust.

3. Bake 35 to 38 minutes, until just set. Transfer to wire rack and cool completely. Cut into bars.

VARIATION *for Margarita Bars*

BOURBON BARS: Prepare as directed but use a caramel cake mix, replace tequila and lime juice with ⅓ cup bourbon or whiskey, and replace orange peel with 1 teaspoon vanilla extract.

Cake Mix
WHITE

WHITE CHOCOLATE CANDY CANE BARS

Got leftover candy canes? Then you've got good reason to make these bars. Part cookie, part cream, part candy, they are guaranteed pleasers for kids of every age.

PREHEAT OVEN TO 350°F

MAKES 3 DOZEN BARS

13 x 9-INCH BAKING PAN, GREASED OR LINED WITH FOIL (SEE PAGE 16)

1 (18.25-ounce) package white cake mix

4 large eggs

¾ cup (1½ sticks) butter, melted, divided

1 cup sour cream (not reduced fat)

1½ cups white chocolate chips

1 cup crushed peppermint candy canes or red and white-striped peppermint candies

1. Reserve 1 cup cake mix. Mix the remaining cake mix, 1 egg, and ¼ cup (½ stick) melted butter in a large bowl. Blend for 1 to 2 minutes with electric mixer on low speed until blended. Press mixture into prepared pan.

2. Mix the sour cream, reserved cake mix, remaining 3 eggs, and remaining ½ cup (1 stick) melted butter in medium bowl with electric mixer on low speed 1 to 2 minutes until blended. Stir in the white chocolate chips and crushed peppermint candy. Pour over prepared crust.

3. Bake 35 to 38 minutes, until just set. Transfer to wire rack and cool completely. Cut into bars.

Tip: To easily crush the candy canes, place the wrapped canes in a large, heavy-duty zipper-top bag. Close bag, pressing out extra air, then pound with a mallet or rolling pin. Open the bag and remove the candy cane wrappers.

ITALIAN RICOTTA CHEESECAKE BARS

For anyone who loves Italian cheesecake—rich with ricotta, Marsala or dark rum, and golden raisins or chocolate—these bars offer the perfect combination, but in an easy-to-make, handheld form.

PREHEAT OVEN TO 350°F

MAKES 3 DOZEN BARS

13 x 9-INCH BAKING PAN, GREASED OR LINED WITH FOIL (SEE PAGE 16)

1 (18.25-ounce) package white cake mix, divided

¼ cup (½ stick) butter, melted

4 large eggs

1 (16-ounce) container (2 cups) ricotta cheese

1 (14-ounce) can sweetened condensed milk (not evaporated)

¼ cup Marsala or dark rum

1 cup golden raisins or miniature semisweet chocolate chips

1. Reserve ½ cup cake mix. Mix the remaining cake mix, melted butter, and 1 egg in a large bowl with electric mixer on medium speed 1 to 2 minutes until blended. Press into prepared pan.
2. Mix the ricotta cheese, condensed milk, and Marsala or rum in a large bowl with electric mixer on medium speed for 1 minute until blended. Mix in the reserved ½ cup cake mix and remaining 3 eggs on medium speed for 1 to 2 minutes until blended. Stir in the raisins with a wooden spoon. Spread evenly over prepared crust.
3. Bake 45 to 50 minutes or until center is just barely set when pan is jiggled (do not overbake). Transfer to wire rack and cool completely. Chill at least 4 hours or overnight. Cut into bars.

CANNOLI BARS

Cannoli are Sicilian pastries that have become an Italian-American classic. Cannoli means "little tubes," which aptly describes the cone or tube pastries that are filled with a ricotta cheese mixture, sweetened with candied fruits, pistachios, or chocolate. These bars capture both the flavor and spirit of the favorite dessert.

PREHEAT OVEN TO 350°F

MAKES 3 DOZEN BARS

13 x 9-INCH BAKING PAN, GREASED OR LINED WITH FOIL (SEE PAGE 16)

1 (18.25-ounce) package white cake mix, divided

¼ cup (½ stick) butter, melted

4 large eggs

1 (16-ounce) container (2 cups) ricotta cheese

1 (14-ounce) can sweetened condensed milk (not evaporated)

1½ teaspoons almond extract

1½ cups miniature semisweet chocolate chips

1 cup roasted, lightly salted shelled pistachios, chopped

1. Reserve ½ cup cake mix. Mix the remaining cake mix, melted butter, and 1 egg in a large bowl with electric mixer on medium speed 1 to 2 minutes until blended. Press into prepared pan.
2. Mix the ricotta cheese, condensed milk, and almond extract in a large bowl with electric mixer on medium speed for 1 minute until blended. Mix in the reserved ½ cup cake mix and remaining 3 eggs on medium speed for 1 to 2 minutes until blended. Stir in the chocolate chips and pistachios with a wooden spoon. Spread evenly over prepared crust.
3. Bake 45 to 50 minutes or until center is just barely set when pan is jiggled (do not overbake). Transfer to wire rack and cool completely. Chill at least 4 hours or overnight. Cut into bars.

Cake Mix
LEMON

LEMON-RICOTTA BARS

These creamy, cheesecake-like bars have a sweet-tangy zing from both fresh lemon juice and lemon cake mix.

PREHEAT OVEN TO 350°F

MAKES 3 DOZEN BARS

13 x 9-INCH BAKING PAN, GREASED OR LINED WITH FOIL (SEE PAGE 16)

1 (18.25-ounce) package lemon cake mix, divided

¼ cup (½ stick) butter, melted

4 large eggs

1 (16-ounce) container (2 cups) ricotta cheese

1 (14-ounce) can sweetened condensed milk (not evaporated)

⅓ cup lemon juice

1. Reserve ½ cup cake mix. Mix the remaining cake mix, melted butter, and 1 egg in a large bowl with electric mixer on medium speed 1 to 2 minutes until blended. Press into prepared pan.
2. Mix the ricotta cheese, condensed milk, and lemon juice in a large bowl with electric mixer on medium speed for 1 minute until blended. Mix in reserved ½ cup cake mix and remaining 3 eggs on medium speed for 1 to 2 minutes until blended. Spread evenly over prepared crust.
3. Bake 45 to 50 minutes or until center is just barely set when pan is jiggled (do not overbake). Transfer to wire rack and cool completely. Chill at least 4 hours or overnight. Cut into bars.

Cake Mix
DEVIL'S FOOD

PEPPERMINT BARK BARS

These indulgent, candy-like bars owe their inspiration to one of my favorite Christmas treats, peppermint bark, a white and dark chocolate confection topped with crushed peppermint candy.

PREHEAT OVEN TO 350°F

MAKES 4 DOZEN BARS

13 x 9-INCH BAKING PAN, GREASED OR LINED WITH FOIL (SEE PAGE 16)

1 (18.25-ounce) package devil's food cake mix

½ cup (1 stick) butter, melted

1 large egg

1 teaspoon peppermint extract

1½ cups semisweet chocolate chips

1½ cups white chocolate chips

1 cup crushed peppermint candy canes or red and white-striped peppermint candies

1. Mix the cake mix, melted butter, egg, and peppermint extract in a large bowl with electric mixer on medium speed until blended. Pat the dough evenly into the prepared pan.
2. Bake 21 to 25 minutes until just set at center. Remove from oven and sprinkle with the semi-sweet chocolate chips, white chocolate chips, and crushed peppermint candies.
3. Bake 5 minutes longer. Transfer to wire rack and cool completely. Cut into small bars.

Cake Mix
WHITE

HAZELNUT BLONDIES

A traditional favorite throughout Europe, chocolate-hazelnut spread is combined here with crunchy hazelnuts and a decadent blondie dough to create an incredible cookie experience.

PREHEAT OVEN TO 350°F

MAKES 3 DOZEN BARS

13 x 9-INCH BAKING PAN, GREASED OR LINED WITH FOIL (SEE PAGE 16)

1 (18.25-ounce) package white cake mix

½ cup (1 stick) butter, melted

¼ cup packed dark brown sugar

2 large eggs

1½ cups chopped hazelnuts, toasted

½ cup chocolate-hazelnut spread (e.g., Nutella)

1. Mix the cake mix, melted butter, brown sugar, and eggs in a large bowl with a wooden spoon until blended. Stir in the hazelnuts. Spread in prepared pan.
2. Dollop top of dough with teaspoonfuls of the chocolate-hazelnut spread. Swirl into dough with tip of kitchen knife (note: the spread will sink further and blend into dough as the blondies bake).
3. Bake 19 to 24 minutes or until edges are light golden brown. Transfer to wire rack and cool completely. Cut into bars.

BITTERSWEET CHOCOLATE-ESPRESSO BARS

Any chocolate hedonist worthy of the title will request seconds—perhaps thirds—of these butter-rich, bittersweet espresso bars.

PREHEAT OVEN TO 350°F

MAKES 3 DOZEN BARS

13 x 9-INCH BAKING PAN, GREASED OR LINED WITH FOIL (SEE PAGE 16)

1 (18.25-ounce) package devil's food cake mix

½ cup (1 stick) butter, melted

¼ cup packed dark brown sugar

2 large eggs

2 teaspoons instant espresso powder or 4 teaspoons instant coffee powder

1 (12-ounce) package bittersweet or semisweet chocolate chips

1. Mix the cake mix, butter, brown sugar, eggs, and espresso powder in a large bowl with a wooden spoon until blended. Stir in the chocolate chips. Press dough in pan with moistened fingers.
2. Bake 18 to 23 minutes or until edges are just set. Transfer to wire rack and cool completely. Cut into bars.

POWER BARS WITH DRIED FRUIT, NUTS, AND FLAX

Leave the expensive power bars on the shelf and whip up a batch of your own at home. You can vary the dried fruits and nuts or seeds to suit your taste or mood—it's impossible to go wrong.

PREHEAT OVEN TO 350°F

MAKES 3 DOZEN BARS

13 x 9-INCH BAKING PAN, GREASED OR LINED WITH FOIL (SEE PAGE 16)

1 (18.25-ounce) package yellow cake mix

½ cup whole wheat flour

½ cup mashed banana (about 1 large banana)

⅓ cup vegetable oil

2 large eggs

3 tablespoons ground flax seeds (flaxseed meal)

2 teaspoons vanilla extract

1½ cups dried cranberries, raisins, or other chopped dried fruit

1½ cups roasted, lightly salted mixed nuts or seeds, coarsely chopped

1. Mix the cake mix, flour, banana, oil, eggs, ground flax seeds, and vanilla in a large bowl with a wooden spoon until blended. Stir in the dried fruit and nuts (dough will be stiff). Press dough in pan with moistened fingers.
2. Bake 18 to 23 minutes or until edges are light golden brown. Transfer to wire rack and cool completely. Cut into bars.

Cake Mix DEVIL'S FOOD
CHOCOLATE-NUT POWER BARS

You won't know (nor will anyone else who eats these bars) that they're packed with good-for-you ingredients, including carrots, flax seeds, and nuts. You'll just be thrilled by the taste.

PREHEAT OVEN TO 350°F

MAKES 3 DOZEN BARS

13 x 9-INCH BAKING PAN, GREASED OR LINED WITH FOIL (SEE PAGE 16)

1 (18.25-ounce) package devil's food cake mix

½ cup ground flax seeds (flaxseed meal)

1 (4-ounce) jar strained carrots baby food

⅓ cup vegetable oil

2 large eggs

2 teaspoons vanilla extract

1½ cups roasted, lightly salted mixed nuts, coarsely chopped

¾ cup miniature semisweet chocolate chips

1. Mix the cake mix, ground flax seeds, baby food, oil, eggs, and vanilla in a large bowl with a wooden spoon until blended. Stir in the nuts and chocolate chips (dough will be stiff). Press dough in pan with moistened fingers.
2. Bake 18 to 23 minutes or until just set at center. Transfer to wire rack and cool completely. Cut into bars.

VEGAN FRUIT AND SEED BARS

Cake Mix
WHITE

Cake mixes aren't just for no-holds-barred treats: they can also be used as a starting point for a great-tasting, nutrition-packed power bar. These are great travelers for trips near and far, and are made entirely from pantry ingredients (i.e., no eggs or dairy products).

PREHEAT OVEN TO 350°F

MAKES 3 DOZEN BARS

13 x 9-INCH BAKING PAN, GREASED OR LINED
   WITH FOIL (SEE PAGE 16)

1 (18.25-ounce) package white cake mix
   (check the label for egg or milk products)

½ cup quick-cooking oats

2 teaspoons ground cinnamon

1 teaspoon baking powder

⅔ cup vegan margarine, melted

⅓ cup applesauce

⅓ cup molasses

1 cup chopped dried fruit (any combination)

1 cup roasted, lightly salted sunflower seeds
   or pepitas (green pumpkin seeds), or a
   combination

1. Whisk the cake mix, oats, cinnamon, and baking powder in a large bowl. Add the melted margarine, applesauce, and molasses, stirring with a wooden spoon until blended. Stir in the dried fruit and seeds. Spread dough in prepared pan.
2. Bake 18 to 23 minutes or until edges are light golden brown. Transfer to wire rack and cool completely. Cut into bars.

228   THE ULTIMATE CAKE MIX COOKIE BOOK

BETWIXT BARS

Inspired by the caramel, cookie, and milk chocolate bar of similar name, these no-holds-barred bars *have a wealth of luscious components.*

PREHEAT OVEN TO 350°F

MAKES 3 DOZEN BARS

13 x 9-INCH BAKING PAN, GREASED OR LINED WITH FOIL (SEE PAGE 16)

1 (18.25-ounce) package white cake mix

⅓ cup butter, melted

2 large eggs

32 caramels, unwrapped

1 (14-ounce) can sweetened condensed milk (not evaporated)

½ cup (1 stick) butter

1½ cups milk chocolate chips

1. Mix the cake mix, melted butter, and eggs in a large bowl with a wooden spoon until blended. Press half of dough into prepared pan. Bake 10 minutes.
2. Meanwhile, melt caramels, condensed milk, and butter in a medium heavy saucepan, stirring over medium-low heat until blended and smooth. Pour evenly over partially baked crust and sprinkle with the milk chocolate chips. Crumble remaining dough over chips.
3. Bake 25 to 28 minutes or until the topping is golden and firm to the touch. Transfer to wire rack. Run knife around edges of pan to loosen and cool completely. Cut into bars.

ALMOND JOYFUL BARS

This variation on a popular candy bar of similar name has the perfect proportion of coconut to milk chocolate. Consider yourself warned, though: they are habit-forming.

PREHEAT OVEN TO 350°F

MAKES 4 DOZEN BARS

15 x 10 x 1-INCH JELLY ROLL PAN, GREASED OR LINED WITH FOIL (SEE PAGE 16)

1 (18.25-ounce) package white cake mix

½ cup (1 stick) butter, melted

1 large egg

4 cups sweetened flake coconut

1 (10-ounce) bag (1¾ cups) milk chocolate chips

1 (14-ounce) can sweetened condensed milk

1 cup sliced almonds

1. Mix the cake mix, melted butter, and egg in large bowl with a wooden spoon until blended. Press into prepared pan. Sprinkle with the coconut and chocolate chips.
2. Drizzle condensed milk evenly over coconut and chocolate chips. Sprinkle with almonds.
3. Bake at 18 to 25 minutes or until light golden brown. Transfer to wire rack and cool completely.

CHAPTER THREE	# formed and filled cookies

Formed and filled cookies encompass an enticing assortment of delectable options, including, but not limited to, hand-shaped classics (such as crinkles, crackles, and balls), biscotti (twice-baked crunchy cookies, perfect with coffee drinks), madeleines (French cookies that are formed and baked in a shell-shaped tin), rolled cut-outs (think ginger people and sugar cookies), sandwich cookies, whoopies (part cake, part cookie, plus frosting), and thumbprints (a cookie and a tart all in one). One thing all of the selections in this chapter share in common is that they're delicious, memorable, and will make any occasion all the more splendid.

FAVORITE CHOCOLATE COOKIES

Cake Mix
CHOCOLATE FUDGE

This may be the recipe you turn to most from this entire collection. I've offered a short list of variations, but you can use any flavor cake mix. The same holds true for the chocolate chips: use any variety of chocolate chips (e.g., white, milk, bittersweet, chocolate-mint), or use an equal amount of flavored baking chips (e.g., cinnamon, peanut butter, butterscotch), toffee bits, crushed candies, dried fruit, or chopped nuts.

PREHEAT OVEN TO 375°F

MAKES 4 DOZEN COOKIES

COOKIE SHEETS, UNGREASED OR LINED WITH
    PARCHMENT PAPER

1 (18.25-ounce) package chocolate fudge
  cake mix

½ cup vegetable oil

2 large eggs

1 cup semisweet chocolate chips

½ cup sugar or 1 cup confectioners' sugar

1. Mix the cake mix, oil, and eggs in large bowl with wooden spoon until blended. Stir in chocolate chips.

2. Place the sugar in small, shallow dish. Shape dough into 1-inch balls, roll in sugar, and place 2 inches apart on ungreased cookie sheet.

3. Bake 9 to 12 minutes or until set around edges. Cool 1 minute on sheets, then remove cookies with spatula to wire racks to cool completely.

VARIATIONS *for Favorite Chocolate Cookies*

FAVORITE MOCHA COOKIES: Prepare as directed, but dissolve 2 teaspoons instant coffee powder in 2 teaspoons water before adding.

FAVORITE VANILLA COOKIES: Prepare as directed, but use a vanilla cake mix and use vanilla baking chips or white chocolate chips.

SNICKERDOODLES

Cake Mix
WHITE

Snickerdoodles, favorite American cookies dating back to nineteenth-century New England, are likely beloved for their whimsical name as much as their old-fashioned good taste. Whatever the case, these cinnamon-spiked, crisp-soft cookies have never been easier to prepare than with a package of cake mix.

PREHEAT OVEN TO 350°F

MAKES 4 DOZEN COOKIES

COOKIE SHEETS, GREASED OR LINED WITH
PARCHMENT PAPER

1 (18.25-ounce) package white cake mix

¼ cup vegetable oil

2 large eggs

¼ teaspoon ground nutmeg

½ cup sugar

2 teaspoons ground cinnamon

1. Mix the cake mix, oil, eggs, and nutmeg in a large bowl with a wooden spoon until blended.
2. Combine the sugar and cinnamon in small, shallow dish. Roll the dough into 1-inch balls, roll in cinnamon sugar, then place 2 inches apart on ungreased cookie sheets.
3. Bake 9 to 12 minutes or until centers are just barely set. Cool 5 minutes on sheets, then remove cookies with spatula to wire racks to cool completely.

WHIPPERSNAPPERS (WHIPPED TOPPING COOKIES)

Cake Mix
ANY FLAVOR

I've often wondered, while making these cookies, who had the strange notion to mix frozen whipped topping into a cake mix to make cookies. Hats off to them, because it was a stroke of genius. Use any variety of cake mix and let the fun begin.

PREHEAT OVEN TO 350°F

MAKES 3 DOZEN COOKIES

COOKIE SHEETS, UNGREASED OR LINED WITH
PARCHMENT PAPER

1 (18.25-ounce) package cake mix, any flavor

2 large eggs

1 (8-ounce) container frozen whipped
topping (e.g., Cool Whip), thawed

1 cup confectioners' sugar

1. Mix the cake mix, thawed whipped topping, and eggs in a large bowl with an electric mixer on medium speed 1 to 2 minutes until blended.
2. Place the confectioners' sugar in small, shallow bowl. Roll the dough into 1-inch balls, roll in confectioners' sugar, then place on ungreased cookie sheets.

3. Bake 9 to 12 minutes or until cookies are puffed and edges are firm. Cool 2 minutes on sheets, then remove cookies with spatula to wire racks to cool completely.

ICED LEMON COOKIES

Whenever I'm in a pinch to bake a dessert for a potluck, after-church coffee hour, or bake sale, I whip up these cookies. A snap to make, their bright lemon flavor and sunny color makes them instant hits with one and all.

PREHEAT OVEN TO 350°F

MAKES 5 DOZEN COOKIES

COOKIE SHEETS, UNGREASED OR LINED WITH PARCHMENT PAPER

1 (18.25-ounce) package lemon cake mix

⅓ cup butter, softened

¼ cup vegetable shortening

1 large egg

3 cups confectioners' sugar

2 tablespoons fresh lemon juice

1. Place the cake mix, butter, shortening, and egg in a large bowl. Blend with an electric mixer on medium speed 1 minute until blended (dough will be stiff).

2. Roll the dough into 1-inch balls and place on ungreased cookie sheets.

3. Bake 9 to 12 minutes or until centers are just set. Cool 1 minute on sheets, then remove cookies with spatula to wire racks to cool completely.

4. Mix the confectioners' sugar and lemon juice in a small bowl with a wooden spoon until smooth. Drizzle or spread icing over cooled cookies.

CREAM CHEESE BUTTONS

If cheesecake were recreated as a butter cookie, this is what it would taste like. In other words, perfect.

PREHEAT OVEN TO 375°F

MAKES 3½ DOZEN COOKIES

COOKIE SHEETS, GREASED OR LINED WITH PARCHMENT PAPER

1 (8-ounce) package cream cheese, softened

¼ cup (1 stick) butter, softened

1 large egg yolk

1 teaspoon vanilla extract

1 (18.25-ounce) package white cake mix

1. Place the cream cheese, butter, egg yolk, and vanilla in large bowl. Beat with an electric mixer on medium-high speed 1 to 2 minutes until light and fluffy. Mix in the cake mix with a wooden spoon until blended.
2. Roll the dough into 1-inch balls and place on prepared cookie sheets.
3. Bake 9 to 12 minutes or until centers are just set. Cool 1 minute on sheets, then remove cookies with spatula to wire racks to cool completely.

VARIATION *for Cream Cheese Buttons*

CHOCOLATE CHIP CREAM CHEESE BUTTONS: Prepare as directed but add ¾ cup miniature semisweet chocolate chips.

SNOW-CAPPED CHOCOLATE CRINKLES

Mayonnaise may sound like an unusual ingredient for cookies, but when you think of its components—eggs and oil—it makes perfect sense. These easy cookies are loved by one and all and are a last-minute saving grace when a batch of cookies is needed in a pinch. They get their "snow-capped" appearance when the confectioners' sugar tops crack as they cool.

PREHEAT OVEN TO 350°F

MAKES 4 DOZEN COOKIES

COOKIE SHEETS, GREASED OR LINED WITH PARCHMENT PAPER

1 (18.25-ounce) package devil's food cake mix

2 (4-serving size) packages cook and stir chocolate pudding mix (not instant)

1¼ cups mayonnaise (not reduced fat)

Optional: 1 cup miniature semisweet chocolate chips

1½ cups confectioners' sugar

1. Mix the cake mix, dry pudding mixes, and mayonnaise in a large bowl with an electric mixer set on medium speed 1 to 2 minutes until blended. Mix in the chocolate chips with a wooden spoon.
2. Place the confectioners' sugar in small, shallow dish. Roll the dough into 1-inch balls, roll in confectioners' sugar, then place 2 inches apart on ungreased cookie sheets.
3. Bake 9 to 10 minutes or until centers are just barely set. Cool 5 minute on sheets, then remove cookies with spatula to wire racks to cool completely.

CRUSHED PEPPERMINT SNOWBALLS

Cake Mix
WHITE

You'll want to stock up on candy canes at the after-Christmas sales so that you can make these easy, but nonetheless amazing, peppermint cookies.

PREHEAT OVEN TO 375°F

MAKES 4 DOZEN COOKIES

COOKIE SHEETS, UNGREASED OR LINED WITH
PARCHMENT PAPER

1 (18.25-ounce) package white cake mix

⅓ cup vegetable shortening

⅓ cup butter, softened

1 large egg

1 crushed peppermint candy canes or red
and white striped peppermint candies

1½ cups confectioners' sugar

1. Place the cake mix, shortening, butter, and egg in large bowl. Beat with electric mixer on medium speed 1 to 2 minutes until blended. Mix in the crushed peppermints with wooden spoon.
2. Shape the dough into 1-inch balls and place 2 inches apart on ungreased cookie sheet.
3. Bake 9 to 12 minutes or until light brown around edges. Cool 1 minute on sheets, then remove with spatula. Place the confectioners' sugar in small bowl and roll warm cookies in the sugar to coat. Place cookies on wire racks to cool completely.

INDIAN-SPICED COCONUT COOKIES

Cake Mix
WHITE

These delicious and slightly exotic Indian-influenced cookies incorporate a blend of coconut and pistachios in a sumptuous butter cookie scented with cardamom and rose water.

PREHEAT OVEN TO 350°F

MAKES 4 DOZEN COOKIES

COOKIE SHEETS, UNGREASED OR LINED WITH
PARCHMENT PAPER

1 (18.25-ounce) package white cake mix

½ cup (½ stick) butter, softened

2 large eggs

1 teaspoon ground cardamom

½ teaspoon rose water

2½ cups sweetened flake coconut, divided

1 cup chopped roasted, lightly salted
shelled pistachios

1. Place the cake mix, butter, eggs, cardamom, and rose water in large bowl. Beat with electric

mixer on medium speed 1 to 2 minutes until blended. Mix in 1¼ cups coconut and the pistachios with a wooden spoon.

2. Place the remaining coconut in a medium, shallow dish. Shape the dough into 1-inch balls, roll in coconut, then place 2 inches apart on ungreased cookie sheet.

3. Bake 10 to 13 minutes or until light brown around edges. Cool 1 minute on sheets, then remove cookies with spatula to wire racks to cool completely.

Cake Mix WHITE — ORANGE-SPICE COOKIES

Orange and spice makes for a favorite cookie when the weather turns cold. A cup of tea and a good book for accompaniments is my idea of a perfect afternoon.

PREHEAT OVEN TO 350°F

MAKES 4 DOZEN COOKIES

COOKIE SHEETS, UNGREASED OR LINED WITH PARCHMENT PAPER

1 (18.25-ounce) package white cake mix

1 (3-ounce) package cream cheese, softened

¼ cup (½ stick) butter, softened

1 large egg

2 tablespoons fresh orange juice

1 tablespoon grated orange peel

1¼ teaspoons pumpkin pie spice, divided

¼ cup granulated sugar

1. Place the cake mix, cream cheese, butter, egg, orange juice, orange peel, and 1 teaspoon pumpkin pie spice in large bowl. Beat with electric mixer on medium speed 1 to 2 minutes until blended.

2. Mix the sugar and remaining ¼ teaspoon pumpkin pie spice in a small, shallow dish. Shape the dough into 1-inch balls, roll in pumpkin spice sugar, then place 2 inches apart on ungreased cookie sheet.

3. Bake 9 to 12 minutes or until light brown around edges. Cool 1 minute on sheets, then remove cookies with spatula to wire racks to cool completely.

CARDAMOM-LIME COOKIES

Inspired by Persian and Indian confections, these cookies highlight the delicate nuances of cardamom in combination with the bright zing of fresh lime.

PREHEAT OVEN TO 375°F

MAKES 4 DOZEN COOKIES

COOKIE SHEETS, UNGREASED OR LINED WITH
   PARCHMENT PAPER

1 (18.25-ounce) package white cake mix

⅓ cup vegetable shortening

¼ cup (½ stick) butter, softened

1 large egg

1 tablespoon grated lime peel

1 teaspoon ground cardamom

1½ cups confectioners' sugar

1. Place the cake mix, shortening, butter, egg, lime peel, and cardamom in large bowl. Beat with electric mixer on medium speed 1 to 2 minutes until blended.
2. Shape the dough into 1-inch balls and place 2 inches apart on ungreased cookie sheet.
3. Bake 9 to 12 minutes or until light brown around edges. Cool 1 minute on sheets, then remove with spatula. Place confectioners' sugar in small bowl and roll warm cookies in the sugar to coat. Place cookies on wire racks to cool completely.

BENNE SEED CRINKLES

"Benne" is the Carolina Low Country word for sesame seeds, which came to the United States from Africa. Because of their high oil content, the seeds begin to turn rancid very easily. For this recipe it is important that they be very fresh. Taste them before adding to the recipe to make sure they are fresh.

PREHEAT OVEN TO 350°F

MAKES 5 DOZEN COOKIES

COOKIE SHEETS, UNGREASED OR LINED WITH
   PARCHMENT PAPER

1 (18.25-ounce) package white cake mix

⅓ cup butter, softened

⅓ cup vegetable shortening

¼ cup packed light brown sugar

1 large egg

1 teaspoon vanilla extract

½ cup sesame seeds

1. Place the cake mix, butter, shortening, brown sugar, egg, and vanilla in a large bowl. Blend with an electric mixer on medium speed 1 to 2 minutes until blended (dough will be stiff).
2. Place the sesame seeds in small, shallow dish. Roll the dough into 1-inch balls, roll in sesame seeds, then place 2 inches apart on ungreased cookie sheets.
3. Bake 9 to 12 minutes or until centers are just set. Cool 1 minute on sheets, then remove cookies with spatula to wire racks to cool completely.

CAKE BALLS

Who would have thought that a box of cake mix, a can of frosting, and some chocolate chips could rise to superstar status? Part candy, part cake, I think these incredible miniatures belong in a cake-mix cookie book, too. They are so darn cute, easy to make, and endlessly variable by changing out the flavors of cake mix, frosting, and chocolate chips. I've made my triple-chocolate version the starting point, but I've followed it up with a slew of variations I know you will love.

MAKES 4 DOZEN CAKE BALLS

13 x 9-INCH BAKING PAN (FOR BAKING CAKE)

COOKIE SHEETS, LINED WITH WAX PAPER

1 (18.25-ounce) package cake mix (any flavor)

1 (16-ounce) tub ready-to-spread frosting (any flavor)

3 cups chocolate chips (semisweet, bittersweet, milk, or white)

1 tablespoon vegetable shortening

1. Prepare and bake the cake mix as directed on package for a 13 x 9-inch cake. Cool completely. Crumble the cooled cake into a large bowl. Add the frosting. With an electric mixer on medium-low speed, mix until blended. Chill 1 hour.
2. Roll the mixture into 1-inch balls (use a cookie scoop for evenly sized balls). Place on an ungreased cookie sheet. Chill 3 to 4 hours until very firm.
3. Line a second cookie sheet with wax paper. Melt the chocolate chips and shortening in a medium bowl in the microwave according to directions on package.
4. Using a candy-dipping fork or kitchen fork, drop balls in melted chocolate to coat. Lift ball from chocolate, tapping off excess, and place on prepared cookie sheet. Repeat with remaining balls. Store, loosely covered, in refrigerator.

VARIATIONS *for Cake Balls*

CAKE MIX POPS: Prepare cake balls as directed. Dip the end of a lollipop stick in the melted chocolate and then insert into each ball (this ensures the stick will stay in). Dip pops in chocolate coating, gently tapping off excess. Place stick-side up on lined cookie sheet and chill as directed.

NOTE: To stand pops upright, place pieces of styrofoam or floral foam on a cookie sheet. Stick the coated pops into the foam so they can stand upright as the coating sets.

RED VELVET CAKE BALLS: Prepare as directed, but use a red velvet cake mix and cream cheese frosting. Use white chocolate chips for the coating. Suggested garnish: sprinkle of red colored sugar.

LEMON CAKE BALLS: Prepare as directed, but use a lemon cake mix and lemon frosting. Add 3 tablespoons fresh lemon juice to the cake mix-frosting mixture. Use white chocolate chips for the coating. Suggested garnish: sprinkle of yellow colored sugar.

PEANUT BUTTER CAKE BALLS: Prepare as directed, but use a yellow cake mix and 1¾ cups creamy or chunky peanut butter. Use white or milk chocolate chips for the coating. Suggested garnish: chopped, roasted, salted peanuts.

PEANUT BUTTER CUP CAKE BALLS: Prepare as directed, but use a chocolate or devil's food cake mix and 1¾ cups creamy or chunky peanut butter. Use semisweet or milk chocolate chips for the coating. Suggested garnish: chopped, roasted, salted peanuts.

CHEESECAKE BALLS: Prepare as directed, but use a vanilla cake mix. In place of the full can of frosting, use half a can of cream cheese frosting plus 1 (8-ounce) package softened cream cheese. Use semisweet, milk, or white chocolate chips for the coating.

MAPLE CAKE BALLS: Prepare as directed, but use a butter pecan cake mix, 1½ cups vanilla frosting, and ⅓ cup pure maple syrup. Use white chocolate chips for the coating. Suggested garnish: finely chopped toasted pecans.

GERMAN CHOCOLATE CAKE BALLS: Prepare as directed, but use a German chocolate cake mix and coconut pecan frosting. Use milk chocolate chips for the coating. Suggested garnish: toasted coconut.

BERRIES-AND-CREAM CAKE BALLS: Prepare as directed, but use a white cake mix. In place of the full can of frosting, use half of a can of vanilla frosting plus 1 cup seedless raspberry jam. Use white chocolate chips for the coating. Suggested garnish: pink sprinkles or pink colored sugar.

CINNAMON ROLL CAKE BALLS: Prepare as directed, but use a yellow cake mix and vanilla frosting. Add 2 teaspoons ground cinnamon and ¼ cup packed dark brown sugar to the cake-frosting mixture. Use white chocolate chips for the coating. Suggested garnish: sprinkle of ground cinnamon.

CHOCOLATE CHIP COOKIE CAKE BALLS: Prepare as directed, but use a yellow cake mix and caramel frosting. Add ¾ cup miniature chocolate chips to the cake-frosting mixture. Use semisweet chocolate chips for the coating.

WEDDING CAKE BALLS: Prepare as directed, but use a white cake mix and cream cheese or white frosting. Add 1 teaspoon almond extract to the cake mix-frosting mixture. Use white chocolate chips for the coating. Suggested garnishes: white sprinkles, edible glitter, silver dragees, or candied flowers.

ITALIAN CHOCOLATE-HAZELNUT CAKE BALLS: Prepare as directed, but use a devil's food cake mix and a 13-ounce jar chocolate-hazelnut spread (e.g., Nutella) in place of frosting. Use semisweet chocolate chips for the coating. Suggested garnish: toasted chopped hazelnuts.

ENGLISH TOFFEE CAKE BALLS: Prepare as directed, but use a vanilla cake mix and vanilla frosting. Add 1 cup toffee baking bits to the cake-frosting mixture. Use milk chocolate chips for the coating. Suggested garnish: toffee baking bits.

BIRTHDAY CAKE BALLS: Prepare as directed, but use a yellow cake mix and vanilla frosting. Use semisweet chocolate chips for the coating. Suggested garnish: multicolored sprinkles.

CANDY CANE CAKE BALLS: Prepare as directed, but use a vanilla cake mix and vanilla frosting. Add 1 cup crushed candy canes to the cake-frosting mixture. Use semisweet, milk, or white chocolate chips for the coating. Suggested garnish: crushed candy canes.

MOCHA CAKE BALLS: Prepare as directed, but use a vanilla cake mix and chocolate frosting. Dissolve 1 tablespoon espresso powder in 1 tablespoon hot water, and then add to the cake-frosting mixture. Use semisweet or milk chocolate chips for the coating. Suggested garnish: sprinkle of ground cinnamon, unsweetened cocoa powder, or chocolate sprinkles.

CAPPUCCINO CAKE BALLS: Prepare as directed, but use a vanilla cake mix and vanilla frosting. Dissolve 1 tablespoon espresso powder in 1 tablespoon hot water, and then add to the cake-frosting mixture. Use white chocolate chips for the coating. Suggested garnish: sprinkle of ground cinnamon or unsweetened cocoa powder.

CRANBERRY-ORANGE CAKE BALLS: Prepare as directed, but use an orange cake mix and cream cheese frosting. Add 1 cup chopped dried cranberries and 1 tablespoon finely grated orange peel to the cake-frosting mixture. Use white chocolate chips for the coating. Suggested garnish: finely grated orange peel, orange sprinkles, or orange and red colored sugars.

GINGERBREAD CAKE BALLS: Prepare as directed, but use a spice cake mix and 1¾ cups vanilla frosting. Add ¼ cup dark molasses, 2 teaspoons ground ginger, and 1 teaspoon cinnamon to the cake-frosting mixture. Use white chocolate chips for the coating. Suggested garnish: finely chopped crystallized ginger.

CARROT CAKE BALLS: Prepare as directed, but use a carrot cake mix and cream cheese frosting. Add 1 teaspoon ground cinnamon and 2 tablespoons orange juice to the cake mix-frosting mixture. Use white chocolate chips for the coating. Suggested garnish: sweetened flake coconut, orange sprinkle, or orange-colored sugar.

KEY LIME CAKE BALLS: Prepare as directed, but use a vanilla cake mix and vanilla frosting. Add 3 tablespoons lime juice and 2 teaspoons grated lime peel to the cake mix-frosting mixture. Use white chocolate chips for the coating. Suggested garnish: graham cracker crumbs.

BOURBON BALLS

Variations of bourbon balls abound, and it's no wonder: they are easy to make, delicious to eat, and their flavor intensifies for days after they're made. I think they are best made with a baked, cooled, chocolate cake (as opposed to vanilla wafers or chocolate cookies)—the chocolate flavor is intense and the finished bourbon balls are moist and dense.

MAKES 5 DOZEN COOKIES
COOKIE SHEETS, LINED WITH WAX PAPER

1 (18.25 ounce) package chocolate or devil's food cake mix, baked and cooled
1 cup finely chopped toasted pecans
2 cups confectioners' sugar, sifted
⅓ cup unsweetened cocoa powder, sifted
2 tablespoons bourbon, whiskey, or rum
Optional: sifted confectioners' sugar, finely chopped nuts or chocolate sprinkles

1. Crumble the baked, cooled cake into a large bowl. Break into very fine crumbs with a fork. Mix in the pecans, confectioners' sugar, cocoa powder, and bourbon with a wooden spoon until blended.
2. Shape into 1-inch balls. If desired, roll in confectioners' sugar, chopped nuts, or sprinkles, then place on prepared cookie sheets. Chill at least 1 hour before serving.

GIANT APPLE-PIE PIZZA COOKIE

Two great American classics—apple pie and pizza—come together for one perfect dessert.

PREHEAT OVEN TO 350°F
MAKES 1 EXTRA-LARGE COOKIE (16 SERVINGS)
12-INCH PIZZA PAN, UNGREASED

1 (18.25-ounce) package white cake mix
1¼ cups quick-cooking oats, divided
½ cup (1 stick) butter, softened
½ cup chopped walnuts or pecans
½ cup packed light brown sugar
1 large egg
1 teaspoon ground cinnamon
2 tablespoons vegetable oil
1 (21-ounce) can apple pie filling
Optional: ½ cup raisins or dried cranberries

1. Mix the cake mix, 1 cup of the oats, and butter in a large bowl with a wooden spoon until blended and crumbly. Reserve 1 cup of crumbs. Press the remaining crumbs into ungreased pizza pan, forming a narrow rim around edge of pan. Bake 10 minutes.
2. Mix the walnuts, brown sugar, egg, cinnamon, oil, and remaining ¼ cup oats into reserved 1 cup crumbs with a wooden spoon until blended.
3. Remove crust from oven and spread with apple pie filling. If desired, sprinkle with raisins or cranberries, then sprinkle with reserved crumb mixture.
4. Bake 18 to 23 minutes longer until crumb topping is golden brown. Transfer to wire rack and cool 30 minutes. Serve warm or cool completely. Cut into slices.

GIANT COOKIE PIZZA

Cake Mix
WHITE

If you're looking for a fun baking project to make with the kids, this is it. Let little hands choose the toppings and sprinkle them on top. But don't limit this sweet treat to the kids—adults love eating pizza for dessert, too!

PREHEAT OVEN TO 350°F
MAKES 1 EXTRA-LARGE COOKIE (16 SERVINGS)
12-INCH PIZZA PAN, UNGREASED

1 (18.25-ounce) package white cake mix
⅓ cup butter, softened
1 large egg
2 cups assorted toppings (e.g., candy-coated chocolate candies, candy corn, chocolate chips, roasted, salted nuts, sweetened flake coconut, etc.)
1 cup miniature marshmallows
½ cup semisweet or white chocolate chips

1. Mix the cake mix, butter, and egg in large bowl with electric mixer on medium speed 1 to 2 minutes until blended. Press the dough into ungreased pizza pan, forming a narrow rim around edge of pan.
2. Sprinkle the 2 cups assorted toppings on dough. Bake 18 minutes. Sprinkle the marshmallows over toppings.
3. Bake 5 to 8 minutes longer or until marshmallows are puffed and golden. Transfer to wire rack and cool 30 minutes.
4. Microwave chocolate chips in small microwaveable bowl on High 1 minute, stirring after 30 seconds, until melted and smooth. Drizzle over pizza. Serve warm or cool completely. Cut into slices.

GIANT CHOCOLATE CHIP COOKIE

Cake Mix
WHITE

Looking for a perfect present? Bake a special someone a giant chocolate cookie. You can't go wrong serving it plain, but for extra fun, purchase tubes of colored decorating icing to write a special message on top of the cooled cookie.

PREHEAT OVEN TO 350°F

MAKES 1 EXTRA-LARGE COOKIE (16 SERVINGS)

12-INCH PIZZA PAN, UNGREASED

1 (18.25-ounce) package white cake mix

⅓ cup butter, softened

¼ cup packed light brown sugar

1 large egg

1 teaspoon vanilla extract

1¼ cups semisweet chocolate chips

Optional: ½ cup chopped pecans, walnuts, or macadamia nuts

1. Mix the cake mix, butter, brown sugar, egg, and vanilla in large bowl with electric mixer on medium speed 1 to 2 minutes until blended. Mix in the chocolate chips and (optional) nuts with wooden spoon.
2. Press the dough into ungreased pan, forming a narrow rim around edge of pan.
3. Bake 20 to 25 minutes or until cookie is golden at edges. Transfer to wire rack and cool 30 minutes. Serve warm or cool completely. Cut into slices.

COOKIES-AND-CREAM HIDDEN TREASURE COOKIES

Cake Mix
DEVIL'S FOOD

This is my kind of hidden treasure: a cookies-and-cream white chocolate bar, nestling inside dark chocolate cookie dough. Don't forget the tall glass of ice-cold milk!

PREHEAT OVEN TO 350°F

MAKES 3 DOZEN COOKIES

COOKIE SHEETS, GREASED OR LINED WITH PARCHMENT PAPER

1 (18.25-ounce) package devil's food cake mix

¼ cup (½ stick) butter, melted

2 large eggs

18 cookies-and-cream white chocolate mini rectangular white chocolate candy bars, unwrapped

1 cup semisweet chocolate chips

2 teaspoons vegetable shortening

1. Mix the cake mix, melted butter, and eggs in a large bowl with a wooden spoon until blended.
2. Cut the candy bars in half crosswise (36 pieces total). Mold a level tablespoon of dough around each candy, covering completely. Place, 2 inches apart, onto prepared cookie sheets.
3. Bake 8 to 11 minutes or until dough looks slightly dry and cracked. Cool 1 minute on sheets, then remove cookies with spatula to wire racks to cool completely.
4. In small microwaveable bowl, microwave the chocolate chips and vegetable shortening uncovered on High 60 to 90 seconds, stirring every 30 seconds until melted and smooth. Drizzle the melted chocolate over tops of cooled cookies. Chill 10 to 15 minutes to set the chocolate.

Cake Mix
DEVIL'S FOOD

CARAMEL-PECAN TURTLE COOKIES

Turtles are caramel and pecan candy clusters that are then covered in a thick swath of milk chocolate. To caramel lovers, like me, they are heaven. Here's a quick and easy cookie version of the irresistible treat. Warning: do not leave yourself alone with a fresh batch.

PREHEAT OVEN TO 350°F

MAKES 4½ DOZEN COOKIES

COOKIE SHEETS, GREASED OR LINED WITH
    PARCHMENT PAPER

1 (18.25-ounce) package devil's food cake mix

¼ cup (½ stick) vegetable shortening

2 large eggs

2 cups whole pecan halves

24 milk caramels, unwrapped

3 tablespoons whole or lowfat milk

1. Mix the cake mix, shortening, and eggs in large bowl with electric mixer on medium speed 1 to 2 minutes until blended.
2. Shape the dough into 1-inch balls. Place 2 inches apart on prepared cookie sheets. Press one whole pecan half in center of each cookie.
3. Bake 9 to 11 minutes or until firm to the touch at the edges. Cool 1 minute on sheets, then remove cookies with spatula to wire racks to cool completely.
4. Melt the caramels with the milk in a small saucepan set over low heat, stirring until smooth; remove from heat. Drizzle the caramel across cooled cookies using spoon or fork.

NUTTY JAM THUMBPRINTS

Thumbprint cookies are all-American favorites for good reason. Made with a rich shortbread-like dough that is formed into balls, they get their "thumbprint" moniker from the fact that you can use your "thumb" to make an indentation into each ball of dough and then fill it with a variety of yummy fillings, from jam to lemon curd to bite-sized candies; for their sheer cuteness alone, they are irresistible. This version gets added flavor and crunch by rolling the dough in chopped nuts of your choice. Any flavor of jam or preserves will work for the filling; for a colorful variety, fill a batch with a few different types.

PREHEAT OVEN TO 350°F

MAKES 5 DOZEN COOKIES

COOKIE SHEETS, UNGREASED OR LINED WITH PARCHMENT PAPER

1 (18.25-ounce) package white cake mix

⅓ cup vegetable shortening

¼ cup (½ stick) butter, softened

1 large egg

1 teaspoon vanilla extract

1½ cups finely chopped nuts (e.g., peanuts, almonds, pistachios, walnuts, pecans, etc.)

½ cup jam, preserves, or marmalade (e.g., raspberry, strawberry, or orange marmalade)

1. Place the cake mix, shortening, butter, egg, and vanilla in a large bowl. Blend with an electric mixer on medium speed 1 minute until blended (dough will be stiff).
2. Place the nuts in small, shallow dish. Roll the dough into 1-inch balls, roll in nuts, then place on ungreased cookie sheets. Using thumb, make small impression in center of each ball and fill with ¼ teaspoon jam.
3. Bake 9 to 12 minutes or until centers are just set. Cool 1 minute on sheets, then remove cookies with spatula to wire racks to cool completely.

RASPBERRY CHEESECAKE THUMBPRINTS

Cake Mix
WHITE

If you love cheesecake, you have to try these cookies. With only five simple ingredients, no one will believe they are so easy to make.

PREHEAT OVEN TO 375°F

MAKES 4 DOZEN COOKIES

COOKIE SHEETS, UNGREASED OR LINED WITH PARCHMENT PAPER

1 (18.25-ounce) package white cake mix

1 (4-serving size) package cheesecake-flavor instant pudding and pie filling

½ cup (1 stick) butter, softened

1 large egg

½ cup seedless raspberry jam

1. Place the cake mix, dry pudding mix, butter, and egg in large bowl. Beat with electric mixer on medium speed 1 to 2 minutes until blended.
2. Shape the dough into 1-inch balls and place 2 inches apart on ungreased cookie sheet. Make small indentation in center of each cookie with thumb and fill with ½ teaspoon jam.
3. Bake 9 to 12 minutes or until light brown around edges. Cool 1 minute on sheets, then remove cookies with spatula to wire racks to cool completely.

DOUBLE-LEMON THUMBPRINTS

Cake Mix
LEMON

Sinking your teeth into these tender, golden cookies, with their gooey, lemon centers is citrus heaven. One simply won't be enough!

PREHEAT OVEN TO 375°F

MAKES 4 DOZEN COOKIES

COOKIE SHEETS, UNGREASED OR LINED WITH PARCHMENT PAPER

1 (18.25-ounce) package lemon cake mix

⅓ cup vegetable shortening

¼ cup (½ stick) butter, softened

1 large egg

⅓ cup sugar

½ cup store-bought lemon curd

1. Place the cake mix, shortening, butter, and egg in large bowl. Beat with electric mixer on medium speed 1 to 2 minutes until blended.
2. Place the sugar in small, shallow dish. Shape the dough into 1-inch balls, roll in sugar, and

place 2 inches apart on ungreased cookie sheet. Make small indentation in center of each cookie with thumb and fill with ½ teaspoon lemon curd.

3. Bake 9 to 12 minutes or until light brown around edges. Cool 1 minute on sheets, then remove cookies with spatula to wire racks to cool completely.

Cake Mix WHITE
CARAMEL-MACCHIATO THUMBPRINTS

Sometimes you just have to go overboard with indulgence, and when you do, this is the cookie to make. Coffee, caramel, and chocolate, in one petite cookie…be sure to prop up your feet and savor every extravagant bite.

PREHEAT OVEN TO 375°F

MAKES 4 DOZEN COOKIES

COOKIE SHEETS, UNGREASED OR LINED WITH PARCHMENT PAPER

1 (18.25-ounce) package white cake mix

⅓ cup vegetable shortening

¼ cup (½ stick) butter, softened

1 large egg

4 teaspoons instant coffee powder, dissolved in 1 tablespoon water

1 cup miniature semisweet chocolate chips

42 chocolate-covered caramel candies (e.g., Rolos)

1. Add the cake mix, shortening, butter, egg, and coffee mixture in large bowl. Beat with electric mixer on medium speed 1 to 2 minutes until blended. Mix in the miniature chocolate chips with a wooden spoon.

2. Shape the dough into 1-inch balls and place 2 inches apart on ungreased cookie sheet. Gently press a chocolate-caramel candy in center of each cookie.

3. Bake 8 to 11 minutes or until light brown around edges. Cool 1 minute on sheets, then remove cookies with spatula to wire racks to cool completely.

| Cake Mix YELLOW | # CARAMEL-GRAHAM THUMBPRINTS |

Prepare to hand out the recipe for this one. Reminiscent of s'mores, these dainty graham cracker thumbprints are made irresistible with a dot of gooey chocolate caramel in the center.

PREHEAT OVEN TO 375°F

MAKES 3½ DOZEN COOKIES

COOKIE SHEETS, GREASED OR LINED WITH
    PARCHMENT PAPER

1 (18.25-ounce) package yellow cake mix

1 (3-ounce) package cream cheese, softened

¼ cup (½ stick) butter, softened

1 large egg

1 cup graham cracker crumbs

42 chocolate-covered caramel candies
    (e.g., Rolos)

1. Place the cake mix, cream cheese, butter, and egg in large bowl. Beat with an electric mixer on low speed 1 to 2 minutes until blended. Stir in the graham cracker crumbs with a wooden spoon.
2. Shape dough into 1-inch balls and place 2 inches apart on ungreased cookie sheet. Gently press chocolate-caramel candy in center of each cookie.
3. Bake 9 to 12 minutes or until light brown around edges. Cool 1 minute on sheets, then remove cookies with spatula to wire racks to cool completely.

| Cake Mix VANILLA | # CITRUS-FIG THUMBPRINTS |

These orange-scented vanilla cookies, dotted with fig preserves, will make you think you've made an escape to Tuscany.

PREHEAT OVEN TO 375°F

MAKES 4 DOZEN COOKIES

COOKIE SHEETS, UNGREASED OR LINED WITH
    PARCHMENT PAPER

1 (18.25-ounce) package vanilla cake mix

⅓ cup vegetable shortening

¼ cup (½ stick) butter, softened

1 large egg

1 tablespoon grated orange peel

½ cup fig preserves

1. Place the cake mix, shortening, butter, egg, and orange peel in large bowl. Beat with electric mixer on medium speed 1 to 2 minutes until blended.

2. Shape the dough into 1-inch balls and place 2 inches apart on ungreased cookie sheet. Make small indentation in center of each cookie with thumb and fill with ½ teaspoon fig preserves.

3. Bake 9 to 12 minutes or until light brown around edges. Cool 1 minute on sheets, then remove cookies with spatula to wire racks to cool completely.

Cake Mix WHITE — STRAWBERRY CREAM CHEESE THUMBPRINTS

These sweet cookies are pretty-as-a-picture perfect, as welcome in a lunch box as they are at a bridal shower. You can use the basic dough as a blueprint for your own thumbprint designs, varying the cake mix flavor and filling choice in endless permutations.

PREHEAT OVEN TO 350°F

MAKES 4 DOZEN COOKIES

COOKIE SHEETS, UNGREASED OR LINED WITH PARCHMENT PAPER

1 (18.25-ounce) package white cake mix

1 cup all-purpose flour

1 (3-ounce) package cream cheese, softened

¼ cup (½ stick) butter, softened

1 large egg

1 teaspoon almond extract

1⅔ cup strawberry jam, stirred to loosen

1. Mix the cake mix, flour, cream cheese, butter, egg, and almond extract in a large bowl with an electric mixer on medium speed 1 to 2 minutes until mixture is blended and crumbly.

2. Shape dough into 1-inch balls and place, 2 inches apart, on ungreased sheets. Push an indentation in center of each cookie with thumb and fill with ¼ teaspoon jam.

3. Bake 9 to 12 minutes or until firm to the touch at the edges and slightly puffed in appearance. Cool for 1 minute on cookie sheets. Transfer to wire racks with metal spatula and cool completely.

VARIATIONS *for Strawberry Cream Cheese Thumbprints*

CHOCOLATE CHIP STRAWBERRY THUMBPRINTS: Prepare as directed but add ¾ cup miniature semisweet chocolate chips to the dough along with the egg.

LEMON CURD THUMBPRINTS: Prepare as directed but use lemon cake mix in place of white cake mix, 2 teaspoons grated lemon peel in place of almond extract, and jarred lemon curd in place of jam.

OLD-FASHIONED BLACKBERRY THUMBPRINTS

Wheat germ lends an extra-toasty, old-fashioned flavor to these tea-wonderful cookies. Be sure to use toasted wheat germ as opposed to raw wheat germ—the latter will impart an unpleasant flavor to the dough. Blackberry is a delicious flavor contrast to the rich dough, but you can substitute the jam, preserves, or jelly of your choice.

PREHEAT OVEN TO 375°F

MAKES 3½ DOZEN COOKIES

COOKIE SHEETS, GREASED OR LINED WITH
    PARCHMENT PAPER

1 (18.25-ounce) package spice cake mix

1 (3-ounce) package cream cheese, softened

¼ cup (½ stick) butter, softened

1 large egg

1 teaspoon vanilla extract

1 cup toasted wheat germ

½ cup blackberry jam, stirred to loosen

1. Mix the cake mix, cream cheese, butter, egg, and vanilla in large bowl with an electric mixer on medium speed 1 to 2 minutes until blended. Stir in the wheat germ with a wooden spoon.
2. Shape dough into 1-inch balls and place 2 inches apart on ungreased cookie sheet. Make small indentation in center of each cookie with thumb and fill with ½ teaspoon jam.
3. Bake 9 to 12 minutes or until light brown around edges. Cool 1 minute on sheets, then remove cookies with spatula to wire racks to cool completely.

CHOCOLATE-COVERED MARSHMALLOW PILLOWS

Take an already fabulous chocolate cookie, top it with a large marshmallow half, bake until melt-y, then top all with a thick layer of chocolate icing. It's a recipe for a fabulous cookie, but also a recipe for bite-size bliss.

PREHEAT OVEN TO 375°F

MAKES 4 DOZEN COOKIES

COOKIE SHEETS, UNGREASED OR LINED WITH
   PARCHMENT PAPER

1 (18.25-ounce) package chocolate fudge
   cake mix

½ cup vegetable oil

2 large eggs

2 cups miniature semisweet chocolate
   chips, divided

24 large marshmallows, cut in half crosswise

½ cup heavy whipping cream

⅔ cup confectioners' sugar

1. Mix the cake mix, oil, and eggs in large bowl with wooden spoon until blended. Mix in ⅔ cup chocolate chips.
2. Shape the dough into 1-inch balls, then place 2 inches apart on ungreased cookie sheet.
3. Bake 9 minutes. Remove from oven and immediately press marshmallow half, cut side down, into each cookie. Bake 1 to 2 minutes longer until marshmallow softens slightly. Cool 2 minutes on sheets, then remove cookies with spatula to wire racks to cool completely.
4. Heat whipping cream and remaining chocolate chips in small saucepan set over medium-low heat, stirring until melted and smooth. Remove from heat and whisk in confectioners' sugar.
5. Spoon and gently spread frosting over each cookie. Let stand at least 20 minutes until set.

ANISE BISCOTTI

Despite a reputation as a temperamental treat, biscotti are simply a few basic ingredients blended into dough and baked twice to create impressive cookies perfect for dunking or nibbling along with a favorite hot drink. This version of biscotti has what is perhaps the most traditional Italian flavor combination: aniseed and almond. One bite and you'll instantly appreciate why it's a classic.

PREHEAT OVEN TO 350°F

MAKES 3 DOZEN COOKIES

COOKIE SHEETS, GREASED OR LINED WITH
    PARCHMENT PAPER

1 (18.25-ounce) package white cake mix

1 cup all-purpose flour

½ cup light olive oil or vegetable oil

2 large eggs

1 tablespoon aniseed, crushed

¼ teaspoon ground cinnamon

1 teaspoon almond extract

1 cup slivered almonds

1. Mix the cake mix, flour, oil, eggs, crushed aniseed, cinnamon, and almond extract in a large bowl with an electric mixer on medium speed 1 to 2 minutes until well blended (dough will be very stiff). Mix in the almonds with wooden spoon.

2. On prepared cookie sheet, shape dough into two 12 x 3-inch rectangles, using moistened hands.

3. Bake 25 to 30 minutes until golden and center is set. Cool on cookie sheet on cooling rack 15 minutes.

4. Cut rectangles crosswise into ½-inch slices. Place slices, cut sides down, on cookie sheet. Bake 10 to 12 minutes longer or until edges are dark golden. Cool 1 minute on sheets, then remove cookies with spatula to wire racks to cool completely.

ANISEED

Although used in a variety of European desserts, aniseed is a native of the Middle East. It imparts a subtle licorice flavor to baked goods.

DELUXE CHOCOLATE CHIP BISCOTTI

Crisp and crunchy, biscotti are tailor-made for dunking into your drink of choice, from tea to coffee to ice-cold milk. Tart-sweet dried cherries or blueberries, along with chopped hazelnuts, elevate these chocolate chip biscotti from fine and dandy to deluxe.

PREHEAT OVEN TO 350°F

MAKES 3 DOZEN COOKIES

COOKIE SHEETS, GREASED OR LINED WITH
    PARCHMENT PAPER

1 (18.25-ounce) package white cake mix

1 cup all-purpose flour

½ cup (1 stick) butter, melted

2 large eggs

1½ cups semisweet chocolate chips

½ cup dried cherries or dried cranberries,
    coarsely chopped

½ cup chopped hazelnuts

1. Mix the cake mix, flour, melted butter, and eggs in a large bowl with an electric mixer on medium speed 1 to 2 minutes until well blended (dough will be very stiff). Mix in the chocolate chips, dried cherries or cranberries, and hazelnuts with wooden spoon.

Tip! **TIPS FOR BAKING BISCOTTI**

1. Use a ruler when forming the logs of dough. The specified lengths and widths of the dough are important. If a log is too long or too wide, for example, the cookies will be small and flat, and will bake too quickly.

2. Be sure to slice the logs of dough after the first bake while they are still warm, but not hot; if the logs cool completely, they will crumble when sliced.

3. A sharp chef's knife is the perfect cutting tool for biscotti after the first bake; a serrated knife can tear and crumble the dough.

4. The second bake is where you can control the final crispness of your biscotti. A bit of brown on the underside of the cookie is generally a good indication that it's done. If you prefer biscotti that aren't quite so crunchy, bake them for less time.

2. On prepared cookie sheet, shape the dough into two 12 x 3-inch rectangles, using moistened hands.

3. Bake 25 to 30 minutes until golden and center is set. Cool on cookie sheet on cooling rack 15 minutes.

4. Cut rectangles crosswise into ½-inch slices. Place slices, cut sides down, on cookie sheet. Bake 10 to 12 minutes longer or until edges are dark golden. Cool 1 minute on sheets, then remove cookies with spatula to wire racks to cool completely.

Cake Mix
WHITE

DOUBLE-GINGER BISCOTTI

One of my favorite family rituals is afternoon tea. We stop what we're doing, plug in the kettle, and load up a tray with an assortment of nibbles. These biscotti are favorites of my ginger-loving parents and siblings. Don't be put off by the addition of black pepper to the dough—it enhances the peppery bite of the ginger.

PREHEAT OVEN TO 350°F

MAKES 3 DOZEN COOKIES

COOKIE SHEETS, GREASED OR LINED WITH PARCHMENT PAPER

1 (18.25-ounce) package white cake mix

1 cup all-purpose flour

½ cup (1 stick) butter, melted

2 large eggs

2½ teaspoons ground ginger

⅔ cup finely chopped crystallized ginger

1. Mix the cake mix, flour, melted butter, eggs, and ginger in a large bowl with an electric mixer on medium speed 1 to 2 minutes until well blended (dough will be very stiff). Mix in the crystallized ginger with wooden spoon.

2. On prepared cookie sheet, shape the dough into two 12 x 3-inch rectangles, using moistened hands.

3. Bake 25 to 30 minutes until golden and center is set. Cool on cookie sheet on cooling rack 15 minutes.

4. Cut rectangles crosswise into ½-inch slices. Place slices, cut sides down, on cookie sheet. Bake 10 to 12 minutes longer or until edges are dark golden. Cool 1 minute on sheets, then remove cookies with spatula to wire racks to cool completely.

CHOCOLATE CHUNK BISCOTTI

A cup of espresso. An inspiring view. And one of these very chocolate biscotti. These cookies can make a coffee break a quick escape.

PREHEAT OVEN TO 350°F

MAKES 3 DOZEN COOKIES

COOKIE SHEETS, GREASED OR LINED WITH
    PARCHMENT PAPER

1 (18.25-ounce) package devil's food or
    chocolate cake mix

½ cup all-purpose flour

½ cup unsweetened cocoa powder

½ cup (1 stick) butter, melted and cooled

2 large eggs

1 (12-ounce) bag (2 cups) semisweet
    chocolate chunks or chips

1. Mix the cake mix, flour, cocoa powder, melted butter, and eggs in a large bowl with an electric mixer on medium speed 1 to 2 minutes until well blended (dough will be very stiff). Mix in the chocolate chunks with wooden spoon.
2. On prepared cookie sheet, shape dough into two 12 x 3-inch rectangles, using moistened hands.
3. Bake 25 to 30 minutes until center is set. Cool on cookie sheet on cooling rack 15 minutes.
4. Cut rectangles crosswise into ½-inch slices. Place slices, cut sides down, on cookie sheet. Bake 10 to 12 minutes longer or until edges are dry and crisp-looking. Cool 1 minute on sheets, then remove cookies with spatula to wire racks to cool completely.

VARIATIONS *for Chocolate Chunk Biscotti*

MINT CHIP CHOCOLATE BISCOTTI: Prepare as directed but add 1½ teaspoons peppermint extract. Use chocolate-mint chips (e.g., Andes brand) in place of chocolate chunks.

CHUNKY CHOCOLATE WALNUT BISCOTTI: Prepare as directed but decrease chocolate chunks to 1¼ cups and add 1 cup chopped walnuts.

APRICOT-ALMOND BISCOTTI

My afternoon cup of tea wouldn't be complete without a dunkable cookie. These particular biscotti, accented with bits of dried apricot and almond in each bite, are at the top of my list of favorites.

PREHEAT OVEN TO 350°F

MAKES 3 DOZEN COOKIES

COOKIE SHEETS, GREASED OR LINED WITH PARCHMENT PAPER

1 (18.25-ounce) package white cake mix

1 cup all-purpose flour

½ cup (1 stick) butter, melted

2 large eggs

1 teaspoon almond extract

1 cup chopped dried apricots

1 cup coarsely chopped almonds

1. Mix the cake mix, flour, melted butter, eggs, and almond extract in a large bowl with an electric mixer on medium speed 1 to 2 minutes until well blended (dough will be very stiff). Mix in the apricots and almonds with wooden spoon.
2. On prepared cookie sheet, shape dough into two 12 x3-inch rectangles, using moistened hands.
3. Bake 25 to 30 minutes until golden and center is set. Cool on cookie sheet on cooling rack 15 minutes.
4. Cut rectangles crosswise into ½-inch slices. Place slices, cut sides down, on cookie sheet. Bake 10 to 12 minutes longer or until edges are dark golden. Cool 1 minute on sheets, then remove cookies with spatula to wire racks to cool completely.

CARIBBEAN BISCOTTI

The flavors of the Caribbean—toasted coconut, ginger, and lime—enrich this simple biscotti dough for a unique crispy-crunchy cookie.

PREHEAT OVEN TO 350°F

MAKES 2½ DOZEN COOKIES

COOKIE SHEETS, GREASED OR LINED WITH
    PARCHMENT PAPER

1 (18.25-ounce) package white cake mix

2 large eggs

1 tablespoon vegetable oil

1 tablespoon grated lime peel

2 teaspoons ground ginger

1 cup sweetened flaked coconut, lightly
    toasted

½ cup chopped macadamia nuts

1. Mix the cake mix, eggs, oil, lime peel, and ginger in a large bowl with an electric mixer on medium speed 1 to 2 minutes until well blended (dough will be very stiff). Mix in the coconut and nuts with wooden spoon.
2. On prepared cookie sheet, shape dough into 15 x 4-inch rectangle, using moistened hands.
3. Bake 20 to 25 minutes until golden and center is set. Cool on cookie sheet on cooling rack 15 minutes.
4. Cut rectangle crosswise into ½-inch slices. Place slices, cut sides down, on cookie sheet. Bake 10 to 12 minutes longer or until edges are dark golden. Cool 1 minute on sheets, then remove cookies with spatula to wire racks to cool completely.
5. Drizzle or spread cooled biscotti with lime icing. Chill 10 to 15 minutes to set icing.

CAFÉ BRÛLOT BISCOTTI

Café Brûlot is a traditional New Orleans coffee drink, often served flaming, flavored with spices, orange peel, lemon peel, and brandy. Here it is in crunchy biscotti form.

PREHEAT OVEN TO 350°F

MAKES 3 DOZEN COOKIES

COOKIE SHEETS, GREASED OR LINED WITH
   PARCHMENT PAPER

1 (18.25-ounce) package white cake mix

1 cup all-purpose flour

½ cup (1 stick) butter, melted and cooled

2 large eggs

1 tablespoon instant coffee powder,
   dissolved in 1 tablespoon water

1 tablespoon grated lemon or orange peel

2 teaspoons brandy-flavored extract

¼ teaspoon ground cloves

1. Mix the cake mix, flour, melted butter, eggs, coffee mixture, lemon or orange peel, brandy extract, and cloves in a large bowl with an electric mixer on medium speed 1 to 2 minutes until well blended (dough will be very stiff).
2. On prepared cookie sheet, shape dough into two 12 x 3-inch rectangles, using moistened hands.
3. Bake 25 to 30 minutes until golden and center is set. Cool on cookie sheet on cooling rack 15 minutes.
4. Cut rectangles crosswise into ½-inch slices. Place slices, cut sides down, on cookie sheet. Bake 10 to 12 minutes longer or until edges are dark golden. Cool 1 minute on sheets, then remove cookies with spatula to wire racks to cool completely.

COFFEE-TOFFEE BISCOTTI

These toffee-studded biscotti, enriched further with both coffee and nuts, stand strong on their own but are even finer alongside a favorite coffee or espresso drink.

PREHEAT OVEN TO 350°F

MAKES 3 DOZEN COOKIES

COOKIE SHEETS, GREASED OR LINED WITH PARCHMENT PAPER

1 (18.25-ounce) package white cake mix

1 cup all-purpose flour

½ cup (1 stick) butter, melted and cooled

2 large eggs

1 tablespoon instant coffee powder, dissolved in 1 tablespoon water

½ teaspoon almond extract

1 cup toffee baking bits

1 cup slivered almonds

1. Mix the cake mix, flour, melted butter, eggs, coffee mixture, and almond extract in a large bowl with an electric mixer on medium speed 1 to 2 minutes until well blended (dough will be very stiff). Mix in the toffee bits and almonds with a wooden spoon.
2. On prepared cookie sheet, shape dough into two 12 x 3-inch rectangles, using moistened hands.
3. Bake 25 to 30 minutes until golden and center is set. Cool on cookie sheet on cooling rack 15 minutes.
4. Cut rectangles crosswise into ½-inch slices. Place slices, cut sides down, on cookie sheet. Bake 10 to 12 minutes longer or until edges are dark golden. Cool 1 minute on sheets, then remove cookies with spatula to wire racks to cool completely.

LEMON POPPY SEED BISCOTTI

Poppy seeds have a natural charm—*perhaps due to their polka-dotting potential—that always appeals. Here they grace lemon-scented biscotti that come together with ease. Like all biscotti, they are good candidates for a picnic since they travel well, and deliciously.*

PREHEAT OVEN TO 350°F

MAKES 3 DOZEN COOKIES

COOKIE SHEETS, GREASED OR LINED WITH
    PARCHMENT PAPER

1 (18.25-ounce) package lemon cake mix

1 cup all-purpose flour

½ cup (1 stick) butter, melted and cooled

2 large eggs

¼ cup poppy seeds

1 tablespoon grated lemon peel

1. Mix the cake mix, flour, melted butter, eggs, poppy seeds, and lemon peel in a large bowl with an electric mixer on medium speed 1 to 2 minutes until well blended (dough will be very stiff).
2. On prepared cookie sheet, shape dough into two 12 x 3-inch rectangles, using moistened hands.
3. Bake 25 to 30 minutes until golden and center is set. Cool on cookie sheet on cooling rack 15 minutes.
4. Cut rectangles crosswise into ½-inch slices. Place slices, cut sides down, on cookie sheet. Bake 10 to 12 minutes longer or until edges are dark golden. Cool 1 minute on sheets, then remove cookies with spatula to wire racks to cool completely.

VARIATIONS *for Lemon Poppy Seed Biscotti*

ORANGE POPPY SEED BISCOTTI: Prepare as directed but use an orange cake mix and orange peel.

ALMOND POPPY SEED BISCOTTI: Prepare as directed but use a white cake mix and 1 teaspoon almond extract in place of lemon peel.

PISTACHIO-CHERRY BISCOTTI

Cultivated in Mediterranean climates, pale green pistachios have a delicate flavor that pairs perfectly with lemon. Either raw or roasted unsalted pistachios can be used here with equally successful results.

PREHEAT OVEN TO 350°F

MAKES 3 DOZEN COOKIES

COOKIE SHEETS, GREASED OR LINED WITH PARCHMENT PAPER

1 (18.25-ounce) package white cake mix

1 cup all-purpose flour

½ cup (1 stick) butter, melted and cooled

2 large eggs

½ teaspoon almond extract

1 cup shelled natural pistachios

1 cup dried cherries or dried cranberries, roughly chopped

1. Mix the cake mix, flour, melted butter, eggs, and almond extract in a large bowl with an electric mixer on medium speed 1 to 2 minutes until well blended (dough will be very stiff). Mix in the pistachios and cherries or cranberries with wooden spoon.

2. On prepared cookie sheet, shape dough into two 12 x 3-inch rectangles, using moistened hands.

3. Bake 25 to 30 minutes until golden and center is set. Cool on cookie sheet on cooling rack 15 minutes.

4. Cut rectangles crosswise into ½-inch slices. Place slices, cut sides down, on cookie sheet. Bake 10 to 12 minutes longer or until edges are dark golden. Cool 1 minute on sheets, then remove cookies with spatula to wire racks to cool completely.

WHITE CHOCOLATE AND CRANBERRY BISCOTTI

These biscotti are as beautiful as they are delicious and make an especially appealing gift. You can transform this recipe into a dark chocolate treat by substituting chocolate cake mix for the vanilla cake mix and semisweet chocolate chips for the white chocolate chips.

PREHEAT OVEN TO 350°F

MAKES 3 DOZEN COOKIES

COOKIE SHEETS, GREASED OR LINED WITH PARCHMENT PAPER

1 (18.25-ounce) package white cake mix

1 cup all-purpose flour

½ cup (1 stick) butter, melted and cooled

2 large eggs

1 tablespoon grated orange peel

1⅓ cups dried cranberries, coarsely chopped

1½ cups white chocolate chips

1 tablespoon vegetable shortening

1. Mix the cake mix, flour, melted butter, eggs, and orange peel in a large bowl with an electric mixer on medium speed 1 to 2 minutes until well blended, scraping down sides of bowl (dough will be very stiff). Mix in cranberries with wooden spoon.
2. On prepared cookie sheet, shape dough into two 12 x 3-inch rectangles, using moistened hands.
3. Bake 25 to 30 minutes until golden and center is set. Cool on cookie sheet on cooling rack 15 minutes.
4. Cut rectangles crosswise into ½-inch slices. Place slices, cut sides down, on cookie sheet. Bake 10 to 12 minutes longer or until edges are dark golden. Cool 1 minute on sheets, then remove cookies with spatula to wire racks to cool completely.
5. Melt the white chocolate chips with shortening in small microwaveable bowl 60 to 90 seconds until melted; stir until smooth. Drizzle, spread, or dunk cooled biscotti with or into melted chocolate. Place on wax paper-lined cookie sheet and chill 30 minutes to set chocolate.

Cake Mix YELLOW
WHOLE WHEAT BISCOTTI

Your favorite coffee-time treat just got a makeover. Packed with good-for-you whole wheat flour and walnuts, these cookies are a snack you can feel good about eating.

PREHEAT OVEN TO 350°F

MAKES 3 DOZEN COOKIES

COOKIE SHEETS, GREASED OR LINED WITH PARCHMENT PAPER

1 (18.25-ounce) package yellow cake mix

¾ cup whole wheat flour

½ cup light olive oil or vegetable oil

2 large eggs

1 teaspoon vanilla

½ teaspoon ground cinnamon

1 cup coarsely chopped walnuts

1. Mix the cake mix, flour, oil, eggs, vanilla, and cinnamon in a large bowl with an electric mixer on medium speed 1 to 2 minutes until well blended, scraping down sides of bowl (dough will be very stiff). Mix in the walnuts with wooden spoon.
2. On prepared cookie sheet, shape dough into two 12 x 3-inch rectangles, using moistened hands.
3. Bake 25 to 30 minutes until golden and center is set. Cool on cookie sheet on cooling rack 15 minutes.
4. Cut rectangles crosswise into ½-inch slices. Place slices, cut sides down, on cookie sheet. Bake 10 to 12 minutes longer or until edges are dark golden. Cool 1 minute on sheets, then remove cookies with spatula to wire racks to cool completely.

Cake Mix WHITE
OATS AND HONEY BISCOTTI

Not too sweet, these crunchy oats and honey biscotti are perfect for an afternoon pick-me-up alongside a cup of tea.

PREHEAT OVEN TO 350°F

MAKES 3 DOZEN COOKIES

COOKIE SHEETS, GREASED OR LINED WITH PARCHMENT PAPER

1 (18.25-ounce) package white cake mix

1 cup quick-cooking oats

½ cup (1 stick) butter, melted

2 large eggs

¼ cup honey

1 cup chopped pecans or raisins

1. Mix the cake mix, oats, melted butter, eggs, and honey in a large bowl with a wooden spoon until well blended. Mix in the pecans or raisins with wooden spoon.
2. On prepared cookie sheet, shape dough into two 12 x 3-inch rectangles, using moistened hands.
3. Bake 22 to 27 minutes until golden and center is set. Cool on cookie sheet on cooling rack 15 minutes.
4. Cut rectangles crosswise into ½-inch slices. Place slices, cut sides down, on cookie sheet. Bake 10 to 12 minutes longer or until edges are dark golden. Cool 1 minute on sheets, then remove cookies with spatula to wire racks to cool completely.

Cake Mix
WHITE

WHEAT GERM AND RAISIN BISCOTTI

Despite their modern form, these whole wheat and raisin biscotti have old-fashioned flavor and charm. The wheat germ is made from whole grains, making this a healthful—as well as tasty—choice of cookie for you or the kids.

PREHEAT OVEN TO 350°F

MAKES 3 DOZEN COOKIES

COOKIE SHEETS, GREASED OR LINED WITH PARCHMENT PAPER

1 (18.25-ounce) package white cake mix

1 cup toasted wheat germ

2 large eggs

½ cup vegetable oil

2 teaspoons vanilla extract

1 cup raisins

1. Mix the cake mix, wheat germ, eggs, oil, and vanilla in a large bowl with a wooden spoon until well blended. Mix in raisins with wooden spoon.
2. On prepared cookie sheet, shape dough into two 12 x 3-inch rectangles, using moistened hands.
3. Bake 22 to 27 minutes until golden and center is set. Cool on cookie sheet on cooling rack 15 minutes.
4. Cut rectangles crosswise into ½-inch slices. Place slices, cut sides down, on cookie sheet. Bake 10 to 12 minutes longer or until edges are dark golden. Cool 1 minute on sheets, then remove cookies with spatula to wire racks to cool completely.

BUTTER PECAN BISCOTTI

Cake Mix
BUTTER PECAN

Butter and pecans are made for each other and deserve to be highlighted in more than just ice cream. Here they find crunchy harmony in brown sugar-sweetened biscotti—the perfect dunk for a mid-morning latte.

PREHEAT OVEN TO 350°F

MAKES 3 DOZEN COOKIES

COOKIE SHEETS, GREASED OR LINED WITH
   PARCHMENT PAPER

1 (18.25-ounce) package butter pecan cake mix

1 cup all-purpose flour

½ cup (1 stick) butter, melted

¼ cup packed dark brown sugar

2 large eggs

1½ cups coarsely chopped pecans

1. Mix the cake mix, flour, melted butter, brown sugar, and eggs in a large bowl with an electric mixer on medium speed 1 to 2 minutes until well blended (dough will be very stiff). Mix in the pecans with wooden spoon.
2. On prepared cookie sheet, shape dough into two 12 x 3-inch rectangles, using moistened hands.
3. Bake 25 to 30 minutes until golden and center is set. Cool on cookie sheet on cooling rack 15 minutes.
4. Cut rectangles crosswise into ½-inch slices. Place slices, cut sides down, on cookie sheet. Bake 10 to 12 minutes longer or until edges are dark golden. Cool 1 minute on sheets, then remove cookies with spatula to wire racks to cool completely.

CORNMEAL-CRANBERRY BISCOTTI

Cake Mix
WHITE

Are you ready for a holiday biscotti recipe? Cornmeal in the dough gives these biscotti a distinctive texture, crispy bite, and gorgeous yellow color. Studded with tart-sweet bits of dried cranberry, they offer the perfect pairing of holiday flavors.

PREHEAT OVEN TO 350°F

MAKES 3 DOZEN COOKIES

COOKIE SHEETS, GREASED OR LINED WITH
   PARCHMENT PAPER

1 (18.25-ounce) package white cake mix

¾ cup yellow cornmeal

½ cup (1 stick) butter, melted

2 large eggs

1 tablespoon grated lemon peel

1¼ cups dried cranberries, coarsely chopped

1. Mix the cake mix, cornmeal, melted butter, eggs, and lemon peel in a large bowl with an electric mixer on medium speed 1 to 2 minutes until well blended (dough will be very stiff). Mix in cranberries with wooden spoon.
2. On prepared cookie sheet, shape dough into two 12 x 3-inch rectangles, using moistened hands.
3. Bake 25 to 30 minutes until golden and center is set. Cool on cookie sheet on cooling rack 15 minutes.
4. Cut rectangles crosswise into ½-inch slices. Place slices, cut sides down, on cookie sheet. Bake 10 to 12 minutes longer or until edges are dark golden. Cool 1 minute on sheets, then remove cookies with spatula to wire racks to cool completely.

Cake Mix WHITE HAZELNUT BISCOTTI

Hazelnuts were difficult to find a few years ago, but now they are readily available, and very afford-able, to home cooks. It's a wonderful offering to home bakers, since hazelnuts add a distinctive sweet-nutty flavor and crisp crunch to cookies, such as these easy biscotti. Look for the hazelnuts, shelled and chopped, in the baking aisle where other nuts are shelved.

PREHEAT OVEN TO 350°F

MAKES 3 DOZEN COOKIES

COOKIE SHEETS, GREASED OR LINED WITH PARCHMENT PAPER

1 (18.25-ounce) package white cake mix

1 cup all-purpose flour

½ cup (1 stick) butter, melted

2 large eggs

¼ cup packed light brown sugar

1½ cups chopped hazelnuts

1. Mix the cake mix, flour, melted butter, eggs, and brown sugar in a large bowl with an electric mixer on medium speed 1 to 2 minutes until well blended (dough will be very stiff). Mix in the hazelnuts with wooden spoon.
2. On prepared cookie sheet, shape dough into two 12 x 3-inch rectangles, using moistened hands.
3. Bake 25 to 30 minutes until golden and center is set. Cool on cookie sheet on cooling rack 15 minutes.
4. Cut rectangles crosswise into ½-inch slices. Place slices, cut sides down, on cookie sheet. Bake 10 to 12 minutes longer or until edges are dark golden. Cool 1 minute on sheets, then remove cookies with spatula to wire racks to cool completely.

ALMOND BISCOTTI: Prepare as directed but add 1 teaspoon almond extract and use 1½ cups coarsely chopped whole almonds in place of hazelnuts.

Cake Mix
DEVIL'S FOOD

CHOCOLATE-CHERRY BISCOTTI

Chocolate and cherry are a classic combination in these simple yet rich biscotti. The addition of almond extract to the batter adds just the right flavor to marry the chocolate and cherry flavors in perfect harmony.

PREHEAT OVEN TO 350°F

MAKES 3 DOZEN COOKIES

COOKIE SHEETS, GREASED OR LINED WITH
    PARCHMENT PAPER

1 (18.25-ounce) package devil's food cake mix

½ cup all-purpose flour

½ cup unsweetened cocoa powder

½ cup (1 stick) butter, melted

2 large eggs

1 teaspoon almond extract

1 cup dried cherries

1 cup miniature semisweet chocolate chips

1. Mix the cake mix, flour, cocoa powder, melted butter, eggs, and almond extract in a large bowl with an electric mixer on medium speed 1 to 2 minutes until well blended (dough will be very stiff). Mix in the dried cherries and chocolate chips with wooden spoon.
2. On prepared cookie sheet, shape dough into two 12 x 3-inch rectangles, using moistened hands.
3. Bake 25 to 30 minutes until golden and center is set. Cool on cookie sheet on cooling rack 15 minutes.
4. Cut rectangles crosswise into ½-inch slices. Place slices, cut sides down, on cookie sheet. Bake 10 to 12 minutes longer or until edges are dark golden. Cool 1 minute on sheets, then remove cookies with spatula to wire racks to cool completely.

CINNAMON-SUGAR BISCOTTI

Cinnamon has a unique way of making cookies at once old-fashioned and modern, comforting and cutting-edge; it is little wonder why explorers sailed the world to find it centuries ago. Here it acts as the perfect accent to understated, but oh-so-appealing, biscotti.

PREHEAT OVEN TO 350°F

MAKES 3 DOZEN COOKIES

COOKIE SHEETS, GREASED OR LINED WITH
PARCHMENT PAPER

1 (18.25-ounce) package white cake mix

1 cup all-purpose flour

½ cup (1 stick) butter, melted

2 large eggs

3 teaspoons ground cinnamon, divided

¼ cup granulated sugar

1. Mix the cake mix, flour, melted butter, eggs, and 2 teaspoons cinnamon, in a large bowl with an electric mixer on medium speed 1 to 2 minutes until well blended, scraping down sides of bowl (dough will be very stiff).
2. On prepared cookie sheet, shape dough into two 12 x 3-inch rectangles, using moistened hands. Combine the sugar and remaining 1 teaspoon cinnamon in small bowl, then sprinkle over rectangles.
3. Bake 25 to 30 minutes until golden and center is set. Cool on cookie sheet on cooling rack 15 minutes.
4. Cut rectangles crosswise into ½-inch slices. Place slices, cut sides down, on cookie sheet. Bake 10 to 12 minutes longer or until edges are dark golden. Cool 1 minute on sheets, then remove cookies with spatula to wire racks to cool completely.

VARIATION *for Cinnamon-Sugar Biscotti*

CINNAMON-RAISIN BISCOTTI: Prepare as directed but add 1 cup raisins.

TOASTED COCONUT BISCOTTI

No need to pre-toast the coconut before adding to the dough; it toasts during the second baking of the biscotti, lending tropical flavor and a crisp texture.

PREHEAT OVEN TO 350°F

MAKES 3 DOZEN COOKIES

COOKIE SHEETS, UNGREASED OR LINED WITH
    PARCHMENT PAPER

1 (18.25-ounce) package white cake mix

2 large eggs

3 tablespoons butter, melted

1 teaspoon vanilla extract

1 (7-ounce) package sweetened flake
    coconut

1 cup white or semisweet chocolate chips

2 teaspoons vegetable shortening

1. Mix the cake mix, eggs, melted butter, and vanilla extract in a large bowl with an electric mixer on medium speed 1 to 2 minutes until well blended (dough will be very stiff). Mix in the coconut with wooden spoon.
2. On ungreased cookie sheet, shape dough into 15 x 4-inch rectangle, using moistened hands.
3. Bake 20 to 25 minutes until golden and center is set. Cool on cookie sheet on cooling rack 15 minutes.
4. Cut rectangle crosswise into ½-inch slices. Place slices, cut sides down, on cookie sheet. Bake 10 to 12 minutes longer or until edges are dark golden. Cool 1 minute on sheets, then remove cookies with spatula to wire racks to cool completely.
5. Microwave the chocolate chips and shortening in a medium microwaveable bowl on High 1 minute, stirring after 30 seconds, until melted. Drizzle chocolate over cookies, or dip one end of each cookie into chocolate. Let stand about 30 minutes or until chocolate is set.

DEVIL'S FOOD WHOOPIES

Part cookie, part cake, whoopie pies are 100 percent irresistible. A whoopie pie is like a sandwich, but made with two soft cookies and a fluffy frosting filling. This is the most traditional of whoopie pies: soft, dark chocolate cookies and a vanilla frosting. Always showstoppers, they reward a little bit of work with heaps of praise. Kids can help with the final assembly of the whoopies—they'll love saying the name as much as eating their efforts.

PREHEAT OVEN TO 350°F

MAKES 15 WHOOPIES

COOKIE SHEETS, GREASED OR LINED WITH
    PARCHMENT PAPER

1 (18.25-ounce) package devil's food cake mix

½ cup vegetable oil

3 large eggs

¼ cup unsweetened cocoa powder

Optional: 1 cup miniature semisweet chocolate chips

1¼ cups (from 16-ounce tub) ready-to spread vanilla frosting

1¼ cups (from 8-ounce tub) frozen whipped topping (such as Cool Whip), thawed

1. Mix the cake mix, oil, eggs, and cocoa powder in a large bowl with an electric mixer on medium speed 1 to 2 minutes until blended. If desired, stir in the chocolate chips.
2. Drop by ¼-cupfuls, 3 inches apart, onto prepared cookie sheets.
3. Bake 12 to 15 minutes or until edges are firm and center is just barely set when lightly touched. Cool 1 minute on sheets, then carefully remove cookies with spatula to wire racks to cool completely.
4. Mix the frosting and whipped topping in a medium bowl until blended. Spread flat side of half of cookies with frosting, then sandwich with remaining cookies.

FLUFFERNUTTER WHOOPIES

Fluffernutters—peanut butter and marshmallow fluff sandwiches on white bread—are distinctly American treats. Here I've refashioned them into even more scrumptious whoopie pies. What could be better?

PREHEAT OVEN TO 350°F

MAKES 15 WHOOPIES

COOKIE SHEETS, GREASED OR LINED WITH
    PARCHMENT PAPER

1 (18.25-ounce) package yellow cake mix

1 (8-ounce) container sour cream (not
    reduced fat)

2 large eggs

¼ cup vegetable oil

1 cup marshmallow creme or fluff

1 cup creamy peanut butter

1. Mix the cake mix, sour cream, eggs, and oil in a large bowl with an electric mixer on medium speed 1 to 2 minutes until blended.
2. Drop by ¼-cupfuls, 3 inches apart, onto prepared cookie sheets.
3. Bake 12 to 15 minutes or until edges are firm and center is just barely set when lightly touched. Cool 1 minute on sheets, then carefully remove cookies with spatula to wire racks to cool completely.
4. Spread bottoms of half of cooled cookies with marshmallow creme. Spread bottoms of second half of cooled cookies with peanut butter. Sandwich the cookies together.

Tip! ### ADD FLAVOR AND CRUNCH TO SANDWICH COOKIES AND WHOOPIES

Add some extra flair to cookie sandwiches or whoopies by dipping the frosting edge into one of these scrumptious embellishments:

- Finely chopped toasted nuts
- Crushed toffee
- Crushed candy canes
- Toasted coconut
- Miniature chocolate chips
- Candy sprinkles
- Chopped dried fruit
- Crushed cereal
- Chopped chocolate

RED VELVET WHOOPIES

Red velvet cake is a traditional Southern cake, made flavorful with a hint of cocoa powder, tinted a deep, gorgeous red, and then slathered with cream cheese frosting. My favorite version also includes fresh berries on top, so in this whoopie pie recreation of the beloved dessert, I've added a thin layer of raspberry jam to the cream cheese filling. Whoopee!

PREHEAT OVEN TO 350°F

MAKES 15 WHOOPIES

COOKIE SHEETS, GREASED OR LINED WITH PARCHMENT PAPER

1 (18.25-ounce) package devil's food cake mix

1 (4-serving size) package chocolate instant pudding and pie filling mix

¾ cup plus 2 tablespoons sour cream, (not reduced fat), divided

½ cup vegetable oil

3 large eggs

2 tablespoons (2 1-ounce bottles) red food coloring

1½ cups (from 16-ounce tub) ready-to-spread cream cheese frosting

¾ cup seedless raspberry jam

1. Mix the cake mix, pudding mix, ¾ cup sour cream, oil, eggs, and red food coloring in a large bowl with an electric mixer on medium speed 1 to 2 minutes until blended.
2. Drop by ¼-cupfuls, 3 inches apart, onto prepared cookie sheets.
3. Bake 12 to 15 minutes or until edges are firm and center is just barely set when lightly touched. Cool 1 minute on sheets, then carefully remove cookies with spatula to wire racks to cool completely.
4. Mix the frosting and remaining 2 tablespoons sour cream in a medium bowl until blended. Spread flat side of half of cookies with frosting. Spread flat side of remaining cookies with raspberry jam. Sandwich the cookies together.

EGGNOG WHOOPIES WITH TIPSY BRANDY FILLING

Even if you're not an eggnog aficionado, you will love these whoopies. Nutmeg and cinnamon coupled with the rounded complexity of brandy in the filling lend them grown-up flair and flavor, perfect for a tree-trimming party or a cozy dessert by the fire.

PREHEAT OVEN TO 350°F

MAKES 15 WHOOPIES

COOKIE SHEETS, GREASED OR LINED WITH
   PARCHMENT PAPER

1 (18.25-ounce) package white food cake mix

1 (4-serving size) package vanilla instant
   pudding and pie filling mix

¾ cup sour cream (not reduced fat)

½ cup vegetable oil

3 large eggs

¾ teaspoon ground nutmeg

1½ cups (from 16-ounce tub) ready-to-
   spread cream cheese frosting

1½ tablespoons brandy or dark rum

1 teaspoon ground cinnamon

1. Mix the cake mix, pudding mix, sour cream, oil, eggs, and nutmeg in a large bowl with an electric mixer on medium speed 1 to 2 minutes until blended.
2. Drop by ¼-cupfuls, 3 inches apart, onto prepared cookie sheets.
3. Bake 12 to 15 minutes or until edges are firm and center is just barely set when lightly touched. Cool 1 minute on sheets, then carefully remove cookies with spatula to wire racks to cool completely.
4. Mix the frosting, brandy, and cinnamon in a medium bowl until blended. Spread flat side of half of cookies with frosting. Sandwich with remaining cookies.

GINGERBREAD WHOOPIES WITH LEMON FILLING

My mother always served gingerbread with a tart lemon sauce, so in my mind, the two flavors are meant for each other. Here they star in a playful whoopie-pie variation. Prepare yourself for the critical acclaim!

PREHEAT OVEN TO 350°F

MAKES 15 WHOOPIES

COOKIE SHEETS, GREASED OR LINED WITH PARCHMENT PAPER

1 (18.25-ounce) package spice cake mix

1 (8-ounce) container sour cream (not reduced fat)

2 large eggs

¼ cup vegetable oil

2½ teaspoons ground ginger

1½ teaspoons ground cinnamon

1½ cups (from 16-ounce tub) ready-to-spread cream cheese frosting

2 tablespoons fresh lemon juice

1 teaspoon grated lemon peel

1. Mix the cake mix, sour cream, eggs, oil, ginger, and cinnamon in a large bowl with an electric mixer on medium speed 1 to 2 minutes until blended.
2. Drop by ¼-cupfuls, 3 inches apart, onto prepared cookie sheets.
3. Bake 12 to 15 minutes or until edges are firm and center is just barely set when lightly touched. Cool 1 minute on sheets, then carefully remove cookies with spatula to wire racks to cool completely.
4. Mix the frosting, lemon juice, and lemon peel in a medium bowl until blended. Spread flat side of half of cookies with frosting, then sandwich with remaining cookies.

CHOCOLATE-WHISKEY WHOOPIES

Pull out all the stops! These triple-chocolate whoopies (chocolate cake, chocolate chips, and a tangy, tipsy chocolate-sour cream filling) are a spectacular treat, despite the brief list of ingredients and easy-as-(whoopie)-pie preparation.

PREHEAT OVEN TO 350°F

MAKES 15 WHOOPIES

COOKIE SHEETS, GREASED OR LINED WITH PARCHMENT PAPER

1 (18.25-ounce) package chocolate or chocolate fudge cake mix

1½ cups sour cream (not reduced fat), divided

2 large eggs

¼ cup vegetable oil

1 (12-ounce) package miniature semisweet chocolate chips, divided

1 teaspoon vegetable shortening

2 tablespoons whiskey or bourbon

1. Mix the cake mix, 1 cup sour cream, eggs, and oil in a large bowl with an electric mixer on medium speed 1 to 2 minutes until blended. Stir in 1 cup chocolate chips.
2. Drop by ¼-cupfuls, 3 inches apart, onto prepared cookie sheets.
3. Bake 12 to 15 minutes or until edges are firm and center is just barely set when lightly touched. Cool 1 minute on sheets, then carefully remove cookies with spatula to wire racks to cool completely.
4. Microwave the remaining chocolate chips and shortening in a medium microwaveable bowl on High 1 minute, stirring after 30 seconds, until melted and smooth. Whisk in the whiskey and remaining ½ cup sour cream. Chill 30 minutes.
5. Spread bottoms of half of cooled cookies with chocolate mixture. Sandwich with remaining cookies.

TOFFEE-BUTTERSCOTCH WHOOPIES

We all know about chocoholics, but an equal number of us are diehard butterscotch-toffee-caramel connoisseurs. To all in the latter camp, I offer these scrumptious whoopie pies, an over-the-top homage.

PREHEAT OVEN TO 350°F

MAKES 15 WHOOPIES

COOKIE SHEETS, GREASED OR LINED WITH
   PARCHMENT PAPER

1 (18.25-ounce) package white cake mix

1 (4-serving size) package butterscotch
   instant pudding and pie filling mix

¾ cup whole or lowfat milk

½ cup (1 stick) butter, melted

3 large eggs

1½ cups (from 16-ounce tub) ready-to-
   spread vanilla frosting

1 cup toffee baking bits

1. Mix the cake mix, dry pudding mix, milk, melted butter, and eggs in a large bowl with an electric mixer on medium speed 1 to 2 minutes until blended.
2. Drop by ¼-cupfuls, 3 inches apart, onto prepared cookie sheets.
3. Bake 12 to 15 minutes or until edges are firm and center is just barely set when lightly touched. Cool 1 minute on sheets, then carefully remove cookies with spatula to wire racks to cool completely.
4. Mix the frosting and toffee bits in a medium bowl until blended. Spread flat side of half of cookies with frosting, then sandwich with remaining cookies.

CARAMEL LATTE WHOOPIES

Cake Mix
WHITE

The oh-so-popular coffee drink of the same name is transformed here into a scrumptious and easy-to-make whoopie. If you cannot find caramel frosting, use vanilla frosting and dissolve a tablespoon of dark brown sugar in the hot water along with the coffee powder.

PREHEAT OVEN TO 350°F

MAKES 15 WHOOPIES

COOKIE SHEETS, GREASED OR LINED WITH
   PARCHMENT PAPER

1 (18.25-ounce) package white cake mix

1 (8-ounce) container sour cream (not
   reduced fat)

⅓ cup packed dark brown sugar

2 large eggs

¼ cup (½ stick) butter, melted

1½ cups (from 16-ounce tub) ready-to-
   spread caramel frosting

1 tablespoon instant coffee powder,
   dissolved in 1 tablespoon hot water

1. Mix the cake mix, sour cream, brown sugar, eggs, and melted butter in a large bowl with an electric mixer on medium speed 1 to 2 minutes until blended.
2. Drop by ¼-cupfuls, 3 inches apart, onto prepared cookie sheets.
3. Bake 12 to 15 minutes or until edges are firm and center is just barely set when lightly touched. Cool 1 minute on sheets, then carefully remove cookies with spatula to wire racks to cool completely.
4. Mix the frosting and coffee mixture in a medium bowl until blended. Spread flat side of half of cookies with frosting, then sandwich with remaining cookies.

VARIATIONS *for Caramel Latte Whoopies*

MOCHA LATTE WHOOPIES: Prepare as directed, but use a chocolate cake mix and milk chocolate frosting.

VANILLA LATTE WHOOPIES: Prepare as directed, but use a vanilla cake mix and vanilla frosting.

Cake Mix
BUTTER PECAN

MAPLE WHOOPIES

All you need to make these amazing maple whoopies is a simple-to-mix and bake top and bottom with a layer of yum in the center.

PREHEAT OVEN TO 350°F

MAKES 15 WHOOPIES

COOKIE SHEETS, GREASED OR LINED WITH PARCHMENT PAPER

1 (18.25-ounce) package butter pecan cake mix

1 cup sour cream, divided

2 large eggs

¼ cup butter, melted

4 teaspoons maple-flavored extract, divided

1½ cups (from a 16-ounce tub) ready-to-spread white frosting

1. Mix the cake mix, sour cream, eggs, melted butter, and 2 teaspoons maple extract in a large bowl with an electric mixer on medium speed 1 to 2 minutes until blended.
2. Drop by ¼-cupfuls, 3 inches apart, onto prepared cookie sheets.
3. Bake 12 to 15 minutes or until edges are firm and center is just barely set when lightly touched. Cool 1 minute on sheets, then carefully remove cookies with spatula to wire racks to cool completely.
4. Mix the frosting and remaining 2 teaspoons maple extract in a medium bowl until blended. Spread flat side of half of cookies with frosting, then sandwich with remaining cookies.

LEMON BUTTERMILK WHOOPIES

Buttermilk bestows these whoopies with a delicious tang that both complements and enhances the lemon in the cookies and the filling. It also makes the tops and bottoms especially tender.

PREHEAT OVEN TO 350°F

MAKES 15 WHOOPIES

COOKIE SHEETS, GREASED OR LINED WITH
    PARCHMENT PAPER

1 (18.25-ounce) package lemon cake mix

1 (4-serving size) package vanilla instant
    pudding and pie filling mix

¾ cup buttermilk

½ cup vegetable oil

3 large eggs

3 tablespoons lemon juice, divided

1½ cups (from a 16-ounce tub) ready-to-
    spread lemon frosting

1. Mix the cake mix, dry pudding mix, buttermilk, oil, eggs, and 2 tablespoons lemon juice in a large bowl with an electric mixer on medium speed 1 to 2 minutes until blended.
2. Drop by ¼-cupfuls, 3 inches apart, onto prepared cookie sheets.
3. Bake 12 to 15 minutes or until edges are firm and center is just barely set when lightly touched. Cool 1 minute on sheets, then carefully remove cookies with spatula to wire racks to cool completely.
4. Mix the frosting and remaining tablespoon lemon juice in a medium bowl until blended. Spread flat side of half of cookies with frosting, then sandwich with remaining cookies.

PEANUT BUTTER WHOOPIES

These peanut butter whoopies are perfect for a casual get-together, backyard party—or any celebration!

PREHEAT OVEN TO 350°F

MAKES 15 WHOOPIES

COOKIE SHEETS, GREASED OR LINED WITH
    PARCHMENT PAPER

1 (18.25-ounce) package yellow cake mix

1¼ cups creamy peanut butter, divided

½ cup sour cream (not reduced fat)

2 large eggs

¼ cup vegetable oil

1 (12-ounce) tub whipped vanilla frosting

1. Mix the cake mix, ½ cup peanut butter, sour cream, eggs, and oil in a large bowl with an electric mixer on medium speed 1 to 2 minutes until blended.
2. Drop by ¼-cupfuls, 3 inches apart, onto prepared cookie sheets.
3. Bake 12 to 15 minutes or until edges are firm and center is just barely set when lightly touched. Cool 1 minute on sheets, then carefully remove cookies with spatula to wire racks to cool completely.
4. Mix the frosting and remaining ¾ cup peanut butter in a medium bowl until blended. Spread flat side of half of cookies with frosting, then sandwich with remaining cookies.

VARIATION *for Peanut Butter Whoopies*

CHOCOLATE PEANUT BUTTER WHOOPIES: Prepare as directed but use a chocolate cake mix and whipped chocolate frosting.

Cake Mix
CHOCOLATE

CHOCOLATE-PEPPERMINT WHOOPIES

These pretty whoopies are just the thing to get you in the festive mood—especially since you'll be in and out of the kitchen in a flash. Gather up the youngsters in your family for some hands-on fun—they can help mix and drop the batter and spread and sandwich the whoopies with the peppermint frosting.

PREHEAT OVEN TO 350°F

MAKES 15 WHOOPIES

COOKIE SHEETS, GREASED OR LINED WITH PARCHMENT PAPER

1 (18.25-ounce) package chocolate cake mix

1 (8-ounce) container sour cream

2 large eggs

¼ cup vegetable oil

1 teaspoon peppermint extract

1½ cups (from a 16-ounce tub) ready-to-spread vanilla frosting

1 cup crushed peppermint candy canes or red and white striped peppermint candies

1. Mix the cake mix, sour cream, eggs, oil, and peppermint extract in a large bowl with an electric mixer on medium speed 1 to 2 minutes until blended.
2. Drop by ¼-cupfuls, 3 inches apart, onto prepared cookie sheets.
3. Bake 12 to 15 minutes or until edges are firm and center is just barely set when lightly touched. Cool 1 minute on sheets, then carefully remove cookies with spatula to wire racks to cool completely.

4. Mix the frosting and crushed candy in a medium bowl until blended. Spread flat side of half of cookies with frosting, then sandwich with remaining cookies.

VARIATION *for Chocolate-Peppermint Whoopies*

VANILLA-MINT WHOOPIES: Prepare as directed but use a vanilla cake mix.

DOUBLE-CHOCOLATE-MINT WHOOPIES: Prepare as directed, but use chocolate frosting.

Cake Mix
SPICE

BANANA WHOOPIES

You'll want to buy extra bananas at the grocery store merely to have the excuse for making another batch of these banana whoopies. Let the little ones help make them by stirring the batter and forming the whoopies into sandwiches—baking with them provides a perfect way to teach, share, and connect.

PREHEAT OVEN TO 350°F

MAKES 15 WHOOPIES

COOKIE SHEETS, GREASED OR LINED WITH
    PARCHMENT PAPER

1 (18.25-ounce) package spice cake mix

1 cup mashed ripe banana (about 2 large)

½ cup plus 2 tablespoons sour cream (not
    reduced fat), divided

⅓ cup butter, softened

2 large eggs

1½ cups (from a 16-ounce tub) ready-to-
    spread cream cheese frosting

¼ teaspoon ground nutmeg

1. Mix the cake mix, mashed banana, ½ cup sour cream, butter, and eggs in a large bowl with an electric mixer on medium speed 1 to 2 minutes until blended.

2. Drop by ¼-cupfuls, 3 inches apart, onto prepared cookie sheets.

3. Bake 12 to 15 minutes or until edges are firm and center is just barely set when lightly touched. Cool 1 minute on sheets, then carefully remove cookies with spatula to wire racks to cool completely.

4. Mix the frosting, nutmeg, and remaining 2 tablespoons sour cream in a medium bowl until blended. Spread flat side of half of cookies with frosting, then sandwich with remaining cookies.

PUMPKIN WHOOPIES WITH CINNAMON CREAM CHEESE FILLING

These cream-filled, handheld "pies" are festive fun for kids and adults alike. The flavors of pumpkin and cinnamon fit the bill for all sorts of fall festivities from Halloween to hay rides.

PREHEAT OVEN TO 375°F

MAKES 15 WHOOPIES

COOKIE SHEETS, GREASED OR LINED WITH
    PARCHMENT PAPER OR FOIL

1 (18.25-ounce) package spice cake mix

1 cup canned pumpkin purée

½ cup whole or lowfat milk

⅓ cup butter, softened

2 large eggs

1 (16-ounce) tub ready-to-spread cream
    cheese frosting

1 teaspoon ground cinnamon

1. Mix the cake mix, pumpkin, milk, butter, and eggs in a large bowl with an electric mixer on medium speed 1 to 2 minutes until smooth.
2. Drop by the ¼-cupfuls, 3 inches apart, onto cookie sheet.
3. Bake 15 minutes or until set and lightly browned around edges. Cool 3 minutes on sheets, then transfer to wire rack. Cool completely.
4. Mix the frosting and cinnamon in a small bowl until blended. Spread flat side of half of cookies with generous amount of frosting, then sandwich with remaining cookies.

CARAMEL APPLE WHOOPIES

**Cake Mix
YELLOW**

When the weather turns chilly and the leaves begin to fall from the trees, make a batch of these caramel apple treats. Make them for a Halloween party, too—among the most coveted treats on the table, these are usually the first to disappear.

PREHEAT OVEN TO 350°F

MAKES 15 WHOOPIES

COOKIE SHEETS, GREASED OR LINED WITH
    PARCHMENT PAPER

1 (18.25-ounce) yellow cake mix

1 cup applesauce

⅓ cup packed dark brown sugar

¼ cup (½ stick) butter, melted

2 large eggs

1 teaspoon ground cinnamon

1 cup dried apples, chopped

1½ cups (from a 16-ounce tub) ready-to-
    spread caramel frosting

1. Mix the cake mix, applesauce, brown sugar, butter, eggs, and cinnamon in a large bowl with an electric mixer on medium speed 1 to 2 minutes until blended. Mix in the chopped dried apples with a wooden spoon.

2. Drop by ¼-cupfuls, 3 inches apart, onto prepared cookie sheets.

3. Bake 12 to 15 minutes or until edges are firm and center is just barely set when lightly touched. Cool 1 minute on sheets, then carefully remove cookies with spatula to wire racks to cool completely.

4. Spread flat side of half of cookies with frosting, then sandwich with remaining cookies.

CHOCOLATE CHIP COOKIE WHOOPIES

For chocolate chip cookie lovers everywhere, this is an exciting new way to indulge—chocolate chip-flecked mini-cakes with chocolate chip-flecked filling, too. Be forewarned: if the kids are helping to assemble them, they may start disappearing before they even hit the table!

PREHEAT OVEN TO 350°F

MAKES 15 WHOOPIES

COOKIE SHEETS, GREASED OR LINED WITH PARCHMENT PAPER

1 (18.25-ounce) package yellow cake mix

1 (8-ounce) container sour cream

¼ cup packed light brown sugar

2 large eggs

¼ cup (½ stick) butter, melted

1½ cups miniature semisweet chocolate chips, divided

1½ cups chocolate or vanilla prepared frosting

1. Mix the cake mix, sour cream, brown sugar, eggs, and melted butter in a large bowl with an electric mixer on medium speed 1 to 2 minutes until blended. Mix in 1 cup chocolate chips with a wooden spoon.

2. Drop by ¼-cupfuls, 3 inches apart, onto prepared cookie sheets.

3. Bake 12 to 15 minutes or until edges are firm and center is just barely set when lightly touched. Cool 1 minute on sheets, then carefully remove cookies with spatula to wire racks to cool completely.

4. Mix the frosting and remaining ½ cup chocolate chips in a medium bowl. Spread flat side of half of cookies with frosting, then sandwich with remaining cookies.

BERRIES-AND-CREAM WHOOPIES

Dried blueberries, raspberry jam, tender cake, and creamy vanilla filling are a sublime combination. They make great mini-desserts for bridal showers, baby showers, or graduation parties.

PREHEAT OVEN TO 350°F

MAKES 15 WHOOPIES

COOKIE SHEETS, GREASED OR LINED WITH
    PARCHMENT PAPER

1 (18.25-ounce) package white cake mix

1 (8-ounce) container sour cream

2 large eggs

¼ cup (½ stick) butter, melted

1 teaspoon almond extract

¾ cup dried blueberries or dried
    cranberries, chopped

1 cup (½ a 16-ounce tub) ready-to-spread
    vanilla frosting

¾ cup seedless raspberry jam

1. Mix the cake mix, sour cream, eggs, melted butter, and almond extract in a large bowl with an electric mixer on medium speed 1 to 2 minutes until blended. Mix in the chopped dried blueberries or dried cranberries with a wooden spoon.

2. Drop by ¼-cupfuls, 3 inches apart, onto prepared cookie sheets.

3. Bake 12 to 15 minutes or until edges are firm and center is just barely set when lightly touched. Cool 1 minute on sheets, then carefully remove cookies with spatula to wire racks to cool completely.

4. Spread flat side of half of cookies with frosting. Spread flat side of remaining cookies with raspberry jam, then sandwich with remaining cookies.

CRANBERRY WHOOPIES WITH ORANGE-SPICE FILLING

Cranberries and oranges are classic seasonal Christmas fruits and nowhere better than in these pretty red-flecked whoopies with a luscious orange-spice filling.

PREHEAT OVEN TO 375°F

MAKES 15 WHOOPIES

COOKIE SHEETS, GREASED OR LINED WITH PARCHMENT PAPER

1 (18.25-ounce) package yellow cake mix

1 cup applesauce (not chunky)

⅓ cup butter, softened

2 large eggs

1 cup dried cranberries, roughly chopped

1 (12-ounce) tub ready-to-spread whipped fluffy white frosting

2 teaspoons grated orange peel

½ teaspoon pumpkin pie spice or ground cinnamon

1. Mix the cake mix, applesauce, butter, and eggs in a large bowl with an electric mixer on medium speed 1 to 2 minutes until blended. Stir in the cranberries with a wooden spoon.
2. Drop by ¼-cupfuls, 3 inches apart, onto prepared cookie sheets.
3. Bake 12 to 15 minutes or until edges are firm and center is just barely set when lightly touched. Cool 1 minute on sheets, then carefully remove cookies with spatula to wire racks to cool completely.
4. Mix the frosting, orange peel, and pumpkin pie spice or cinnamon in a medium bowl until blended. Spread flat side of half of cookies with frosting, then sandwich with remaining cookies.

VARIATION *for Cranberry Whoopies with Orange-Spice Filling*

SPICED CURRANT WHOOPIES: Prepare as directed but use a spice cake mix and dried currants in place of the dried cranberries. Add 1 teaspoon pumpkin pie spice or ground cinnamon to cookie batter and omit orange peel and spice from filling.

BUTTERY CUTOUT COOKIES

You can't please all of the people all of the time—unless, that is, you're a warm butter cookie, fresh from the oven.

PREHEAT OVEN TO 375°F

MAKES 3½ DOZEN 3-INCH COOKIES

COOKIE SHEETS, UNGREASED OR LINED WITH
    PARCHMENT PAPER

1 (18.25-ounce) package white cake mix

½ cup vegetable shortening

⅓ cup butter, softened

1 large egg

1 teaspoon vanilla extract

Optional: sugar or colored sugar

1. Mix the cake mix, shortening, butter, egg, and vanilla with electric mixer on low speed 1 minute to blend. Increase speed to high and beat 1 minute longer.
2. Divide dough into 4 equal portions. Roll 1 portion of dough to ⅛-inch thickness on lightly floured surface. Cut with 3-inch cookie cutters into desired shapes. Transfer shapes with pancake turner to ungreased cookie sheets, placing 2 inches apart. If desired, sprinkle with sugar.
3. Bake 5 to 7 minutes or until golden. Cool 1 minute on sheets, then remove cookies with spatula to wire racks to cool completely.

VARIATIONS *for Buttery Cutout Cookies*

BUTTERY ALMOND CUTOUTS: Prepare as directed but use ½ teaspoon almond extract in place of vanilla extract.

BUTTERY LEMON CUTOUTS: Prepare as directed but use ¾ teaspoon lemon extract or 1½ teaspoons grated lemon peel in place of vanilla extract.

GINGERBREAD PEOPLE

An afternoon spent making, baking, and decorating these nostalgic cutout cookies is perfect for preheating memories, folding in both friends and family, and baking up good times.

PREHEAT OVEN TO 375°F

MAKES 2 DOZEN 4-INCH COOKIES

COOKIE SHEETS, UNGREASED OR LINED WITH
    PARCHMENT PAPER

1 (18.25-ounce) package spice cake mix

¾ cup all-purpose flour

⅓ cup vegetable oil

⅓ cup molasses

2 large eggs

2½ teaspoons ground ginger

1 teaspoon ground cinnamon

Optional: 1 cup (½ a 16-ounce tub) ready-to-spread vanilla frosting

Optional: Red Hots cinnamon candies or raisins

1. Mix the cake mix, flour, oil, molasses, eggs, ginger, and cinnamon in a large bowl with a wooden spoon until blended. Chill, covered, 4 hours or up to overnight.
2. Roll ¼ of the chilled dough on floured surface (cover and return remaining dough to refrigerator) to ¼-inch thickness. Cut out shapes with 4-inch floured cutters. Transfer dough to prepared cookie sheets with spatula. Re-roll any scraps, then repeat with remaining dough, rolling ¼ at a time.
3. Bake 8 to 11 minutes until center is puffed and sinks back. Cool 1 minute on sheets, then remove cookies with spatula to wire racks to cool completely. If desired, decorate cookies with frosting and candies or raisins, if desired.

Tip! **COOKIE CUTTING TIP**

Cookie cutters are fun to use, and the options are almost endless. For perfectly cut cookies, roll out your dough on a lightly floured surface and dip the cutter in flour each time (or every other time) you press it into the dough. You may need to lightly flour the rolling pin, too.

CHOCOLATE-VANILLA PINWHEEL COOKIES

These pretty cookies may take a few more steps than other options in this book, but the results are well worth it. Get ready for the compliments!

PREHEAT OVEN TO 350°F

MAKES 3½ DOZEN COOKIES

COOKIE SHEETS, GREASED OR LINED WITH
    PARCHMENT PAPER

½ cup vegetable shortening

⅓ cup plus 1 tablespoon butter, softened,
    divided

2 large egg yolks

1 teaspoon vanilla extract

1 (18.25-ounce) package vanilla cake mix

2½ tablespoons unsweetened cocoa
    powder

1. Beat the shortening, ⅓ cup softened butter, egg yolks, and vanilla extract in a large bowl with an electric mixer on medium-high speed for 1 to 2 minutes until blended. Mix in the cake mix on low speed 1 to 2 minutes until blended.

2. Divide dough in half. Knead in cocoa powder and remaining tablespoon butter to half of dough until thoroughly blended.

3. Roll vanilla dough between 2 pieces of wax paper into 18 x 12-inch rectangle, ⅛-inch thick. Repeat process with chocolate dough. Remove top piece of wax paper from each piece of dough. Place one rectangle on top of the other and roll up like a jelly roll, beginning with long side. Tightly wrap in plastic wrap and chill at least 2 hours.

4. Slice dough into ⅛-inch thick slices and place 1 inch apart on prepared cookie sheets. Bake 9 to 11 minutes. Cool 2 minutes on cookie sheets. Transfer to wire racks with metal spatula and cool completely.

SLICE-AND-BAKE CINNAMON COOKIES

When these cookies are baking in the oven, it's easy to understand why the ancient Romans used cinnamon as a perfume—the scent is decidedly aphrodisiacal.

PREHEAT OVEN TO 350°F

MAKES 5 DOZEN COOKIES

COOKIE SHEETS, UNGREASED OR LINED WITH PARCHMENT PAPER

1 (18.25-ounce) package spice cake mix

½ cup vegetable shortening

⅓ cup butter, softened

1 large egg

2 teaspoons ground cinnamon

Optional: 1½ cups turbinado (raw) sugar

1. Place the cake mix, shortening, butter, egg, and cinnamon in a large bowl. Blend with an electric mixer on low speed 1 minute (dough will be stiff).
2. Divide dough in half, shaping each half into 12 x 2-inch roll.
3. If desired, place raw sugar on a shallow plate. Roll each log in the sugar, pressing gently to adhere. Wrap each roll in plastic wrap and chill at least 3 hours.
4. Cut rolls into ¼-inch slices with a sharp knife, then place 2 inches apart on ungreased cookie sheets.
5. Bake 7 to 8 minutes or until edges are lightly browned. Cool 1 minute on sheets, then remove cookies with spatula to wire racks to cool completely.

VARIATION *for Slice-and-Bake Cinnamon Cookies*

CARAMEL-SPICE SANDWICH COOKIES: Prepare cookies as directed. Spread 1 tablespoon ready-to-spread caramel frosting on flat sides of half of the cookies. Sandwich with remaining cookies.

VANILLA MADELEINES

French writer Marcel Proust praised the tender, buttery sponge cakes known as madeleines in his work Remembrance of Things Past. *You, too, will sing their praises once you give this recipe a try. A few standard pantry items transform a box of cake mix into these classic cookies, worthy of a Parisian patisserie.*

PREHEAT OVEN TO 350°F

MAKES 2½ DOZEN MADELEINES

LARGE MADELEINE PAN (3 x 1¼-INCH SHELL MOLDS), SPRAYED WITH NONSTICK BAKING SPRAY WITH FLOUR (E.G., PAM WITH FLOUR OR BAKER'S JOY)

1 (18.25-ounce) package white cake mix

½ cup (1 stick) butter, melted

¼ cup whole or lowfat milk

4 large eggs, separated

1 teaspoon vanilla extract

2–3 tablespoons confectioners' sugar

1. Place the cake mix, melted butter, milk, egg yolks, and vanilla in large bowl. Blend 1 to 2 minutes with electric mixer on medium speed until well blended and smooth. Set aside momentarily. Clean beaters.

BEATING EGG WHITES

When beating egg whites, make sure the bowl and beaters have absolutely no traces of grease (e.g., egg yolks, butter, oil) or the whites will not whip. Ceramic or metal bowls are better than plastic, which is more susceptible to retaining traces of grease.

2. Beat the egg whites in another large bowl with electric mixer on high speed until soft peaks form. Stir ¼ of the beaten egg whites into the cake batter, then fold in remaining whites.

3. Spoon 1 heaping tablespoon batter into each indentation in pan (do not overfill; batter will spread as it bakes).

4. Bake 8 to 10 minutes until puffed and set at center. Cool in pan 5 minutes, then gently remove madeleines to wire rack. Repeat process with remaining batter. Sift confectioners' sugar over cooled cookies.

VARIATION *for Vanilla Madeleines*

ALMOND MADELEINES: Prepare as directed but omit the vanilla and add ¾ teaspoon almond extract to the batter.

FRESH ORANGE MADELEINES

I love these madeleines for their lightness and intense orange flavor. The most difficult thing about making them is remembering to take it easy when folding the egg whites into the batter—the gentler the folding, the airier the madeleines. For a fancier final flourish, consider dipping each madeleine in melted white chocolate instead of dusting with confectioners' sugar.

PREHEAT OVEN TO 350°F

MAKES 2½ DOZEN MADELEINES

LARGE MADELEINE PAN (3 x 1¼-INCH SHELL MOLDS), SPRAYED WITH NONSTICK BAKING SPRAY WITH FLOUR (E.G., PAM WITH FLOUR OR BAKER'S JOY)

1 (18.25-ounce) package white cake mix

½ cup (1 stick) butter, melted

¼ cup orange juice

4 large eggs, separated

1 tablespoon grated orange peel

2–3 tablespoons confectioners' sugar

1. Beat the cake mix, melted butter, orange juice, egg yolks, and orange peel in a large bowl with an electric mixer on medium speed 1 to 2 minutes, until well blended and smooth. Clean beaters.
2. Beat the egg whites in a separate large bowl with electric mixer on high speed until soft peaks form. Stir ¼ of egg whites into cake batter, then fold in remaining whites.
3. Spoon 1 heaping tablespoon batter into each indentation in pan (do not overfill; batter will spread as it bakes).
4. Bake 8 to 10 minutes until puffed and set at center. Cool in pan 5 minutes, then gently remove madeleines to wire rack. Repeat process with remaining batter. Sift confectioners' sugar over cooled cookies.

VARIATION *for Fresh Orange Madeleines*

LEMON MADELEINES: Prepare as directed but replace the orange juice with 2 tablespoons water plus 2 tablespoons fresh lemon juice and use grated lemon peel in place of the orange peel.

CHOCOLATE MINT CHIP MADELEINES

Peppermint gives these tender, double-chocolate madeleines a cool accent of refreshing flavor. Be sure to use miniature chocolate chips in the recipe—regular-size chips will sink in the batter.

PREHEAT OVEN TO 350°F

MAKES 2½ DOZEN MADELEINES

LARGE MADELEINE PAN (3 x 1¼-INCH SHELL MOLDS), SPRAYED WITH NONSTICK BAKING SPRAY WITH FLOUR (E.G., PAM WITH FLOUR OR BAKER'S JOY)

1 (18.25-ounce) package devil's food cake mix

½ cup (1 stick) butter, melted

4 large eggs, separated

¼ cup whole or lowfat milk

1 teaspoon peppermint extract

1 cup miniature semisweet chocolate chips

2–3 tablespoons confectioners' sugar

1. Place the cake mix, melted butter, egg yolks, milk, and peppermint extract in large bowl. Blend 1 to 2 minutes with electric mixer on medium speed until well blended and smooth. Stir in the chocolate chips with wooden spoon. Set aside momentarily. Clean beaters.

2. Beat the egg whites in another large bowl with electric mixer on high speed until soft peaks form. Stir ¼ of the beaten egg whites into the cake batter, then fold in remaining whites.

3. Spoon 1 heaping tablespoon batter into each indentation in pan (do not overfill; batter will spread as it bakes).

4. Bake 8 to 10 minutes until puffed and set at center. Cool in pan 5 minutes, then gently remove madeleines to wire rack. Repeat process with remaining batter. Sift confectioners' sugar over cooled cookies.

VARIATION *for Chocolate Mint Chip Madeleines*

MOCHA CHIP MADELEINES: Prepare as directed but omit the peppermint extract, and add 1 tablespoon instant coffee powder that has been dissolved in 1½ teaspoons vanilla extract.

COCONUT-RUM MADELEINES

Spiked with rum and sweetened with coconut, these tender madeleines are decidedly adult, but all tropical fun and games. For an extra flourish, consider drizzling the cooled cookies with melted white or dark chocolate.

PREHEAT OVEN TO 350°F

MAKES 3 DOZEN MADELEINES

LARGE MADELEINE PAN (3 x 1¼-INCH SHELL MOLDS), SPRAYED WITH NONSTICK BAKING SPRAY WITH FLOUR (E.G., PAM WITH FLOUR OR BAKER'S JOY)

1 (18.25-ounce) package white cake mix

½ cup (1 stick) butter, melted

4 large eggs, separated

¼ cup dark rum

1 cup sweetened flake coconut

2–3 tablespoons confectioners' sugar

1. Place the cake mix, melted butter, egg yolks, and rum in large bowl. Blend 1 to 2 minutes with electric mixer on medium speed until well blended and smooth. Stir in the coconut with a wooden spoon. Set aside momentarily. Clean beaters.
2. Beat the egg whites in another large bowl with electric mixer on high speed until soft peaks form. Stir ¼ of the beaten egg whites into the cake batter, then fold in remaining whites.
3. Spoon 1 heaping tablespoon batter into each indentation in pan (do not overfill; batter will spread as it bakes).
4. Bake 8 to 10 minutes until puffed and set at center. Cool in pan 5 minutes, then gently remove madeleines to wire rack. Repeat process with remaining batter. Sift confectioners' sugar over cooled cookies.

MOCHA-JAVA SANDWICH COOKIES

Filled with a super-quick, creamy coffee filling, these mocha sandwich cookies call to mind a celebrated coffeehouse espresso drink. If you can't get enough chocolate, use chocolate frosting in place of the vanilla for the coffee filling.

PREHEAT OVEN TO 350°F

MAKES 3 DOZEN SANDWICH COOKIES

COOKIE SHEETS, UNGREASED OR LINED WITH PARCHMENT PAPER

2 tablespoons instant coffee powder, divided

2 tablespoons water, divided

1 (18.25-ounce) package chocolate cake mix

½ cup (1 stick) butter, softened

2 large eggs

1 cup miniature semisweet chocolate chips

1½ cups (from 16-ounce tub) ready-to-spread vanilla frosting

1. Stir together 1 tablespoon coffee powder and 1 tablespoon water in large bowl until coffee dissolves. Mix in the cake mix, butter, and eggs with a wooden spoon until blended. Stir in chocolate chips.
2. Drop by teaspoonfuls, 2 inches apart, onto prepared cookie sheets.
3. Bake 7 to 10 minutes or until edges are firm and center is just barely set when lightly touched. Cool 1 minute on sheets, then remove cookies with spatula to wire racks to cool completely.
4. Stir together remaining 1 tablespoon water and remaining 1 tablespoon coffee powder in a small bowl. Mix in frosting until blended. Spread flat side of half of cookies with frosting, then sandwich with remaining cookies.

OLD-FASHIONED PEANUT BUTTER SANDWICH COOKIES

Cake Mix YELLOW

Peanut butter cookies plus peanut butter filling equals modern bliss in old-fashioned form.

PREHEAT OVEN TO 350°F

MAKES 3 DOZEN COOKIE SANDWICHES

COOKIE SHEETS, GREASED OR LINED WITH
PARCHMENT PAPER

1 (18.25-ounce) package yellow cake mix

1¾ cups creamy peanut butter, divided

½ cup (1 stick) butter, melted

¼ cup packed dark brown sugar

2 large eggs

5 tablespoons whole or lowfat milk, divided

1 cup quick-cooking oats

1 cup (½ a 16-ounce tub) vanilla ready-to-
spread frosting

1. Place the cake mix, 1 cup peanut butter, melted butter, brown sugar, eggs, and 4 tablespoons (¼ cup) milk in a large bowl. Mix with an electric mixer on low speed 1 minute until blended. Mix in the oats until blended.
2. Drop by tablespoonfuls, 2 inches apart, onto prepared cookie sheets. Flatten with spatula.
3. Bake 9 to 12 minutes or until edges are firm and center is just barely set when lightly touched. Cool 1 minute on sheets, then remove cookies with spatula to wire racks to cool completely.
4. Mix the frosting, remaining ¾ cup peanut butter, and remaining 1 tablespoon milk in a small bowl until blended. Generously spread flat sides of half of the cookies with peanut butter frosting, then sandwich with remaining cookies.

CHOCOLATE PEANUT BUTTER SANDWICH COOKIES

Cake Mix CHOCOLATE

Chocolate and peanut butter are a favorite combination any time, and nowhere better than in these indulgent sandwich cookies with peanut butter in the cookies as well as the filling.

PREHEAT OVEN TO 375°F

MAKES 3 DOZEN SANDWICH COOKIES

COOKIE SHEETS, GREASED OR LINED WITH
PARCHMENT PAPER

1 (18.25-ounce) package chocolate cake mix

1¾ cups creamy peanut butter, divided

⅓ cup water

4 large eggs

1½ cups semisweet chocolate chips

1 (12-ounce) tub whipped fluffy white frosting

1. Place the cake mix, ¾ cup peanut butter, water, and eggs in a large bowl. Beat with an electric mixer on medium speed 1 to 2 minutes until blended. Stir in chocolate chips with a wooden spoon.
2. Drop by teaspoonfuls, 2 inches apart, onto prepared cookie sheets.
3. Bake 7 to 10 minutes or until edges are firm and center is just barely set when lightly touched. Cool 1 minute on sheets, then remove cookies with spatula to wire racks to cool completely.
4. Mix the frosting and remaining 1 cup peanut butter in a medium bowl with a wooden spoon until blended. Spread flat side of half of cookies with frosting, then sandwich with the remaining cookies.

Cake Mix SPICE
OATMEAL-CARROT COOKIE SANDWICHES

Who wants to choose between an oatmeal cookie and carrot cake? Not I, so I created these yummy cookies, sandwiched with a cinnamon-cream cheese filling. You might even convince yourself that, with oats and carrots in the mix, these are health food!

PREHEAT OVEN TO 375°F

MAKES 2½ DOZEN SANDWICH COOKIES

COOKIE SHEETS, UNGREASED OR LINED WITH PARCHMENT PAPER

1 (18.25-ounce) package spice cake mix

½ cup (1 stick) butter, melted

2 large eggs

1 cup quick-cooking oats

¾ cup grated carrots

¾ cup dried cranberries or raisins

1 (16-ounce) tub ready-to-spread cream cheese frosting

1 teaspoon ground cinnamon

1. Mix the cake mix, melted butter, and eggs in a large bowl with a wooden spoon until blended. Mix in the oats, carrots, and cranberries or raisins.
2. On ungreased cookie sheets, drop the dough by teaspoonfuls 2 inches apart.
3. Bake 9 to 10 minutes or until edges are light golden brown. Cool 2 minutes; remove from cookie sheets to cooling racks. Cool completely, about 30 minutes.
4. Mix the frosting and cinnamon in a small bowl until blended. Spread flat side of half of cookies with frosting, then sandwich with remaining cookies.

MOCHA-HAZELNUT SANDWICH COOKIES

An elegant, contemporary cookie with European flair thanks to the chocolate-hazelnut spread. *Look for the spread in one of two places in the supermarket: in the international foods section or the aisle where peanut butter can be found.*

PREHEAT OVEN TO 350°F

MAKES 3 DOZEN SANDWICH COOKIES

COOKIE SHEETS, GREASED OR LINED WITH PARCHMENT PAPER

1 (18.25-ounce) package chocolate cake mix

⅓ cup vegetable oil

2 large eggs

2 teaspoons instant coffee powder, dissolved in 1 tablespoon water

¾ cup chocolate-hazelnut spread (e.g., Nutella)

1. Mix the cake mix, oil, eggs, and coffee mixture in large bowl with a wooden spoon until blended.
2. Drop by tablespoonfuls, 2 inches apart, onto prepared cookie sheets.
3. Bake 8 to 11 minutes or until just barely set at center when lightly touched. Cool 1 minute on sheets, then remove cookies with spatula to wire racks to cool completely.
4. Spread flat side of half of cookies with chocolate-hazelnut spread, then sandwich with remaining cookies.

TOASTED COCONUT AND LEMON SANDWICH COOKIES

No need to pre-toast the coconut here—because the cookies are sliced thin, the coconut toasts in *the dough as it bakes. To-die-for when sandwiched with a tart lemon filling, the crisp cookies are also tops served solo.*

PREHEAT OVEN TO 350°F

MAKES 5 DOZEN COOKIES

COOKIE SHEETS, UNGREASED OR LINED WITH PARCHMENT PAPER

1 (18.25-ounce) package white cake mix

½ cup vegetable shortening

⅓ cup butter, softened

1 large egg

1 teaspoon coconut extract

1½ cups sweetened flaked coconut

1½ cups (from a 16-ounce tub) ready-to-spread lemon frosting

Juice and grated peel from 1 large lemon

1. Mix the cake mix, shortening, butter, egg, and coconut extract in a large bowl with an electric mixer on medium speed 1 to 2 minutes until smooth. Mix in coconut with a wooden spoon.
2. Divide dough in half, shaping each piece into a 12 x 2-inch roll. Wrap each in plastic food wrap. Chill at least 4 hours.
3. Cut rolls into ¼-inch slices with a sharp knife. Place 2 inches apart on ungreased cookie sheets.
4. Bake 7 to 8 minutes or until edges are lightly browned. Let stand on cookie sheets for 1 minute. Transfer to wire rack and cool completely.
5. Mix the frosting, lemon juice, and lemon peel in a small bowl until blended. Spread flat sides of half of cookies with frosting, then sandwich with remaining cookies.

Cake Mix
VANILLA

TIRAMISU SANDWICH COOKIES

Combining the best of both worlds—creamy and rich with crisp and crunchy—these petite tiramisu-inspired sandwiches elevate cookies to new heights of deliciousness.

PREHEAT OVEN TO 350°F

MAKES 2 DOZEN SANDWICH COOKIES

COOKIE SHEETS, GREASED OR LINED WITH
    PARCHMENT PAPER

1 (18.25-ounce) package vanilla cake mix

½ cup (1 stick) butter, melted

2 large eggs

1 tablespoon instant coffee powder, dissolved in 1 tablespoon hot water

⅓ cup unsweetened cocoa powder

1 (12-ounce) tub ready-to-spread fluffy vanilla frosting

1 tablespoon dark rum

1. Mix the cake mix, butter, eggs, and coffee mixture in a large bowl with an electric mixer on medium speed 1 to 2 minutes until blended (dough will be stiff).
2. Place cocoa powder in small, shallow dish. Roll the dough into 1-inch balls, roll in cocoa, then place 2 inches apart on ungreased cookie sheets.
3. Bake 9 to 12 minutes or until centers are just set. Cool 1 minute on sheets, then remove cookies with spatula to wire racks to cool completely.
4. Whisk frosting and rum in a small bowl until blended. Spread frosting on flat sides of half of the cookies. Sandwich with remaining cookies. Store in refrigerator.

Cake Mix WHITE	# VANILLA TEA SANDWICH COOKIES

These petite confections are perfect for teatime, but they also make ideal treats for bridal and baby showers. You can tint the filling pastel colors by adding a drop or two of red, yellow, blue, or green food coloring (or a drop each of red and blue for my favorite, lavender).

PREHEAT OVEN TO 350°F

MAKES 4 DOZEN SANDWICH COOKIES

COOKIE SHEETS, GREASED OR LINED WITH
    PARCHMENT PAPER

2 (18.25-ounce) packages white cake mix

4 large eggs

⅔ cup vegetable oil

2 teaspoons vanilla extract, divided

1 (8-ounce) package cream cheese, softened

½ cup (1 stick) butter, softened

3 cups confectioners' sugar

Optional: 1 to 2 drops red or blue food
    coloring

1. Mix the cake mixes, eggs, oil, and 1 teaspoon vanilla in a large bowl with an electric mixer on medium speed 1 to 2 minutes until blended (dough will be stiff).
2. Roll the dough into 1-inch balls. Place 2 inches apart on ungreased cookie sheets. Flatten dough balls slightly with spatula.
3. Bake 9 to 12 minutes or until centers are just set. Cool 1 minute on sheets, then remove cookies with spatula to wire racks to cool completely.
4. Beat the cream cheese and butter in a medium bowl with an electric mixer on medium until light and fluffy. Beat in the confectioners' sugar, remaining 1 teaspoon vanilla, and (optional) food coloring until blended.
5. Spread cream cheese mixture onto bottom halves of half of the cookies. Sandwich with remaining cookies.

CREAM CHEESE AND CANDY CANE COOKIES

These whimsical cookies are as cute as they are delicious. For an added flavor twist, add a drop or two of peppermint extract to the dough along with the cream cheese and butter.

PREHEAT OVEN TO 350°F

MAKES 3 DOZEN COOKIES

COOKIE SHEETS, UNGREASED OR LINED WITH
    PARCHMENT PAPER

1 (3-ounce) package cream cheese, softened

¼ cup (½ stick) butter, softened

1 large egg

1 (18.25-ounce) package white cake mix

¼ teaspoon red gel or paste icing color

1. Beat the cream cheese, butter, and egg in large bowl with an electric mixer on medium until blended. Mix in the cake mix with a wooden spoon until blended.
2. Divide dough in half. Add the food color to half of the dough, mixing with a wooden spoon until well blended for even red color.
3. Measure 1 teaspoon white dough and 1 teaspoon red dough for each cookie. Roll out each into 4-inch rope. Place ropes side by side. Lightly roll together into twist. Place cookie twists 2 inches apart on ungreased cookie sheet, then shape each into a hook to resemble candy cane.
4. Bake 7 to 9 minutes or just until edges are golden brown. Immediately remove cookies with spatula to wire racks to cool completely.

GINGERSNAP CRINKLES

Turbinado sugar (sometimes called "raw" sugar) adds a sophisticated sparkle and crunch to these spicy favorites. If you cannot find it, regular sugar works just fine as a substitute. Be sure to make these in fall and serve with mugfuls of hot apple cider.

PREHEAT OVEN TO 350°F

MAKES 4 DOZEN COOKIES

COOKIE SHEETS, UNGREASED OR LINED WITH
    PARCHMENT PAPER

1 (18.25-ounce) package spice cake mix

⅓ cup vegetable shortening

⅓ cup butter, softened

1 large egg

2¼ teaspoons ground ginger

1 teaspoon ground cinnamon

⅔ cup turbinado (raw) sugar or granulated
    sugar

1. Mix the cake mix, shortening, butter, egg, ginger, and cinnamon in a large bowl with electric mixer on medium speed 1 minute until blended.
2. Place the sugar in small, shallow bowl. Roll the dough into 1-inch balls, roll in sugar, then place on ungreased cookie sheets.
3. Bake 9 to 12 minutes or until centers are just set. Cool 1 minute on sheets, then remove cookies with spatula to wire racks to cool completely.

Cake Mix
DEVIL'S FOOD

GLOREOS

Think of a favorite sandwich cookie that rhymes with "gloreo" and you'll know what these yummy treats are all about. The cookies are softer than their store-bought cousins, making for a homey, old-fashioned cookie.

PREHEAT OVEN TO 350°F
MAKES 2½ DOZEN SANDWICH COOKIES
COOKIE SHEETS, GREASED OR LINED WITH
   PARCHMENT PAPER

1 (18.25-ounce) package devil's food cake mix
2 large eggs
2 tablespoons cold water
2 tablespoons vegetable oil
1 (12-ounce) tub ready-to-spread fluffy white frosting

1. Mix the cake mix, eggs, water, and oil in a large bowl with an electric mixer on medium speed 1 to 2 minutes until blended (dough will be stiff).
2. Roll the dough into 1-inch balls. Place on prepared cookie sheets and flatten slightly with spatula or palm.
3. Bake 9 to 12 minutes or until centers are just set. Cool 1 minute on sheets, then remove cookies with spatula to wire racks to cool completely.
4. Spoon a heaping teaspoon of frosting on bottom sides of half of the cookies. Sandwich with remaining cookies.

MELTAWAYS

These are refined little cookies with a delicate crunch and slightly fruity essence, both thanks to the olive oil.

PREHEAT OVEN TO 350°F

MAKES 3 DOZEN COOKIES

COOKIE SHEETS, UNGREASED OR LINED WITH
    PARCHMENT PAPER

1¼ cups quick-cooking oats

½ cup light-flavor olive oil or vegetable oil

1 (18.25-ounce) package white cake mix

2 large eggs

1 teaspoon vanilla extract

½ cup finely chopped, lightly toasted walnuts

1½ cups confectioners' sugar

1. Combine the oats and olive oil in a medium bowl. Let stand 5 minutes. Mix in the cake mix, eggs, and vanilla with a wooden spoon until well blended. Mix in the walnuts.
2. Form the dough into 1-inch balls and place about 2 inches apart on ungreased cookie sheets.
3. Bake 9 to 12 minutes or until cookies are puffed and edges are firm. Cool 1 minute on sheets.
4. Place confectioners' sugar in small, shallow bowl. Roll cookies in sugar while still warm, then remove cookies to wire racks to cool completely.

LEMON CORNMEAL COOKIES

Bright with a double dose of citrus, these very easy, very citrus-y cookies are hands-down winners. Be sure to use real butter for optimal results.

PREHEAT OVEN TO 350°F

MAKES 3½ DOZEN COOKIES

COOKIE SHEETS, UNGREASED OR LINED WITH
    PARCHMENT PAPER

1 (18.25-ounce) package white cake mix

¾ cup (1½ sticks) butter, softened

1 large egg

1 tablespoon grated lemon peel

1 cup yellow cornmeal

½ cup granulated sugar

1. Mix the cake mix, butter, egg, and lemon peel in a large bowl with an electric mixer on medium speed 1 to 2 minutes until blended. Mix in cornmeal with a wooden spoon.

2. Place the sugar in small, shallow bowl. Roll the dough into 1-inch balls, then roll in sugar. Place on prepared cookie sheets and flatten slightly with spatula or palm.
3. Bake 9 to 12 minutes or until centers are just set. Cool 1 minute on sheets, then remove cookies with spatula to wire racks to cool completely.

VARIATIONS *for Lemon Cornmeal Cookies*

LEMON-THYME CORNMEAL COOKIES: Prepare as directed but add 1½ teaspoons chopped fresh thyme leaves to the dough.

ROSEMARY POLENTA COOKIES: Prepare as directed but use white cake mix, orange peel in place of lemon peel, and add 2 teaspoons minced fresh rosemary leaves.

Cake Mix
WHITE

LOLLIPOP COOKIES

Looking for a great birthday party activity for a group of little girls or boys? Make several batches of these cookies, set out the icing, candies, and sprinkles, and you'll have a great party all wrapped up. For an even fancier, festive option, buy extra-long wooden sticks (found in craft stores), place the finished cookies in small vases, and tie with ribbon.

PREHEAT OVEN TO 375°F

MAKES 2 DOZEN COOKIE POPS

COOKIE SHEETS, UNGREASED OR LINED WITH
    PARCHMENT PAPER

1 (18.25-ounce) package white cake mix

⅓ cup vegetable oil

2 large eggs

1 teaspoon vanilla extract

24 wooden sticks with rounded ends

1 cup (½ a 16-ounce tub) frosting, any flavor

Assorted decorating candies, colored
    sprinkles, and nonpareils

1. Mix the cake mix, oil, eggs, and vanilla in a large bowl with an electric mixer on low speed 1 to 2 minutes until blended.
2. Drop the dough by heaping tablespoonfuls, 3 inches apart, onto cookie sheet. Insert wooden stick into edge of dough until tip is in center.
3. Bake 8 to 11 minutes or until puffed and just barely set at center. Cool 1 minute on cookie sheet. Transfer to wire rack and cool completely. Frost and decorate as desired.

CAPPUCCINO CRINKLES

Here old-fashioned crinkles take a sophisticated turn. The flavors here—brown sugar, coffee, vanilla, and cocoa—are luxurious, luscious, and decidedly adult.

PREHEAT OVEN TO 350°F

MAKES 3 DOZEN COOKIES

COOKIE SHEETS, GREASED OR LINED WITH PARCHMENT PAPER

1 (18.25-ounce) package white cake mix

⅓ cup vegetable shortening

¼ cup (½ stick) butter, softened

¼ cup packed light brown sugar

1 large egg

1 tablespoon instant coffee powder

2 teaspoons vanilla extract

¼ cup unsweetened cocoa powder

1. Mix the cake mix, shortening, butter, brown sugar, egg, coffee powder, and vanilla in a large bowl with electric mixer on medium speed 1 minute until blended.
2. Place the cocoa powder in a small, shallow bowl. Roll the dough into 1-inch balls and place on ungreased cookie sheets.
3. Bake 9 to 12 minutes or until centers are just set. Cool 1 minute on sheets, then remove cookies with spatula to wire racks to cool completely.

HONEY-WALNUT CRISPS

Sweet with honey and crunchy with walnuts, these cookies have cozy tea break written all over them.

PREHEAT OVEN TO 375°F

MAKES 3½ DOZEN COOKIES

COOKIE SHEETS, GREASED OR LINED WITH PARCHMENT PAPER

1 (18.25-ounce) package white cake mix

⅓ cup vegetable shortening

⅓ cup honey

1 large egg

1 cup chopped walnuts

½ cup sugar

1. Mix the cake mix, shortening, honey, and egg in a large bowl with electric mixer on medium speed 1 minute until blended. Mix in walnuts with a wooden spoon.

2. Place the sugar in small, shallow bowl. Roll the dough into 1-inch balls and place on ungreased cookie sheets.

3. Bake 8 to 11 minutes or until golden. Cool 1 minute on sheets, then remove cookies with spatula to wire racks to cool completely.

VARIATIONS *for Honey-Walnut Crisps*

HONEY-ROSEMARY CRISPS: Prepare as directed, but add 1½ teaspoon finely chopped fresh rosemary when adding the honey and egg.

LEMON-HONEY CRISPS: Prepare as directed, but use a lemon cake mix.

Cake Mix
WHITE and
DEVIL'S FOOD

MARBLED CHOCOLATE AND VANILLA COOKIES

With a gorgeous presentation and the rich, classic flavor combination of chocolate and vanilla, these cookies are showstoppers.

PREHEAT OVEN TO 350°F

MAKES 6 DOZEN COOKIES

COOKIE SHEETS, UNGREASED OR LINED WITH PARCHMENT PAPER

1 (18.25-ounce) package white cake mix

⅔ cup vegetable oil, divided

½ cup (1 stick) butter, melted, divided

2 large eggs

1½ cups chopped pecans or walnuts, toasted

1 (18.25-ounce) package devil's food cake mix

1. Mix the white cake mix, ⅓ cup oil, ¼ cup melted butter, and 1 egg in medium bowl with a wooden spoon until blended. Stir in ¾ cup nuts.

2. Mix the devil's food cake mix, remaining ⅓ cup oil, remaining ¼ cup melted butter, and remaining egg in medium bowl with a wooden spoon until blended. Stir in ¾ cup nuts.

3. Scoop 1 teaspoon of vanilla dough into ball. Scoop 1 teaspoon of chocolate dough into ball. Gently press dough balls together, then roll gently to form one ball. Place balls 2 inches apart on ungreased cookie sheet.

4. Bake 9 to 12 minutes or until white part of cookie is golden. Cool 1 minute on sheets, then remove cookies with spatula to wire racks to cool completely.

VARIATIONS *for Marbled Chocolate and Vanilla Cookies*

MOCHA CHIP MARBLE COOKIES: Prepare as directed but dissolve 1 tablespoon instant coffee powder in 1 tablespoon water before adding to the white cake mix and substitute 1½ cups miniature semisweet chocolate chips for the chopped nuts.

LEMON-MACADAMIA MARBLE COOKIES: Prepare as directed but use lemon cake mix in place of devil's food cake mix and use toasted macadamia nuts instead of walnuts or pecans.

Cake Mix
SPICE

MOLASSES-CINNAMON COOKIES

Here is an old-fashioned cookie that tastes like home—perfect for feeling cozy on cold days and nights.

PREHEAT OVEN TO 375°F

MAKES 3 DOZEN COOKIES

COOKIE SHEETS, GREASED OR LINED WITH
   PARCHMENT PAPER

1 (18.25-ounce) package spice cake mix

¼ cup dark molasses

1 large egg

2 tablespoons vegetable oil

2 teaspoons ground cinnamon

¼ teaspoon baking soda

½ cup sugar

1. Place the cake mix, molasses, egg, vegetable oil, cinnamon, and baking soda in a large bowl. Blend with an electric mixer on medium speed 1 minute until blended (dough will be stiff).
2. Place the sugar in small, shallow dish. Roll the dough into 1-inch balls, roll in sugar, then place on ungreased cookie sheets.
3. Bake 8 to 11 minutes or until centers are just set. Cool 1 minute on sheets, then remove cookies with spatula to wire racks to cool completely.

MAPLE CUTOUTS

Cake Mix
WHITE

Pure maple syrup is best here, but in a pinch, you can certainly use maple-flavored pancake syrup. I love these plain, but for a quick maple decorating icing, mix 1½ cups (from a 16-ounce tub) ready-to-spread white or vanilla frosting with 2 teaspoons maple-flavored extract. Place the frosting in a plastic zipper-top bag, snip a small hole from one corner of the bag, and begin decorating.

PREHEAT OVEN TO 375°F

MAKES 2 DOZEN 4-INCH COOKIES

COOKIE SHEETS, GREASED OR LINED WITH
    PARCHMENT PAPER

1 (18.25-ounce) package white cake mix

¾ cup all-purpose flour

2 large eggs

⅓ cup butter, melted

⅓ cup pure maple syrup

2 teaspoons maple-flavored extract

1. Mix the cake mix, flour, eggs, melted butter, maple syrup, and maple extract with electric mixer on medium speed 1 to 2 minutes until blended. Increase speed to high and beat 1 minute longer.
2. Divide dough into 4 equal portions. Roll 1 portion of dough to ⅛-inch thickness on lightly floured surface. Cut with 3-inch cookie cutters into desired shapes. Transfer shapes with pancake turner to ungreased cookie sheets, placing 2 inches apart. If desired, sprinkle with sugar.
3. Bake 5 to 7 minutes or until golden. Cool 1 minute on sheets, then remove cookies with spatula to wire racks to cool completely.

PASTEL MINT MELTAWAYS

Cake Mix
WHITE

For a tea party with style, an occasion is required—pretty linens, some fresh flowers, and, of course, an assortment of delicious and delicate cakes and cookies. These pastel mint dainties hit the mark.

PREHEAT OVEN TO 350°F

MAKES 4 DOZEN COOKIES

COOKIE SHEETS, GREASED OR LINED WITH
    PARCHMENT PAPER

1 (18.25-ounce) package white cake mix

1 (8-ounce) package cream cheese, softened

¼ cup (½ stick) butter, softened

1 large egg

1 teaspoon peppermint extract

1½ cups coarsely chopped pastel mints

1. Mix the cake mix, cream cheese, butter, egg, and peppermint extract in large bowl with an electric mixer on medium speed 1 to 2 minutes until blended. Stir in pastel mints with a wooden spoon.
2. Shape dough into 1-inch balls and place 2 inches apart on ungreased cookie sheet.
3. Bake 9 to 12 minutes or until light brown around edges. Cool 1 minute on sheets, then remove cookies with spatula to wire racks to cool completely.

Cake Mix YELLOW PEANUT BUTTER BLOSSOMS

This favorite recipe makes enough to feed a small army of cookie monsters. Although delicious when eaten right away, these cookies taste even better if you have the time to make them a day ahead.

PREHEAT OVEN TO 350°F

MAKES 5 DOZEN COOKIES

COOKIE SHEETS, UNGREASED OR LINED WITH
    PARCHMENT PAPER

1 (18.25-ounce) package yellow cake mix

1 (14-ounce) can sweetened condensed
    milk

1 cup chunky-style peanut butter

1 large egg

60 milk chocolate "kiss" candies, unwrapped

1. Mix the cake mix, condensed milk, peanut butter, and egg in large bowl with an electric mixer on medium speed 1 to 2 minutes until blended.
2. Shape dough into 1-inch balls and place 2 inches apart on ungreased cookie sheet.
3. Bake 9 to 12 minutes or until light brown around edges. Immediately push a kiss candy, flat side down, into the center of each cookie. Transfer to wire racks with spatula and cool completely.

VARIATION *for Peanut Butter Blossoms*

PEANUT BUTTER CARAMEL BLOSSOMS: Prepare as directed but use chocolate-covered caramel candies (e.g., Rolos) in place of the kiss candies.

WHITE AND DARK CHOCOLATE PEANUT BUTTER KISS COOKIES

Cake Mix
CHOCOLATE FUDGE

The ingredients list may be brief, but the resulting cookie is big on flavor and flair. They are very easy to make—a simple peanut butter dough, finished with white and milk chocolate swirled "kisses"—and yet look so delightful that everyone will want to tuck in.

PREHEAT OVEN TO 350°F

MAKES 4 DOZEN COOKIES

COOKIE SHEETS, UNGREASED OR LINED WITH PARCHMENT PAPER

1 (18.25-ounce) package chocolate fudge cake mix

1 cup creamy peanut butter

½ cup vegetable oil

2 large eggs

48 white and milk chocolate swirled "kiss" candies, unwrapped

1. Mix the cake mix, peanut butter, oil, and eggs in large bowl with an electric mixer on medium speed 1 to 2 minutes until blended.
2. Shape dough into 1-inch balls and place 2 inches apart on ungreased cookie sheet.
3. Bake 9 to 12 minutes or until barely firm to the touch. Immediately push a kiss candy, flat side down, into the center of each cookie. Transfer to wire racks with spatula and cool completely.

PECAN SANDIES

Cake Mix
BUTTER PECAN

From Christmastime to summer picnics, these buttery, nutty shortbread-like cookies are perennial crowd-pleasers.

PREHEAT OVEN TO 375°F

MAKES 3½ DOZEN COOKIES

COOKIE SHEETS, UNGREASED OR LINED WITH PARCHMENT PAPER

1 (18.25-ounce) package butter pecan cake mix

¾ cup (1½ sticks) butter, softened

1 large egg

1¼ cups finely chopped pecans

½ cup sugar

1. Mix the cake mix, butter, and egg in large bowl with an electric mixer on medium speed 1 to 2 minutes until blended. Mix in pecans with a wooden spoon.

2. Place the sugar in small, shallow bowl. Shape dough into 1-inch balls and roll in sugar. Place 2 inches apart on ungreased cookie sheet.

3. Bake 9 to 12 minutes or until light brown around edges. Transfer to wire racks with spatula and cool completely.

VARIATIONS *for Pecan Sandies*

ALMOND SANDIES: Prepare as directed but substitute finely chopped almonds for the pecans and add ¾ teaspoon almond extract.

PEANUT BRITTLE SANDIES: Prepare as directed but substitute finely chopped peanuts for the pecans. Just before baking, roll the dough balls in toffee baking bits (you will need approximately 1 cup toffee bits).

Cake Mix
DEVIL'S FOOD

SPICY PECAN-CHOCOLATE CRACKLES

These very chocolate cookies are crispy-crunchy delicious, but it's the addition of smoky, earthy chipotle chili powder that moves these to the adult cookie jar.

PREHEAT OVEN TO 375°F

MAKES 3 DOZEN COOKIES

COOKIE SHEETS, GREASED OR LINED WITH
PARCHMENT PAPER

1 (18.25-ounce) package devil's food cake mix

¼ cup unsweetened cocoa powder

2 large eggs

2 tablespoons (¼ stick) butter, softened

¼ teaspoon chipotle chili powder or cayenne pepper (more or less to taste)

1 cup finely chopped pecans

1. Mix the cake mix, cocoa powder, eggs, butter, and chili powder in a large bowl with an electric mixer on medium speed 1 to 2 minutes until blended.

2. Place pecans in small, shallow bowl. Shape dough into 1-inch balls and roll in pecans, then place 2 inches apart on prepared cookie sheet.

3. Bake 9 to 12 minutes or until light brown around edges. Transfer to wire racks with spatula and cool completely.

SANTA'S WHISKERS COOKIES

These festive cookies are especially handy at holiday time—several batches can be made at once, refrigerated, then sliced and baked as needed.

PREHEAT OVEN TO 350°F

MAKES 5 DOZEN COOKIES

COOKIE SHEETS, UNGREASED OR LINED WITH
    PARCHMENT PAPER

1 (18.25-ounce) package white cake mix

½ cup vegetable shortening

⅓ cup butter, softened

1 large egg

1½ cups sweetened flake coconut

1 cup red or green candied cherries (or
    combination of both), halved

½ cup finely chopped pecans

1. Mix the cake mix, shortening, butter, and egg in a large bowl with an electric mixer on medium speed 1 to 2 minutes until smooth. Mix in the coconut, cherries, and pecans with a wooden spoon.

2. Divide dough in half, shaping each piece into a 12 x 2-inch roll. Wrap each in plastic food wrap. Chill at least 4 hours.

3. Cut rolls into ¼-inch slices with a sharp knife. Place 2 inches apart on ungreased cookie sheets.

4. Bake 7 to 8 minutes or until edges are lightly browned. Let stand on cookie sheets for 1 minute. Transfer to wire rack and cool completely.

SESAME-GINGER COOKIES

Culinary historians contend that sesame is one of the first recorded seasonings, dating back to 3000 B.C. In addition to a traditional role in Middle Eastern and Indian cuisines, sesame also has a rich culinary role in the cuisine of the American South (where it is also known as "benne"). One bite of these cookies reveals that sesame is quintessentially suited to honey, making this recipe an all-American winner.

PREHEAT OVEN TO 375°F

MAKES 4 DOZEN COOKIES

COOKIE SHEETS, GREASED OR LINED WITH PARCHMENT PAPER

1 (18.25-ounce) package white cake mix

1 cup all-purpose flour

½ cup (1 stick) butter, melted

¼ cup honey

2 large eggs

1½ teaspoons ground ginger

½ cup sesame seeds

1. Mix the cake mix, flour, melted butter, honey, eggs, and ginger in a large bowl with an electric mixer on medium speed 1 to 2 minutes until blended (dough will be stiff).
2. Place sesame seeds in small, shallow dish. Roll the dough into 1-inch balls, roll in sesame seeds, then place 2 inches apart on ungreased cookie sheets.
3. Bake 8 to 11 minutes or until centers are just set. Cool 1 minute on sheets, then remove cookies with spatula to wire racks to cool completely.

SNICKER-Y TREASURE COOKIES

These cookies are so easy and so delicious—and you can "hide" just about any variety of chocolate candy bars inside the dough. Do be sure to cool the cookies before eating to avoid burning tender tongues on the hot filling.

PREHEAT OVEN TO 350°F

MAKES 3 DOZEN COOKIES

COOKIE SHEETS, GREASED OR LINED WITH PARCHMENT PAPER

1 (18.25-ounce) package yellow cake mix

2 large eggs

¼ cup vegetable oil

18 chocolate-covered caramel nougat candy bars (e.g., Snickers), unwrapped

1. Mix the cake mix, eggs, and oil in a large bowl with a wooden spoon until blended.

2. Cut the candy bars in half crosswise (36 pieces total). Mold a level tablespoon of dough around each candy, covering completely. Place, 2 inches apart, onto prepared cookie sheets.

3. Bake 8 to 11 minutes or until dough looks slightly dry and cracked. Cool 1 minute on sheets, then remove cookies with spatula to wire racks to cool completely.

VARIATION *for Snicker-y Treasure Cookies*

PEANUT BUTTER CUP COOKIES: Prepare as directed but use chocolate cake mix in place of yellow cake mix and miniature peanut butter cups in place of chocolate-caramel nougat candies.

Cake Mix
SPICE

GINGERBREAD BLOSSOMS

Here is one blossom everyone will want to pick—a gingerbread-scented cookie with a white-and-milk chocolate swirled candy plunged into its middle. You may want to make a double batch, should you need to make enough for a whole gang of sugar and spice fans.

PREHEAT OVEN TO 350°F

MAKES 5 DOZEN COOKIES

COOKIE SHEETS, UNGREASED OR LINED WITH
PARCHMENT PAPER

1 (18.25-ounce) package spice cake mix

1 cup all-purpose flour

¼ cup packed dark brown sugar

2 teaspoons ground ginger

1 teaspoon ground cinnamon

¼ cup (½ stick) butter, softened

1 (3-ounce) package cream cheese, softened

1 large egg

60 white- and milk-chocolate swirled "kiss"
candies, unwrapped

1. Mix the cake mix, flour, brown sugar, ginger, cinnamon, butter, and cream cheese in a large bowl with an electric mixer on medium speed until mixture is blended and crumbly. Add the egg and beat on low speed 1 to 2 minutes longer until dough comes together into a ball.

2. Shape dough into 1-inch balls and place, 2 inches apart, on ungreased sheets.

3. Bake 9 to 12 minutes or until firm to the touch at the edges and slightly puffed in appearance. Immediately push a kiss candy, flat side down, into the center of each cookie. Cool for 1 minute on cookie sheets. Transfer to wire racks with metal spatula and cool completely.

VANILLA CHIP COOKIES

All you need to make and enjoy these cookies is a big sweet tooth and a fondness for vanilla.

PREHEAT OVEN TO 350°F

MAKES 4 DOZEN COOKIES

COOKIE SHEETS, GREASED OR LINED WITH PARCHMENT PAPER

1 (18.25-ounce) package vanilla cake mix

1 (4-serving size) package instant vanilla pudding mix

½ cup vegetable oil

½ cup sour cream (not reduced fat)

1 egg

⅔ cup quick-cooking oats

1½ cups vanilla baking chips or white chocolate chips

1. Mix the cake mix, dry pudding mix, oil, sour cream, and egg in a large bowl with an electric mixer on low speed 1 to 2 minutes until blended and smooth. Stir in the oats and chips with wooden spoon.
2. Shape dough into 1½ inch balls and place, 2 inches apart, on prepared cookie sheets.
3. Bake 11 to 14 minutes until golden at edges and just barely set at center. Cool cookies on cookie sheet for 5 minutes (cookies will firm up as they cool). Transfer to a wire rack; cool completely.

VARIATIONS *for Vanilla Chip Cookies*

BUTTERSCOTCH BLISS COOKIES: Prepare as directed but use butter pecan cake mix, instant butterscotch pudding, and butterscotch baking chips.

CHOCOLATE INTENSITY COOKIES: Prepare as directed but use chocolate cake mix, instant chocolate pudding, and semisweet chocolate chips.

Cake Mix WHITE

PEANUT BUTTERSCOTCHIES

Blending a classic favor duo, these peanut-butterscotch treats are so good you'll want to take an extra-long coffee break to savor them.

PREHEAT OVEN TO 350°F

MAKES 5 DOZEN COOKIES

COOKIE SHEETS, UNGREASED OR LINED WITH PARCHMENT PAPER

1 (18.25-ounce) package white cake mix

1 (4-serving size) package instant butterscotch pudding mix

½ cup (1 stick) butter, melted

½ cup creamy peanut butter

1 egg

⅔ cup quick-cooking oats

1½ cups butterscotch baking chips

1. Mix the cake mix, dry pudding mix, melted butter, peanut butter, and egg in a large bowl with an electric mixer on medium speed 1 to 2 minutes until blended. Mix in the oats and butterscotch chips with a wooden spoon.
2. Roll the dough into 1-inch balls. Place 2 inches apart on ungreased cookie sheets.
3. Bake 9 to 12 minutes or until centers are just set. Cool 1 minute on sheets, then remove cookies with spatula to wire racks to cool completely.

Cake Mix WHITE

PISTACHIO AND CHOCOLATE CHIP COOKIES

Here pistachio pudding and pie filling is blended into a quick cookie dough for an immensely satisfying take on classic chocolate chip cookies.

PREHEAT OVEN TO 350°F

MAKES 4 DOZEN COOKIES

COOKIE SHEETS, GREASED OR LINED WITH PARCHMENT PAPER

1 (18.25-ounce) package white cake mix

1 (4-serving size) package pistachio instant pudding and pie filling mix

¾ cup vegetable oil

¼ cup all-purpose flour

1 large egg

1 cup miniature semisweet chocolate chips

1. Mix the cake mix, pudding mix, oil, flour, and egg in a large bowl with a wooden spoon until well blended. Stir in the chocolate chips (dough will be crumbly).
2. Roll the dough into 1-inch balls. Place balls 2 inches apart on prepared cookie sheets.
3. Bake 10 to 12 minutes or until cookies are golden at the edges and just barely set at center. Cool on sheet 2 minutes. Then transfer to wire racks and cool completely.

<table>
<tr><td>Cake Mix
WHITE</td><td></td></tr>
</table>

MACADAMIA-LEMON COOKIES

Buttery cookies are made all the better with a double dose of lemon and the crisp crunch of macadamia nuts. The combination of flavors makes them completely habit-forming.

PREHEAT OVEN TO 350°F

MAKES 4 DOZEN COOKIES

COOKIE SHEETS, GREASED OR LINED WITH PARCHMENT PAPER

1 (18.25-ounce) package white cake mix

1 (4-serving size) package lemon instant pudding and pie filling mix

¾ cup (1½ sticks) butter, softened

¼ cup all-purpose flour

1 large egg

1 cup chopped macadamia nuts

3 cups confectioners' sugar

2 tablespoons lemon juice

1. Mix the cake mix, pudding mix, butter, flour, and egg in a large bowl with electric mixer on low speed 1 minute until blended. Stir in the macadamia nuts (dough will be crumbly).
2. Roll the dough into 1-inch balls. Place balls 2 inches apart on prepared cookie sheets.
3. Bake 10 to 12 minutes or until cookies are golden at the edges and just barely set at center. Cool on sheet 2 minutes. Then transfer to wire racks and cool completely.
4. Mix the confectioners' sugar and lemon juice in a small bowl until blended. Drizzle or spoon over cooled cookies.

CHOCOLATE-PEPPERMINT DREAMS

Rich, chocolate-y, and filled with a double dose of mint, these cookies will fly off the plate any time of year, but especially on a Christmas cookie tray.

PREHEAT OVEN TO 350°F

MAKES 4 DOZEN COOKIES

COOKIE SHEETS, GREASED OR LINED WITH PARCHMENT PAPER

1 (18.25-ounce) package devil's food cake mix

1 (4-serving size) package chocolate instant pudding and pie filling mix

¾ cup vegetable oil

¼ cup unsweetened cocoa powder

1 large egg

1¼ teaspoons peppermint extract

1½ cups mint chocolate chips (e.g., Guittard or Andes baking chips)

1. Mix the cake mix, pudding mix, oil, cocoa powder, egg, and peppermint extract in a large bowl. Blend with an electric mixer on medium speed 1 to 2 minutes until blended. Mix in the mint chocolate chips with a wooden spoon.
2. Roll the dough into 1-inch balls. Place 2 inches apart on prepared cookie sheets.
3. Bake 9 to 12 minutes or until centers are just set. Cool 1 minute on sheets, then remove cookies with spatula to wire racks to cool completely.

LEBKUCHEN (GERMAN HONEY-SPICE COOKIES)

Lebkuchen are soft, cakey cookies hailing from the German town of Nuremberg. They are revered for their rich blend of spices, nuts, and citrus, all of which I've recreated in this much-simplified cake mix variation.

PREHEAT OVEN TO 375°F

MAKES 4 DOZEN COOKIES

COOKIE SHEETS, GREASED OR LINED WITH
    PARCHMENT PAPER

1 (18.25-ounce) package spice cake mix

¾ cup all-purpose flour

½ cup (1 stick) butter, melted

¼ cup honey

2 large eggs

2 teaspoons pumpkin pie spice

2 teaspoons grated orange peel

1 teaspoon almond extract

½ cup finely chopped hazelnuts or almonds

Optional: 1 cup (½ a 16-ounce tub) vanilla
    frosting

1. Mix the cake mix, flour, melted butter, honey, eggs, pumpkin pie spice, orange peel, and almond extract in a large bowl with an electric mixer on medium speed 1 to 2 minutes until blended. Mix in the nuts with a wooden spoon.
2. Roll the dough into 1-inch balls. Place 2 inches apart on prepared cookie sheets.
3. Bake 9 to 12 minutes or until centers are just set. Cool 1 minute on sheets, then remove cookies with spatula to wire racks to cool completely.
4. If desired, microwave frosting in a small microwave safe bowl 30 seconds or until melted. Spoon over cookies to glaze tops.

MAPLE CRINKLES

Cake Mix
WHITE

These very maple crinkles are instant people-pleasers, delighting cookie lovers of all ages with their old-fashioned flavor and crinkly exteriors.

PREHEAT OVEN TO 375°F

MAKES 4 DOZEN COOKIES

COOKIE SHEETS, GREASED OR LINED WITH
PARCHMENT PAPER

1 (18.25-ounce) package white cake mix

1 cup all-purpose flour

½ cup (1 stick) butter, softened

2 large eggs

¼ cup pure maple syrup or maple-flavored
pancake syrup

2 teaspoons maple-flavored extract

½ cup turbinado (raw) sugar

1. Mix the cake mix, flour, butter, eggs, syrup, and maple extract in a large bowl with an electric mixer on medium speed 1 to 2 minutes until blended.
2. Place the sugar in small, shallow dish. Roll the dough into 1-inch balls, roll in sugar, then place 2 inches apart on prepared cookie sheets.
3. Bake 9 to 12 minutes or until centers are just set. Cool 2 minutes on sheets, then remove cookies with spatula to wire racks to cool completely.

TANGERINE CRISPS

Cake Mix
WHITE

The bright, zingy flavor of winter tangerines is showcased in these easy, elegant cookies. Double the deliciousness by pairing them with the added cheer of a cup of strong black tea.

PREHEAT OVEN TO 350°F

MAKES 3½ DOZEN COOKIES

COOKIE SHEETS, GREASED OR LINED WITH
PARCHMENT PAPER

1 (18.25-ounce) package white cake mix

½ cup (1 stick) butter, melted

1 large egg

4 teaspoons grated tangerine peel

3 cups confectioners' sugar

2 tablespoons fresh tangerine juice

1. Mix the cake mix, melted butter, egg, and 3 teaspoons (1 tablespoon) tangerine peel in a large bowl with an electric mixer on medium speed 1 to 2 minutes until blended (dough will be stiff).

2. Roll the dough into 1-inch balls. Place 2 inches apart on ungreased cookie sheets.
3. Bake 9 to 12 minutes or until centers are just set. Cool 1 minute on sheets, then remove cookies with spatula to wire racks to cool completely.
4. Mix the confectioners' sugar, tangerine juice, and remaining teaspoon tangerine peel in a small bowl until blended. Drizzle or spoon icing over cooled cookies.

Cake Mix
WHITE

AGAVE-LIME COOKIES

Agave nectar (also called agave syrup) is a sweetener produced in Mexico from several species of the agave plant. It has a delightful, subtly floral flavor, and can be used interchangeably with honey in most recipes, or for sweetening teas and drinks. It has become widely available in grocery stores in the past few years, allowing for greater use in a wide range of baked goods, like these fragrant agave-lime cookies.

PREHEAT OVEN TO 375°F

MAKES 4 DOZEN COOKIES

COOKIE SHEETS, GREASED OR LINED WITH
    PARCHMENT PAPER

1 (18.25-ounce) package white cake mix

1 cup all-purpose flour

½ cup (1 stick) butter, softened

2 large eggs

¼ cup agave nectar

1 tablespoon finely grated lime peel

½ cup granulated sugar

1. Mix the cake mix, flour, butter, eggs, agave nectar, and lime peel in a large bowl with an electric mixer on medium speed 1 to 2 minutes until blended (dough will be stiff).
2. Place the sugar in small, shallow dish. Roll the dough into 1-inch balls, roll in sugar, then place 2 inches apart on ungreased cookie sheets.
3. Bake 9 to 12 minutes or until centers are just set. Cool 1 minute on sheets, then remove cookies with spatula to wire racks to cool completely.

GIANDUIA COOKIES

**Cake Mix
DEVIL'S FOOD**

Two very European flavors—chocolate and hazelnut—combine to create one posh cookie.

PREHEAT OVEN TO 375°F

MAKES 4 DOZEN COOKIES

COOKIE SHEETS, GREASED OR LINED WITH
    PARCHMENT PAPER

1 (18.25-ounce) package devil's food cake
    mix

½ cup (1 stick) butter, melted

1 large egg

1½ cups chopped hazelnuts, toasted

1 cup miniature semisweet chocolate chips

1. Mix the cake mix, melted butter, and egg in a large bowl with an electric mixer on medium speed 1 to 2 minutes until blended. Mix in the hazelnuts and chocolate chips with a wooden spoon.
2. Roll the dough into 1-inch balls. Place 2 inches apart on ungreased cookie sheets.
3. Bake 9 to 12 minutes or until centers are just set. Cool 1 minute on sheets, then remove cookies with spatula to wire racks to cool completely.

WHITE CHOCOLATE, PRETZEL, AND PEANUT BUTTER COOKIES

**Cake Mix
WHITE**

Sometimes nothing brings out the perfection of a good cookie like the counterbalance of a little salt. A handful of crushed, salty pretzels to this easy peanut butter-white chocolate dough adds a whole new, and very appealing, dimension.

PREHEAT OVEN TO 375°F

MAKES 4 DOZEN COOKIES

COOKIE SHEETS, GREASED OR LINED WITH
    PARCHMENT PAPER

1 (18.25-ounce) package white cake mix

1 cup creamy peanut butter

2 large eggs

1 tablespoon whole or lowfat milk

1 cup white chocolate chips

1 cup coarsely crushed pretzels

1. Mix the cake mix, peanut butter, eggs, and milk in a large bowl with an electric mixer on medium speed 1 to 2 minutes until blended. Mix in the chocolate chips and pretzels with a wooden spoon.

2. Roll the dough into 1-inch balls. Place 2 inches apart on ungreased cookie sheets.

3. Bake 9 to 12 minutes or until centers are just set. Cool 1 minute on sheets, then remove cookies with spatula to wire racks to cool completely.

 Cake Mix
SPICE

JUMBO GINGER COOKIES (EGG AND DAIRY-FREE)

I love the giant ginger cookies at my favorite coffeehouse, so I decided to come up with an easy version to bake at home. Everyone loves them—even friends who do not eat dairy and eggs, since these amazing cookies have neither!

PREHEAT OVEN TO 375°F

MAKES 10 EXTRA-LARGE COOKIES

COOKIE SHEETS, GREASED OR LINED WITH PARCHMENT PAPER

1 (18.25-ounce) package spice cake mix

2½ teaspoons ground ginger

1 teaspoon ground cinnamon

¼ teaspoon baking soda

¼ cup water

¼ cup molasses

1 tablespoon vanilla extract

¾ cup turbinado (raw) sugar or granulated sugar

1. Mix the cake mix, ginger, cinnamon, and baking soda in a large bowl. Stir in the water, molasses, and vanilla with a wooden spoon until blended.

2. Place the sugar in medium, shallow dish. Shape dough into 10 large balls. Roll in sugar. Place on prepared cookie sheets 3 to 4 inches apart. Flatten slightly with glass coated with cooking spray.

3. Bake 13 to 15 minutes or until cracked in appearance and just barely set at center when lightly touched. Cool for 1 minute on cookie sheets. Transfer to wire racks with metal spatula and cool completely.

CHOCOLATE THIN MINT COOKIES

**Cake Mix
CHOCOLATE**

Make an irresistible Christmas gift from your kitchen that everyone will love. Pack the cookies into small boxes and wrap in cellophane. Don't forget the ribbon!

PREHEAT OVEN TO 350°F

MAKES 3 DOZEN COOKIES

COOKIE SHEETS, UNGREASED OR LINED WITH PARCHMENT PAPER

1 (18.25-ounce) package chocolate cake mix

½ cup (1 stick) butter, softened

2 large eggs

1 tablespoon water

1 cup confectioners' sugar

2 (5-ounce) packages chocolate-covered thin mints (e.g., Andes Thin Mints), unwrapped

1. Mix the cake mix, butter, eggs, and water in a large bowl with an electric mixer on medium speed 1 to 2 minutes until blended (dough will be stiff).
2. Place the confectioners' sugar in a medium, shallow dish. Roll the dough into 1-inch balls, then roll in the confectioners' sugar. Place 2 inches apart on ungreased cookie sheets, pressing a candy into each dough ball.
3. Bake 8 to 11 minutes or until centers are just set. Cool 2 minutes on sheets, then remove cookies with spatula to wire racks to cool completely.

WALNUT-CARDAMOM COOKIES

**Cake Mix
WHITE**

These cookies have a short list of ingredients, but tremendous flavor and sophistication. To buy ground cardamom on a dime, head to your local health food store; most carry spices in bulk, allowing you to purchase a wealth of spices for mere pennies.

PREHEAT OVEN TO 350°F

MAKES 3 DOZEN COOKIES

COOKIE SHEETS, GREASED OR LINED WITH PARCHMENT PAPER

1 (18.25-ounce) package white cake mix

½ cup (1 stick) butter, melted

2 large eggs

1 teaspoon ground cardamom

Optional: ½ teaspoon rose water

1½ cups chopped walnuts

1. Mix the cake mix, melted butter, eggs, cardamom, and optional rose water in a large bowl with an electric mixer on medium speed 1 to 2 minutes until blended (dough will be stiff). Stir in the walnuts with a wooden spoon.
2. Roll the dough into 1-inch balls. Place 2 inches apart on ungreased cookie sheets.
3. Bake 9 to 12 minutes or until centers are just set. Cool 1 minute on sheets, then remove cookies with spatula to wire racks to cool completely.

ALOHA COOKIES

Cake Mix WHITE

Get a taste of the tropical with these pretty cookies packed with island flavor: macadamia nuts, coconut, lime, and ginger.

PREHEAT OVEN TO 350°F

MAKES 3 DOZEN COOKIES

COOKIE SHEETS, GREASED OR LINED WITH
   PARCHMENT PAPER

1 (18.25-ounce) package white cake mix

⅓ cup butter, melted

2 large eggs

2 teaspoons grated lime peel

1 teaspoon ground ginger

1 cup chopped macadamia nuts

1 cup sweetened flake coconut

1. Mix the cake mix, melted butter, eggs, lime peel, and ginger in a large bowl with an electric mixer on medium speed 1 to 2 minutes until blended (dough will be stiff). Stir in the nuts and coconut with a wooden spoon.
2. Roll the dough into 1-inch balls. Place 2 inches apart on prepared cookie sheets.
3. Bake 9 to 12 minutes or until centers are just set. Cool 1 minute on sheets, then remove cookies with spatula to wire racks to cool completely.

GOOEY BUTTER COOKIES

If you love my gooey chess bars, then this recipe needs to move to the top of your to-do list: all the gooey goodness of the bars, but in individual form. Yum!

PREHEAT OVEN TO 350°F

MAKES 3 DOZEN COOKIES

COOKIE SHEETS, UNGREASED OR LINED WITH
    PARCHMENT PAPER

1 (18.25-ounce) package white cake mix

1 (8-ounce) package cream cheese, softened

½ cup (1 stick) butter, softened

1 large egg

1 teaspoon vanilla extract

1 cup confectioners' sugar

Optional: 1 cup white chocolate chips

1. Mix the cake mix, cream cheese, butter, egg, and vanilla in a large bowl with an electric mixer on medium speed 1 to 2 minutes until blended. If desired, stir in the white chocolate chips with a wooden spoon.
2. Place the confectioners' sugar in a shallow, medium dish. Roll the dough into 1-inch balls, then roll in the confectioners' sugar. Place 2 inches apart on ungreased cookie sheets.
3. Bake 9 to 12 minutes or until centers are just set. Cool 1 minute on sheets, then remove cookies with spatula to wire racks to cool completely.

VARIATION *for Gooey Butter Cookies*

CHOCOLATE GOOEY BUTTER COOKIES: Prepare as directed but use a chocolate or devil's food cake mix and semisweet chocolate chips.

LEMON CRISPIES

Bright with citrus, made with only five ingredients, easy as can be, and so delicious—what more could you want from a cookie?

PREHEAT OVEN TO 350°F

MAKES 3 DOZEN COOKIES

COOKIE SHEETS, UNGREASED OR LINED WITH
    PARCHMENT PAPER

1 (18.25-ounce) package lemon cake mix

½ cup (1 stick) butter, melted

1 large egg

1 tablespoon finely grated lemon peel

1 cup crisp rice cereal

1. Mix the cake mix, butter, egg, and lemon peel in a large bowl with an electric mixer on medium speed 1 to 2 minutes until blended. Mix in the rice cereal with a wooden spoon.
2. Roll the dough into 1-inch balls. Place 2 inches apart on ungreased cookie sheets.
3. Bake 9 to 12 minutes or until centers are just set. Cool 1 minute on sheets, then remove cookies with spatula to wire racks to cool completely.

lists

PERFECT FOR PACKING

These cookies and bars pack easily, whether for a care package, lunch box, or backpacks.

- No-Bake Peanut Butter Chewies
- Granola Chocolate Chunkers
- Double-Chocolate Oatmeal Jumbles
- Deluxe Nut Jumbles
- Orange, Date, and Walnut Bars
- Cinnamon Graham Bars
- Chocolate Pretzel Candy Bars
- Shortbread Squares
- Peanut Butter Blondies
- Trail Mix Bars
- Deluxe Chocolate Chip Biscotti

KIDS' FAVORITES

These can't-miss picks are the cookies you love to make and the kids love to eat!

- Applesauce Cookies
- Banana Cookies
- Chocolate Chip Graham Cookies
- Gingerbread Softies
- Crispy Rice and Marshmallow Cookies
- S'mores Bars
- Apple-Cranberry Snack Bars
- Rocky Road Bars
- Snickerdoodles
- Gloreos
- Snicker-y Treasure Cookies

HEALTH-CONSCIOUS COOKIES

It's no mistake: with a handful of healthy ingredients, such as whole wheat flour, dried fruit, nuts, and even vegetables, a box of cake mix can be transformed into healthy, delicious cookies. So leave the energy bars on the supermarket shelf and make a batch of any of these cookies instead!

- Fiber-Wonderful Cookies
- Healthy Chocolate-Pumpkin Cookies
- Blueberry Power Cookies
- Zucchini-Chocolate Cookies
- Whole Wheat Chocolate Chip Cookies
- Whole Wheat Raisin Spice Cookies
- Wheat Germ and Raisin Biscotti
- Whole Wheat Pumpkin Breakfast Cookies
- Good-For-You Double-Chocolate Cookies
- Vegan Fruit and Seed Bars
- Power Bars with Dried Fruit, Nuts, and Flax
- Chocolate-Nut Power Bars
- Whole Wheat Biscotti

BAKESHOP CLASSICS

Your favorite coffee drink just wouldn't be the same without these favorites.

- Chocolate Chip Cookies
- Black-and-White Cookies
- Oatmeal Raisin Cookies
- Peanut Butter Cookies
- Cream Cheese Swirl Brownies
- Favorite Fruit Cobbler Bars
- Carmelitas
- New York Cheesecake Bars
- Date Bars Deluxe
- Nutty Jam Thumbprints
- Jumbo Ginger Cookies
- Anise Biscotti
- Vanilla Madeleines

BAKE SALE BESTSELLERS

Are you ready to be the star of the next bake sale? Bring one or more of any of the following cookies and you will be, guaranteed.

- Orange Dreamsicle Cookies
- Coffee-Toffee Cookies
- Creamy Lemon Bars
- Candy Jumble Bars

- Peanut Butter Chocolate Gooey Bars
- Magic Cookie Bars
- Pecan Pie Bars
- Peanut Butter Fudge Bars

- Cake Balls/Cake Mix Pops
- Iced Lemon Cookies
- Red Velvet Whoopies
- Peanut Butter Blossoms

GROWN-UP COOKIES

These sophisticated treats are perfect for impressing adult palates.

- Dark Chocolate-Dipped Apricot Cookies
- Kahlua Cookies
- Rum-Raisin Cookies
- Tipsy Chocolate Chews
- Vanilla Latte Cookies

- Cinnamon Macchiato Gooey Bars
- Mexican Chocolate Bars
- Tiramisu Bars
- Italian Chocolate-Hazelnut Bars
- Chocolate-Whiskey Whoopies

TRENDSETTER COOKIES

Ready for something new? Then these innovative cookies are for you!

- Spumoni Chunk Cookies
- Potato Chip Cookies
- Pine Nut Cookies
- Cake Mix Pops
- Pistachio and Chocolate Chip Cookies
- Vanilla Malt Gooey Bars
- Salty-Sweet Chewy Peanut Bars

- Candied Ginger Bars
- Cardamom-Lime Cookies
- Fluffernutter Whoopies
- Indian-Spiced Coconut Cookies
- Lemon-Thyme Cornmeal Cookies
- Honey-Rosemary Crisps
- Agave-Lime Cookies

HOLIDAY COOKIES

It's the sweetest time of the year, so make a pledge to bake any or all of the cookies on this list of easy, yet incredible, fall and winter treats.

- Fruitcake Jumbles
- Cranberry Cornmeal Cookies

- Eggnog Cookies
- Marmalade-Spice Cookies

- Holiday Fruit and Spice Cookies
- Pumpkin Gooey Bars
- Crushed Peppermint Snowballs
- Maple Whoopies
- Pistachio-Cherry Biscotti
- Gingerbread People
- Cream Cheese and Candy Cane Cookies
- Santa's Whiskers Cookies

CHOCOLATE-LOVERS COOKIES

All of the chocolate lovers in your life will be thrilled to know that you have a special list just for them. Combining the best of all worlds—chocolate, chocolate, and chocolate—every option on this list is guaranteed to please.

- Black Beauties
- Double-Chocolate Coconut Cookies
- Bittersweet Chocolate Blackout Cookies
- Triple-Chocolate Gooey Bars
- Chocolate Cheesecake Bars
- Chocolate Fudge Crumble Bars
- Chocolate Truffle Bars
- Chocolate and Sour Cream Bars
- Double-Chocolate Magic Cookie Bars
- Bittersweet Chocolate-Espresso Bars
- Chocolate Intensity Cookies

SUMMER COOKIES

Making the most of the bright, fresh flavors of summer, these enchanting cookies will elevate any picnic, backyard bbq, or trip to the beach with impeccable taste.

- Lemon-Blueberry Cookies
- Lime and White Chocolate Cookies
- Piña Colada Cookies
- Mandarin Orange Cookies
- Fresh Raspberry Blondies
- Blackberry Cream Cheese Bars
- Pineapple Gooey Bars
- Key Lime Bars
- Tropical Fruit and Cashew Bars
- Fresh Berry Cheesecake Bars
- Tangerine Bars
- Lemon Buttermilk Whoopies

index

cake mix index

Y

yellow cake mix

about the author

Camilla V. Saulsbury is a food writer, recipe developer, and spokesperson. Her culinary focus is translating food and flavor trends into fresh, innovative, and delicious recipes for the home kitchen. Camilla has been involved in the world of food for more than sixteen years, including catering specialty desserts in the San Francisco Bay Area, writing cookbooks and freelance food articles, and developing recipes for national food companies. She is the winner of several top cooking competitions, including the $100,000 National Chicken Cook-Off, the $50,000 Build a Better Burger Contest, and the Food Network's $25,000 Ultimate Recipe Showdown (Cookies Episode). She has made multiple appearances on The Food Network, has been featured in the *New York Times*, made appearances on the *Today Show* and QVC, and is a member of the International Association of Culinary Professionals (IACP). Her work has appeared in such magazines as *Southern Living*, *Better Homes and Gardens*, *Cooking Light*, *Woman's Day*, *Cosmo Girl*, *Quick & Simple*, and many others. She is the author of twelve cookbooks.